LAND LAW AND THE EXTRACTIVE INDUSTRIES

This book analyses the nexus between land access and the extractive industries in Africa, specifically highlighting the gaps in energy, land and mining laws and the practical solutions needed to settle the increasing number of land disputes in resource-rich areas.

Access to land is essential for the successful operation of energy and mining projects. However, there are often social, environmental and economic issues associated with acquiring land for these projects. Socially, many people are relocated; economically, local communities are not given adequate compensation; environmentally, pollution negatively impacts on the agricultural and fishing industries relied on by over 80 per cent of the local communities.

Against this stark background, and drawing from the author's fieldwork research, this book addresses the important question of whether the different land tenure systems, coupled with administration and registration procedures, are adequate to address the increasing land disputes in oil and mineral-rich African countries.

Global Energy Law and Policy: Volume 7

Global Energy Law and Policy

Energy policy and energy law are undergoing rapid global transformation, characterised by the push in favour of decarbonisation. The 2015 Sustainable Development Goals and the 2015 Paris Agreement on international climate action have forged a consensus for a pathway to a universal just transition towards a low-carbon economy for all states and all societies.

This series publishes conceptual works that help academics, legal practitioners and decision-makers to make sense of these transformational changes. The perspective of the series is global. It welcomes contributions on international law, regional law (for example, from the EU, US and ASEAN regions), and the domestic law of all states with emphasis on comparative works that identify horizontal trends, and including transnational law. The series' scope is comprehensive, embracing both public and commercial law on energy in all forms and sources and throughout the energy life-cycle from extraction, production, operation, consumption and waste management/decommissioning. The series is a forum for innovative interdisciplinary work that uses the insights of cognate disciplines to achieve a better understanding of energy law and policy in the 21st century.

Recent titles in this series:

Decarbonisation and the Energy Industry
edited by Tade Oyewumni, Penelope Crossley, Frédéric Gilles Sourgens and Kim Talus

The Global Energy Transition: Law, Policy and Economics for Energy in the 21st Century
edited by Peter D Cameron, Xiaoyi Mu and Volker Roeben

The Law and Governance of Mining and Minerals: A Global Perspective
by Ana Elizabeth Bastida

National Climate Change Acts: The Emergence, Form and Nature of National Framework Climate Legislation
edited by Thomas L Muinzer

Governing the Extractive Sector: Regulating the Foreign Conduct of International Mining Firms
by Jeffrey Bone

Stability and Legitimate Expectations in International Energy Investments
by Rahmi Kopar

Land Law and the Extractive Industries: Challenges and Opportunities in Africa
by Victoria R Nalule

Land Law and the Extractive Industries

Challenges and Opportunities in Africa

Victoria R Nalule

·HART·

OXFORD · LONDON · NEW YORK · NEW DELHI · SYDNEY

HART PUBLISHING

Bloomsbury Publishing Plc

Kemp House, Chawley Park, Cumnor Hill, Oxford, OX2 9PH, UK

1385 Broadway, New York, NY 10018, USA

29 Earlsfort Terrace, Dublin 2, Ireland

HART PUBLISHING, the Hart/Stag logo, BLOOMSBURY and the Diana logo are trademarks of Bloomsbury Publishing Plc

First published in Great Britain 2021

A catalogue record for this book is available from the British Library.

Library of Congress Cataloging-in-Publication data

Names: Nalule, Victoria R, author.

Title: Land law and the extractive industries : challenges and opportunities in Africa / Victoria R Nalule.

Description: Oxford, UK ; New York, NY : Hart Publishing, an imprint of Bloomsbury Publishing, 2021. | Series: Global energy law and policy ; volume 7 | Includes bibliographical references and index.

Identifiers: LCCN 2021021414 | ISBN 9781509938421 (hardback) | ISBN 9781509952755 (paperback) | ISBN 9781509938438 (pdf) | ISBN 9781509938445 (Epub)

Subjects: LCSH: Land tenure—Law and legislation—Africa. | Land reform—Law and legislation—Africa. | Mineral industries—Law and legislation—Africa. | Petroleum law and legislation—Africa. | Gas—Law and legislation—Africa.

Classification: LCC KQC201 .N35 2021 | DDC 346.604/32—dc23

LC record available at https://lccn.loc.gov/2021021414

ISBN: HB: 978-1-50993-842-1
ePDF: 978-1-50993-843-8
ePub: 978-1-50993-844-5

Typeset by Compuscript Ltd, Shannon

To the African youth!

PREFACE

Not all countries in the African continent are rich in oil, gas and solid minerals. Those countries fortunate enough to possess these resources have come to rely on them as being crucial for their economic development, although most of these countries have fallen prey of the 'resource curse' conundrum, with many of their citizens remaining poor, and depending on less than the equivalent of a dollar per day. Nevertheless, there have been national, regional and global efforts to tackle the resource curse, and it is believed that through good governance, transparency and accountability, countries can still benefit from their extractive industries. This can be seen through the examples of countries such as Nigeria, South Sudan, Angola, Libya and Algeria that are known for their oil resources. In terms of solid minerals production including gold, cobalt, industrial diamond, bauxite, phosphate, vermiculite and zirconium – African countries stand out as major producers, including South Africa, Botswana, Ghana, Zimbabwe, the Democratic Republic of the Congo, Equatorial Guinea.

There is a growing body of scholarly articles, and national, regional and international initiatives to ensure that these countries benefit from their resources. Law, policies and regulations have been at the centre of these initiatives. Whilst the issue of land has always been highlighted as crucial in the successful operation of the extractives industries, the sector has continued to fall prey to land grabbing, little or no compensation, and gender inequalities in land administration. These land issues were spotlighted in 2018 during my appearance as an Energy and Mining Expert Witness before the Commission of Inquiry into Land Matters in Uganda. Following the enormous volume of cases the Commission handled on land issues in Uganda, they noted the social, environmental and economic issues associated with acquiring land for oil, gas, and solid minerals projects. These land challenges are not unique only to Uganda, but relate also to other African countries including Kenya, Tanzania, Nigeria, Ghana, South Africa, Namibia and many others. Socially, many people are relocated to unfavourable places; economically, local communities are not given adequate compensation; and environmentally, extractive industries are associated with pollution which negatively impacts the agricultural and fishing industries that many local communities are heavily reliant on.

Throughout history, land in Africa has been characterised by conquest and expropriation, the scars of which are still in evidence in countries such as South Africa, Zimbabwe and Namibia. In recent years, however, conflicts and exploitation are the marked features of the land that makes up the African continent, and these greatly influence the socio-economic and political sphere of the nations of Africa. Consequently, there has been increasing discontent among local people with respect to land procedures, including administration and registration, and this has led to enormous land disputes. Moreover, corruption has marred public institutions responsible for administering land in many African countries. It is on this basis that some African countries such as Uganda established the Commission of Inquiry to investigate land matters in 2017. Although there are laws governing land access to varying degrees throughout Africa, the high level of violence associated with land access and extractives in different countries cannot be ignored. The different land tenures including freehold, leasehold and traditional/ customary land tenures are also noted, given that they greatly influence the extractives industries, especially with respect to artisanal and small-scale mining. There is indeed a significant body of extant literature on the subject matter. However, there is a gap in connecting the nexus between land law, energy law and mining law in Africa. It is against this stark background that this book analyses that nexus between land law, energy law and mining law in selected African countries.

ACKNOWLEDGEMENTS

All glory and appreciation go to God the Almighty for the successful publication of this book. I thank my family and friends for their support. Special thanks to my editor, Dr Geoffrey Wood, for his comments on this book.

CONTENTS

LIST OF ABBREVIATIONS

AfCHPR	African Charter on Human and Peoples Rights
ANC	African National Congress
APEC	Asia-Pacific Economic Cooperation
ASM	Artisanal and Small-scale Mining
ACODE	Advocates Coalition for Development and Environment
ALCs	Area Land Committees
BMAU	Budget Monitoring and Accountability Unit
BITs	Bilateral Investment Treaties
BSA	British South Africa Company
CEDAW	Convention on the Elimination of All Forms of Discrimination against Women
CERD	Convention on Elimination of Racial Discrimination
CESCR	Committee on Economic, Social and Cultural Rights
CLA	Community Land Act (Kenya)
CO_2	Carbon Dioxide
COP	Conference of the Parties
CSR	Corporate Social Responsibility
CGV	Chief Government Valuer
DLBs	District Land Boards
DLTs	District Land Tribunals
DPs	Development Partners
DRC	Democratic Republic of Congo
EAC	East African Community
EACREEE	East African Centre for Renewable Energy and Energy Efficiency

ECs	Extractive Companies
ECOWAS	Economic Community of West African States
ECHR	European Convention on Human Rights
ECT	Energy Charter Treaty
EE	Energy Efficiency
EIA	Environmental Impact Assessment
EITI	Extractives Industry Transparency Initiative
ERU	Emission Reduction Unit
EU	European Union
FDIs	Foreign Direct Investments
FPIC	Free Prior Informed Consent
GDP	Gross Domestic product
GH₵	Ghanaian Cedi
GHEITI	Ghana Extractives Industries Transparency Initiative
GHGs	Greenhouse Gases
HRBA	Human Rights-Based Approach
HRIA	Human Rights Impact Assessment
ICCPR	International Covenant on Civil and Political Rights
ICESCR	International Covenant on Economic, Social and Cultural Rights
ICERD	International Convention on the Elimination of All Forms of Racial Discrimination
ICJ	International Court of Justice
ICSID	International Centre for Settlement of Investment Disputes
IEA	International Energy Agency
IEC	International Energy Charter
ILO	International Labour Organization
IMF	International Monetary Fund
IPCC	Intergovernmental Panel on Climate Change
IUCN	International Union for Conservation of Nature

LAS	League of Arab States
LCR	Local Content Requirements
LDC	Least Developed Countries
LPG	Liquid Petroleum Gas
LRTAP	Convention on Long-Range Transboundary Air Pollution
LSM	Large-scale Mining
LAA	Land Acquisition Act
LC	Local Council
LDHC	Land Division of the High Court
LRD	Land Reform Decree
MDAs	Ministries, Departments and Agencies
MEA	Multilateral Environmental Agreement
MIGA	Multilateral Investment Guarantee Agency
MOU	Memorandum of Understanding
NAFTA	North American Free Trade Agreement
NATO	North Atlantic Treaty Organization
NDP	National Development Plan
NFA	National Forestry Authority
NGOs	Non-Governmental Organizations
NLP	National Land Policy
OAU	Organisation of African Unity
OECD	Organisation of Economic Co-operation and Development
PIC	Prior Informed Consent
PGM	Platinum Group Metals
PLA	Public Lands Act
PV	Photovoltaic (Solar)
RE	Renewable Energy
SADC	Southern African Development Community
SCO	Shanghai Cooperation Organization

SO_2	Sulphur Dioxide
TANU	Tanganyika African National Union
UN	United Nations
UNCLOS	United Nations Convention on the Law of the Sea
UNEP	United Nations Environment Programme
UNFCCC	United Nations Framework Convention on Climate Change
UBoS	Uganda Bureau of Statistics
UGX	Uganda Shillings
ULC	Uganda Land Commission
VCLT	Vienna Convention on the Law of Treaties
WBIP	World Bank Inspection Panel
WHO	World Health Organization
WSSD	World Summit on Sustainable Development
WTO	World Trade Organization
WWF	Worldwide Fund for Nature
ZMDC	Zimbabwe Mining Development Corporation

LIST OF TABLES

1

Introduction to Land Law and Extractives in Africa

I. Introduction

This book sets out to survey the various land legislation and reforms as they impact the extractive industries on the African continent. Land reform is the generic term for modifications in the legal and institutional framework governing land policy.[1] In this respect, this book provides an overview of the legal and regulatory framework governing land administration across the African continent. Indeed, Africa is not a single homogeneous geographical unit. However, there are common challenges that are experienced across the continent. The commonality of both the challenges and opportunities relating to the extractive industries has inspired scholars to advocate for regionalism in tackling some of these energy challenges.[2] To date, there has been some effort for regional cooperation in the energy and mining sectors,[3] but few regional efforts have been made regarding land governance.[4] What is common, however, is the various land reforms that have characterised the continent.

Taking the Southern African Development Community (SADC) as an example, most countries in the region have embraced various land reforms following the various national liberalisation movements of the 1980s and 1990s.[5] Consequently,

[1] Although there are different drivers for land reforms in the different parts of the globe: Land reform is basically intended to implement changes in land policy that are designed to realise desired changes in a changing political, economic and social environment.

[2] Nalule, VR, 'Regionalism in Addressing Energy Access Challenges' in *Energy Poverty and Access Challenges in Sub-Saharan Africa* (Palgrave Macmillan 2018) pp 41–89.

[3] In the mining sector, one of the notable regional/continental policy frameworks is the Africa Mining Vision (AMV). AMV was created by the African Union in 2009 to ensure that Africa utilises its mineral resources strategically for broad-based, inclusive development. The AMV looks broadly and deeply at how development can be achieved through the creation of local value, driven by the strategic use of mineral resources in Africa.

[4] Important to note, the International Land Coalition (ILC). Founded in 1995, ILC is a global alliance of civil society and farmers' organisations, United Nations agencies, NGOs and research institutes. ILC created a Land Matrix database, whereby reported land deals are catalogued and triangulated. The Land Matrix reports that of 203 million hectares of land acquisitions reported worldwide, 134 million hectares are in Africa (as of early 2014).

[5] For instance, the creation of the SADC regional organisation had its origins in the struggle to liberate Rhodesia (now Zimbabwe), South Africa and South-West Africa (now Namibia) from white minority rule, which led to the creation of the Front-Line States (FLS). The FLS was later transformed into the Southern African Development Coordination Conference (SADCC) in 1980, and this was later turned into the SADC. For more information see Nalule, VR, 'Regionalism in Addressing Energy Access Challenges' in Nalule, *Energy Poverty and Access Challenges in Sub-Saharan Africa* (Palgrave Macmillan 2018) pp 41–89.

these countries have experienced a gradual shift in landholding patterns and land tenure systems. These land reforms were characterised by the nationalisation of settler lands and foreign commercial capital. For instance, in Zimbabwe, land has been a source of political conflict since colonisation, when the country was known as Rhodesia.[6] After declaring independence from the British in 1965, the white minority government seized control of the vast majority of good agricultural land, leaving the black peasants landless. After a liberation war, Robert Mugabe, the leader of the Zimbabwe African National Union-Patriotic Front (Zanu-PF), won the elections in 1980. The 1990s were characterised by various land reforms including the enactment of the 1992 Land Acquisition Act, which gave government powers to acquire land for resettlement following 'fair compensation'.[7] By 1999, however, 11 million hectares of the richest land were still in the hands of about 4,500 commercial farmers, the great majority of them white. In an effort to address land inequalities in Zimbabwe, the country enforced a policy of compulsory land expropriation without compensation. This was not an accidental policy, since it was already pondered on during the chimurenga (war of liberation) in Zimbabwe. The main aim of the post-2000 land reforms was to redress the historical anomaly of land inequality in the country.[8] This started in 1998 with land occupations/invasions that were formalised by the Zimbabwean Government in 2001. This was after various attempts to address the land issues, including the willing buyer–willing seller policy, and the British reneging on their colonial responsibility to fund land purchases for resettlement.[9]

With respect to the energy and mining sectors, it is clear that the land reforms have had various impacts on the extractive industries and on general economic development in Zimbabwe. However, the often-ignored impact is how the country's 2000 Fast Track Land Reform Programme (FTLRP) positively, and to some extent, negatively impacted the Artisanal and Small-Scale Mining (ASM) sector. For instance, literature indicates that the FTLRP enabled the newly resettled peasant farmers to access natural resources that were previously enclosed and enjoyed by a minority of white farmers under the dualistic agrarian structure inherited from colonialism: this in essence has driven artisanal gold mining in the country.[10]

[6] The British named Rhodesia after the British coloniser and industrialist Cecil John Rhodes.

[7] These land reforms were possible after the expiration of the Lancaster House Agreement in 1990. The Lancaster House Agreement gave special protections to white Zimbabweans for the first 10 years of independence.

[8] Jenjekwa, V and Barnes, L, 'Changes in the Linguistic Landscape Resulting from Zimbabwe's Post-2000 Land Reforms: Recasting the First and Second Chimurenga Narratives' (2018) 49(3) *Language Matters* 67–85.

[9] The land issues in Zimbabwe date as far back as the 1960s. Under British colonial rule and under the white minority government that in 1965 unilaterally declared its independence from Britain, white Rhodesians seized control of the vast majority of good agricultural land, leaving black peasants landless.

[10] Mkodzongi, G and Spiegel, S, 'Artisanal gold mining and farming: livelihood linkages and labour dynamics after land reforms in Zimbabwe' (2019) 55(10) *The Journal of Development Studies* 2145–61.

Besides Zimbabwe, other SADC countries such as Namibia and South Africa are also still struggling with the land issue. Consequently, these countries have formulated national land policies which are in force in Madagascar, Botswana, Malawi, Mozambique, Namibia, South Africa, Tanzania and Zimbabwe. Outside the SADC region, other African countries have also been taking drastic measures to address land issues. For instance, on 8 December 2016, the President of the Republic of Uganda appointed a Commission to inquire into the effectiveness of law, policies and processes of land acquisition, land administration, land management and land registration in Uganda. The Commission, chaired by Justice Catherine Bamugemereire, handed over its report in July 2020. It is estimated that the Commission received 8,528 complaints from 123 districts out of 135 between 2017 and 2019, which constitutes 91 per cent of the total districts. Some of the key issues tackled by the Commission were land issues associated with energy and mining projects.

There are various drivers for land reforms as stipulated in the examples above, the most common of these being the need to tackle land injustices in different countries. As will be discussed in Chapter two of this book, this research employs the theory of justice to analyse the impact of land access on the energy and mining projects in Africa. With the land justice theory, the key aspects include:

- procedure land justice: this focuses on the legal and regulatory processes for accessing land for energy and mining projects (including relocations of affected communities and fair compensation)
- distributive land justice: concerns the distribution of benefits and also the negatives that accrue from using land for extractive projects (including addressing the environmental damage; sharing the oil and mining revenues equally)
- recognition land justice: entails recognising and protecting the land rights of the different local communities (cultural land has to be respected; community and customary land tenures have to be recognised)
- restorative land justice: entails ensuring that the land is rehabilitated at the end of oil and mining activities (this includes mining closures and decommissioning)
- cosmopolitanism land justice: this stems from the notion that we are all citizens of the world, and as such, we should consider the impact of extractives on land use beyond our borders and from a global perspective.

A. The Origin of Land Injustices in Africa Summarised

Besides the examples above, there are various African countries that have enforced land reforms and endeavoured to address land issues associated with the energy and mining sectors.

In Africa, land injustices, specifically ownership inequality, can be traced back to the colonial era, which was characterised by the appropriation of land for white settlers. This was common in countries such as South Africa, Zimbabwe, Swaziland, Namibia, Kenya and many others. After colonisation, many African countries embraced land reforms with the main aim of redressing colonial and post-independence land ownership inequalities. Besides enacting new land laws and policies, drastic measures were taken in countries such as Zambia and Angola, which nationalised the settler and corporate lands.[11] Other reforms have been common in the administration of customary land, specifically introducing registration options for such land in countries such as Uganda and Kenya.[12]

Although there have been various improvements in land governance, land injustices persist, as many people remain landless in the twenty-first century. These injustices have their root in the inequalities created during apartheid in some African countries. For instance, at the end of apartheid in 1994, approximately 82 million hectares of commercial farmland (86 per cent of all farmland) were held by the white minority (10.9 per cent of the population) in South Africa.[13] Although there were several land reforms in South Africa to address land inequalities, in March 2013, nearly 80 per cent of the land was still owned by white minorities. Lack of access to land remains an issue in African countries such as Zimbabwe, South Africa, Kenya and Liberia.

Land conflicts have been the source of political, social and economic tension between the poor people and the rich people. Industrialisation and an increase in large-scale agriculture in Sub-Saharan Africa (SSA) have increased land tension between investors and the local people in many African countries due to the 'land grabbing', with little or no compensation. Goal one of the UN SDG is focused on poverty eradication.[14] Over 80 per cent of people in rural Africa rely on agriculture for their livelihood. In this respect, secure land tenures, sound land policies, and better land administration and distribution are key in not only tackling poverty in SSA, but also in ensuring food security and economic growth.

Outside Africa, effective land reforms have proved to enhance investment opportunities in different countries. For instance, the 1978 agricultural reforms in China were responsible for reducing poverty and increasing agricultural production in the country. The reforms also dismantled collective farming and conferred land rights on households.[15] In Ethiopia, rural small-holders have been empowered following the land certification programme which started in the

[11] Adams, M, 'Land tenure policy and practice in Zambia: issues relating to the development of the agricultural sector' (Draft) (Mokoro 2003).

[12] Chimhowu, A, 2019. 'The "new" African customary land tenure. Characteristic, features and policy implications of a new paradigm' (2019) 81 *Land Use Policy* 897–903.

[13] For more information on land reforms in South Africa, see Gibson, JL, *Overcoming historical injustices: Land reconciliation in South Africa* (Cambridge University Press 2009).

[14] Goal 1 of the United Nations Sustainable Development Goals.

[15] The reforms were initiated in 1978 by Deng Xiaoping, the leader of the Communist Party of China at the time.

late 1990s. The programme is also responsible for reduced land conflicts, increased investments and improved natural resource management.[16]

Whereas colonisation had an impact on the land administration in different Sub-Saharan African countries, the issues of land injustice can also be traced in countries that were never colonised. Ethiopia is the only SSA country that was not colonised. Historically, land tenure systems in Ethiopia were heterogeneous and highly localised. These were mostly communally managed, but this changed during the Imperial Regimes,[17] when uniform land administration policies were introduced (these favoured ownership of land by the elites).[18] Consequently, the peasants were left landless, hence contributing to the 1960s political activism, where demands were made to give the 'land to the tiller'. In the period between 1974 and 1991, land was nationalised, and all tenure agreements were nullified and land redistributed, thus enabling poor people to access land. In an effort to improve on the land tenure security in Ethiopia, a land certification programme was established and piloted by the Tigray Regional State in 1998.[19] Whereas this is a great initiative, there is an ongoing need to ensure that the land certificates are regularly updated. In addition to the land certification system that emerged in the late 1990s and early 2000s, which involved a paper-based land-use certificate, a second phase using geographic information system (GIS) technology is being implemented (generally referred to as the first stage of land registration and certification and the second stage).[20]

Taking stock of the above, it is obvious that many African countries are embracing different initiatives aimed at ensuring land tenure security. Land security is key in not only promoting foreign investments in agriculture, energy and mining sectors; it is also essential in ensuring that the local communities receive protection and full compensation for their land rights or a fair share of returns from investments on their land. Additionally, effective land policies are responsible for promoting social stability, especially in resource-rich areas, where land conflicts are rampant. Furthermore, land governance has become important given the current climate change threats, which directly impact land use, including fishing and farming. Not to mention the negative impacts associated with oil, gas and mining activities on land use, requiring countermeasures such as carbon offset programmes of reforestation – which in turn require documentation of

[16] See Cochrane, L and Hadis, S, 'Functionality of the land certification program in Ethiopia: Exploratory evaluation of the processes of updating certificates' (2019) 8(10) *Land* 149; Deininger, K, Ali, DA, Holden, S and Zevenbergen, J, 'Rural land certification in Ethiopia: Process, initial impact, and implications for other African countries' (2008) 36(10) *World Development* 1786–1812.

[17] Imperial regimes starting from Tewodros (1855–1968) until Haile Sellasse (1930–74).

[18] Cochrane, L and Hadis, S, 'Functionality of the Land Certification Program in Ethiopia: Exploratory Evaluation of the Processes of Updating Certificates' (2019) 8(10) *Land* 149.

[19] The land certification programme was later adopted by Amhara Regional State in 2003, and then Oromia and the Southern Nations, Nationalities and Peoples' Regional States in 2004.

[20] Cochrane, L and Hadis, S, 'Functionality of the Land Certification Program in Ethiopia: Exploratory Evaluation of the Processes of Updating Certificates' (2019) 8(10) *Land* 149.

land rights to identify and secure the rights of tree plantation owners involved in these programmes.

Whereas various land reforms have been spearheaded at the national level, it is imperative to note that international financial institutions such as the World Bank have been involved in financing and advising on land reforms in different countries.[21] In Malawi for instance, the World Bank funded the 2004 land reform programme. The pilot had three key elements: (1) voluntary acquisition by communities of land sold by willing estate owners; (2) resettlement and on-farm development, including transportation of settlers, establishment of shelter, and purchase of basic inputs such as equipment and necessary advisory services; and (3) survey and registration of redistributed land. The project proved the likely future success of Community-driven land redistribution programmes; the market-assisted willing seller–willing buyer (WSWB) approach.[22]

Moving forward, there is a need to empower local institutions in the administration of land. This is due to the fact that land is ineffably local, and due to the customary ownership in many countries the justification for decentralising land administration is potentially strong. Traditional leaders have always played a major role in addressing land conflicts and disputes in their local territories. However, centralised management may be needed to deliver technology, maintain uniform national standards, or ensure quality of services.[23]

B. A Snapshot of Land Access

Basically, access to land is key for the successful operation of oil, gas, energy and mining projects. But what is land? What does it really entail? Land is not the mere solid portion of the earth's surface. Rather, it comprises the portion of the land on the surface of the earth, the portion of the earth below the surface and the space above, including all easements and appurtenances to the land or reputed to be part of or appurtenant to it. The common law definition of land also agrees with the above definition, which is summed up in the Latin maxim: '*quic quid plantatur solo, solo cedit*', literally translated to mean that everything that attaches to the land goes with it.

The theory of land ownership, also referred to as the *ad coelum* theory of ownership, although not relevant in other sectors, is still being relied upon with

[21] Byamugisha FF (ed), 'Agricultural land redistribution and land administration in sub-Saharan Africa: case studies of recent reforms' (The World Bank 2014).

[22] However, the WSWB approach has seemed difficult to implement in countries such as South Africa, where owners of large holdings are unwilling to sell because they have high incentives to hold on to the land.

[23] Byamugisha FF (ed), 'Agricultural land redistribution and land administration in sub-Saharan Africa: case studies of recent reforms' (The World Bank 2014).

respect to natural resources. Historically, courts relied on the theory of '*cuius est solum, eius est usque ad coelum et ad inferos*' ('whoever owns the soil, owns up to the sky and down to the depths'), which literally means that the owner of the surface owns everything from the skies to the centre of the earth.[24] For instance, in the case of Edward Coke in *Bury v Pope* (1587), the court noted:

> And lastly, the earth hath in law a great extent upwards, not only of water as hath been said, but of air, and all other things even up to heaven, for *cujus est solum, ejus est usque ad coelum*, as it is holden.[25]

Furthermore, in *Kelsen v Imperial Tobacco Co (of Great Britain and Northern Ireland) Ltd*, a mandatory injunction was granted ordering the defendants to remove a sign which projected eight inches over the plaintiff's property on the ground that, applying the above principle, this was a trespass.[26] Although the principle of *cuius est solum, eius est usque ad coelum et ad inferos* is still relevant in the extractives industry, it is noted here that the theory faced greater scrutiny with increased technological advancements. For instance, the US Supreme Court in the case of *United States v Causby* held that the *ad coelum doctrine* had no place in the modern world. In this case, the respondent argued that there was a taking of their property, within the meaning of the Fifth Amendment to the Constitution, by frequent and regular flights of army and navy aircraft over their land at low altitudes.[27] The same direction was taken in the case of *Bernstein of Leigh v Skyviews & General Ltd*, wherein it was noted that the landowner's rights do not extend to an unlimited height.[28]

The above cases notwithstanding, the *ad coelum* doctrine remains relevant in the extractives industry, although issues may arise as to how far into the earth's crust can ownership go?[29] This was a main issue addressed in the case of *Star Energy Weald Basin Limited and Another v Bocardo SA*.[30] In their final ruling, the United Kingdom (UK) Supreme Court unanimously affirmed the *ad coelum* doctrine and upheld both the High Court and the Court of Appeal's decisions that deviational drilling to extract oil constituted trespass. In essence, this decision gave the effect that although property ownership does not extend downward 'indefinitely', the owner of the land owns everything below it including the minerals found therein.[31] There are various theories of ownership, as will be discussed in Chapter two. However, this doctrine of *ad coelum* is also still relevant in some African countries.

[24] Olawuyi, DS, *Extractives Industry Law in Africa* (Springer 2018).
[25] Edward Coke in *Bury v Pope* (1587) Cro Eliz 118.
[26] *Kelsen v Imperial Tobacco Co* [1957] 2 QB 334.
[27] *United States v Causby*, 328 US 256 (1946).
[28] *Bernstein of Leigh v Skyviews & General Ltd* [1978] QB 479.
[29] Olawuyi, DS, *Extractives Industry Law in Africa* (Springer 2018).
[30] *Bocardo SA v Star Energy UK Onshore Ltd and another* [2010] UKSC 35.
[31] Olawuyi, DS, 'Ownership and Control of Extractive Resources' in Olawuyi, *Extractives Industry Law in Africa* (Springer 2018) pp 87–107.

As such, with respect to land access in Africa, the owner of land is entitled to compensation in the event that energy or mining projects are to take place on said land. In essence, ownership of land is key in determining who owns the legal rights and title to such land. In some countries citizens have a right to own land, while in other jurisdictions the ownership of land is vested in the state. In Uganda, for instance, the ultimate ownership of land is vested in the country's citizens. In this respect, the supreme law of the land, which is the Constitution under Article 237(1) and (3), vests the ownership of land in the citizens of Uganda. The article further outlines the different tenure systems under which the land can be held. These include: customary; freehold; mailo; and leasehold.[32]

As will be discussed in Chapter two, African countries have different land tenure systems. However, what is common is the historical background surrounding land ownership across the continent. Historically, land in Africa was customarily held and as such was communal land. The spirit behind communal and customary ownership of land lies in the understanding that land has been inherited from the past generation(s) and therefore must be preserved for the present and future generations. In this respect, customarily, land is managed, controlled and administered in trust for the present and future generations. With the current land reforms, however, land is owned in different categories and is understood differently depending on the location, culture, values and norms of the community concerned.

The different land tenures and land laws notwithstanding, when it comes to the extractives industry, there are some commonalities with respect to land administration. This book therefore provides a multijurisdictional and systemic survey of the legal and institutional frameworks established to govern land administration in the context of the extractives industry.

The extractives industry does not only imply extraction of oil, gas and other minerals from the earth's surface. Behind these activities are people, corporations, governments and financial institutions that support the extraction of the resources. Besides issues of ownership and compensation, the finite nature of the extractives industry implies that countries must employ robust measures to ensure mining closures and decommissioning at the end of the project life cycle.[33] The entire process of the extractives industry has an impact on land rights and land use. In essence, the extractives industry comprises two main subsectors: petroleum; and solid minerals. The processes in these sectors, for instance, oil and gas exploration, solid minerals mining, dredging and quarrying, are associated with environmental concerns which directly affect nearby landowners. This book, therefore, analyses these extractive processes in relation to land law and administration. This chapter provides a conceptual overview of the extractives industry and land law in Africa. Section II summarises the key issues associated with ownership and control of

[32] The Constitution of Uganda, 1995, as amended.

[33] Cameron, PD and Stanley, MC, *Oil, gas, and mining: a sourcebook for understanding the extractive industries* (The World Bank 2017).

the extractive resources, and section III spotlights the legal and regulatory frameworks governing the African extractive industries; section IV briefly explores the nexus between land access and extractives; section V outlines the overall aim and structure of the book; and section VI gives the concluding remarks.

II. Ownership and Control of the Extractive Resources

A. Ownership under National Law

Simply defined, ownership refers to the absolute right to possess, enjoy or freely dispose of a resource or commodity. When discussing ownership over natural resources, it is important to note the distinction between natural resources contained in the subsoil and the final extracted resources. This distinction is key due to the basic fact that a natural resource that is not yet extracted is not clearly known in terms of quality and quantity, and as such it is considered immovable property; the financing requirements for both are also different.[34] There are also other key questions to ask with respect to the ownership of natural resources. These include, among others: who owns and controls oil, gas and mineral resources? Is it the central or federal government? Is it a provincial or State government? Or is there private ownership of the oil, gas and mining resources.

The answer to the above questions varies from one jurisdiction to another.

(i) Ownership in Dominial Jurisdictions

In these jurisdictions, the entire ownership and control of all petroleum and mineral resources in, and under, any lands is generally vested in the state. All African countries exercise dominial control and ownership of natural resources. In many African countries, the Constitution is the supreme law of the land and, as such, is the basis for all other laws including those relating to the oil, gas and mining sectors.[35] In Uganda, for instance, the 1995 Constitution (as amended), under Article 244, provides for the exploitation of minerals. The article is to the effect that the exploitation of minerals should be done in the interest of the people, and should consider the interests of the individual landowners, local government and the central government.[36] It should also be noted that the Constitution provides for sovereignty over natural resources and in this respect, the state owns the minerals as a custodian for the people. Although the state owns the resources on behalf of its citizens, it is relevant to note the power given to the citizens over

[34] Olawuyi, DS, *Extractives Industry Law in Africa* (Springer 2018).

[35] See, for instance, Article 2(1) of the Constitution of Uganda, 1995 (as amended). This article provides that the Constitution is the supreme law of Uganda.

[36] Article 244 of the Constitution of Uganda, 1995 (as amended), Laws of Uganda.

the government. For example, in Uganda this is well stipulated under Article 1 of the 1995 Constitution, which states that:

> All power belongs to the people who shall exercise their sovereignty in accordance with this Constitution … all authority in the State emanates from the people of Uganda; and the people shall be governed through their will and consent.[37]

Besides national constitutions, other laws also affirm the sovereignty of the state over natural resources. For instance, in Rwanda, Article 4(1) of the 2018 Law on Mining and Quarry Operations is to the effect that all the rights of ownership and control of materials or quarry products in Rwanda are vested in the state, notwithstanding personal ownership of land and other rights thereto.[38]

(ii) Ownership in Non-Dominial Jurisdictions

In these jurisdictions, private ownership of natural resources by the surface landowner is possible. A good example is the Province of Alberta in Canada which recognises some forms of private ownership of petroleum and natural gas.[39] In the Unites States, the issue of private ownership of mineral resources was expounded on by the Supreme Court of Texas in the case of *Texas Company v WH Daugherty et al*, wherein the Court held that oil and gas beneath the surface of the earth belonged to the person who owned the land.[40] The ruling in this case is in line with the Latin maxim, '*cuius est solum eius usque ad coelum et ad inferos*' mentioned in section I.B above.[41]

In contrast to African countries, in which resources are owned by the central government, in non-dominial jurisdictions like Canada and the United States the resources are controlled by the States or Provinces. For instance, in Canada, Section 109 of the 1867 Constitution Act vests ownership rights to extractive resources with the Provinces in which they are located. As noted previously, all African countries exercise the dominial ownership. As such, investors who wish to acquire rights over natural resources must deal directly with the relevant government to obtain the required licences or concessions. Most African countries follow the sovereign-inspired system where the natural resources are vested in the custody of the state to be managed on behalf of the citizens of the country. This is the case in countries such as Uganda, Lesotho and Ethiopia.[42] Other countries, including Nigeria, Burkina Faso, Sudan, and Tanzania, have the State land system,

[37] Article 1 of the Constitution of Uganda, 1995 (as amended).

[38] Article 4(1) of the 2018 Law on Mining and Quarry Operations No 58/2018.

[39] Olawuyi, DS, 'Ownership and Control of Extractive Resources' in Olawuyi, *Extractives Industry Law in Africa* (Springer 2018) pp 87–107.

[40] See *Texas Company v WH Daugherty et al*, 107 Tex. 226 (Tex. 1915).

[41] See Olawuyi, DS, 'Ownership and Control of Extractive Resources' in Olawuyi, *Extractives Industry Law in Africa* (Springer 2018) 87–107, p 92.

[42] In Ethiopia, this is stipulated under Article 5(1) of Proclamation no 678/2010 Promoting Sustainable Development of Mineral Resources. In Lesotho, this is stipulated in Section 3 of the Mines and Minerals Act, 2005.

wherein the State or local government owns the resources.[43] Nevertheless, there are various systems that apply to the ownership of natural resources in different countries including: the State land system; the sovereign system; and the accession system.

B. Sovereignty Over Natural Resources under International Law

The starting point with respect to ownership of resources is the doctrine of sovereignty over natural resources. The right of peoples to self-determination and their right to a means of subsistence are two of the justifications for permanent sovereignty over natural resources. Besides appearing in the international instruments, the principle of permanent sovereignty over natural resources is also recognised as a principle of international customary law.[44]

Historically, this principle has been recognised as far back as the 1950s. At the eighth session of the Commission on Human Rights in May 1952, Chile presented a draft resolution asserting the principle of permanent sovereignty of states over their natural resources. Consequently, this right is internationally recognised under United Nations (UN) Resolution 523 (VI) of 12 January 1952 and Resolution 626 (VII) of 21 December 1952. In addition to recognising the right to permanent sovereignty over natural resources, the General Assembly, under Resolution 523 (VI), recommended that Members of the UN, within the framework of their general economic policy, should consider the possibility of facilitating through commercial agreements:

- the movement of machinery, equipment and industrial raw materials needed by the underdeveloped countries for their economic development and for the improvement of their standards of living;
- the development of natural resources which can be utilised for the domestic needs of the underdeveloped countries and also for the needs of international trade.

The resolution, however, is quick to state that such commercial agreements should not contain economic or political conditions violating the sovereign rights of the underdeveloped countries, including the right to determine their own plans for economic development.[45]

Moving forward, Resolution 626 (VII), which was passed during the seventh session of the UN General Assembly, also refers to state sovereignty over natural

[43] In Nigeria, this is stipulated under Section 1(1) of the Mines and Minerals Act, 2007. In Tanzania, this is provided for under Section 5 of the Mining Act, 2010.

[44] Nalule, VR, 'Regulation of mining in Africa' in Nalule, *Mining and the Law in Africa: Exploring the social and environmental impacts* (Palgrave Pivot 2020) pp 19–50.

[45] General Assembly Resolution 523 (VI) of 12 January 1952 – Integrated economic development and commercial agreements. This was passed during the UNGA's Sixth Session.

resources: 'Right to exploit freely natural wealth and resources'.[46] The preamble to the resolution states that the General Assembly bears in mind the need for encouraging the under-developed countries in the proper use and exploitation of their natural wealth and resources, and recognises that universal peace cannot be achieved if the under-developed countries are not economically strengthened. The resolution further recognises the fact that the right of peoples to freely use and exploit their natural wealth and resources is inherent in their sovereignty and is in accordance with the purposes and principles of the Charter of the UN. Accordingly, the General Assembly recommended:

> (1) … all member states in the exercise of their right freely to use and exploit their natural wealth and resources wherever deemed desirable by them for their own progress and economic development, to have due regard, consistently with their sovereignty, to the need for maintaining the flow of capital in conditions of security, mutual confidence and economic co-operation among nations.
>
> (2) Further recommends all member states to refrain from acts, direct or indirect, designed to impede the exercise of the sovereignty of any state over its natural resources.[47]

After six years following the passing of the aforementioned resolutions, on 12 December 1958 the UN created a Commission on Permanent Sovereignty over Natural Resources. This was established pursuant to General Assembly Resolution 1314 (XIII). The Commission was instructed to conduct a full survey of the status of permanent sovereignty over natural wealth and resources as a basic constituent of the right to self-determination.[48]

Additionally, in 1962, the General Assembly passed another resolution focused on the protection of the state's right to permanent sovereignty over natural resources. This is Resolution 1803 (XVII) and it emphasises among other things that:

> 1. The right of peoples and nations to permanent sovereignty over their natural wealth and resources must be exercised in the interest of their national development and of the well-being of the people of the State concerned.
> 2. The exploration, development and disposition of such resources, as well as the import of the foreign capital required for these purposes, should be in conformity with the rules and conditions which the peoples and nations freely consider to be necessary or desirable with regard to the authorisation, restriction or prohibition of such activities.
>
> …
>
> 4. Nationalisation, expropriation or requisitioning shall be based on grounds or reasons of public utility security or the national interest which are recognised as overriding purely individual or private interests, both domestic and foreign.

[46] UN General Assembly, 'Right to Exploit Freely Natural Wealth and Resources', 21 December 1952, A/RES/626, can be accessed at, www.refworld.org/docid/3b00f0853e.html. Last accessed on 3 October 2020.

[47] General Assembly Resolution 626 (VII) of 21 December 1952 – Right to Exploit Freely Natural Wealth and Resources. This was passed during the Seventh Session.

[48] Resolution 1314 (XIII) of the Commission on Permanent Sovereignty over Natural Resources of 12 December 1958.

> In such cases, the owner shall be paid appropriate compensation in accordance with the rules in force in the State taking such measures in the exercise of its sovereignty and in accordance with international law.[49]

Other relevant international instruments affirming the principle of state sovereignty over their natural resources include: the International Covenant on Economic, Social and Cultural Rights, which was adopted in 1966 by General Assembly Resolution 2200 A (XXI);[50] OPEC's 1968 Resolution;[51] and Principle 10 of the Stockholm Declaration of 1972.[52] This follows the UN Conference on the Environment of 1972, and is later reflected in the 1992 Rio Declaration on the Environment and Development – specifically Principle 2 – which is to the effect that states have the sovereign right to exploit their own resources pursuant to their own environmental and developmental policies. In 1974, the principle of sovereignty over natural resources was once more asserted within the framework of the UN through the Charter of Economic Rights and Duties of States of 12 December 1974.[53]

Article 13 of the 1974 Vienna Convention on Succession of States in respect of Treaties also emphasises the state's sovereignty over natural resources. The same right is asserted under Article 21, paragraph (1) of the African Charter on Human and Peoples Rights of 1981. There is indeed case law which interprets Article 21 as stipulated in the case of *Social and Economic Rights Action Center and the Center for Economic and Social Rights v Nigeria*, a case which was decided by the African Commission on Human and People's Rights.[54]

Additionally to the international instruments discussed in this sub-section, national constitutions, and the energy and mining laws of different African countries also affirm sovereignty over natural resources. These will be discussed in detail in the next chapters.

III. Legal and Regulatory Frameworks Governing the Extractive Industries

Having in place laws and regulations is key in the governance of the extractive industries. There are various laws at the national, regional and international

[49] General Assembly Resolution 1803 (XVII) of 14 December 1962 – Permanent Sovereignty over Natural Resources.

[50] Resolution 2200 A (XXI) of 16 December 1966 – International Covenant on Economic, Social and Cultural Rights.

[51] OPEC Resolution XVI.90 of 24 June 1968 – Declaratory Statement of Petroleum Policy in Member Countries.

[52] Stockholm Declaration of 1972.

[53] General Assembly Resolution 3281 (XXIX) of 12 December 1974 – Charter of Economic Rights and Duties of States.

[54] African Commission on Human and People's Rights, Communication no 155–96 of 13 October 2001: *Social and Economic Rights Action Center (SERAC) and Center for Economic and Social Rights v Nigeria.*

levels aimed at regulating the extractive industries. These laws are also categorised depending on the sector concerned. For instance, in most African countries, they have separate laws governing the energy sector, the mining sector, and oil and gas. Recently, countries have also gone ahead to enact climate change laws. Basically, the nexus between climate change and the energy sector lies in the fact that fossil fuels are the main contributor to climate change as they produce around 60 per cent of greenhouse gases (GHGs). As such, Renewable Energy (RE) is seen as not only being essential in tackling energy poverty, but also for addressing climate change.[55] Additionally, the UN Intergovernmental Panel on Climate Change (IPCC) issued a warning in 2018 that humanity had just 12 years to limit global warming to below 2°C.[56]

In sub-section III.C below, a brief overview of the main energy and mining laws and regulations will be discussed. Prior to that, it is imperative to note the role of international law in resource extraction.

A. Role of International Law

The starting point for international law is the preamble of the UN Charter, which notes that 'the peoples of the United Nations aim to … establish conditions under which justice and respect for the obligations arising from treaties and other sources of international law can be maintained'.[57] There are various international instruments with respect to energy governance. The most common one is the Energy Charter Treaty (ECT). The ECT has been recognised as a unique multilateral instrument in the energy sector.[58] The origins of the ECT need to be understood in the European countries' interest to trade with countries in the East following the unexpected collapse of the Soviet Union in 1991.[59] Although the ECT initially covered a limited range of countries, recent developments have seen an expansion in the application of the principles of the ECT to various regions including Asia, Africa, and Latin America, and this expansion

[55] Nalule, VR, *Energy Poverty and Access Challenges in Sub-Saharan Africa: The Role of Regionalism* (Springer 2018).

[56] Intergovernmental Panel on Climate Change (IPCC), 'Global Warming of 1.5°C – A Special Report' (2018). https://www.ipcc.ch/sr15/.

[57] Charter of the United Nations (Adopted June 26 1945, entered into force on 24 October 1945).

[58] See Wälde, TW, 'Investment Arbitration Under the Energy Charter Treaty – From Dispute Settlement to Treaty Implementation' (1996) 12(4) *Arbitration International* 429–66.

[59] The collapse of the Soviet Union in 1991 led to a rise in independent nations (some of which were very rich in energy resources) eager to join the international market. The West responded in several ways including offering the new states membership of the European Union; inviting them to join the General Agreement on Trade and Tariffs (GATT); and an offer of formal cooperation in the energy sector leading to the Energy Charter Treaty, which was signed by some 50 states and the European Community on 17 December 1994. For a full discussion on this, see Cameron, P, *International Energy Investment Law: The Pursuit of Stability* (Oxford University Press 2009) p 152.

was made possible following the adoption of the International Energy Charter (IEC) in 2015.[60]

International energy and mining instruments will be expounded on in Chapter four. However, what is important to note here is that the laws of treaties is set out in the 1969 Vienna Convention of the Law of Treaties (VCLT), which essentially defines a treaty as 'an international agreement concluded between states in written form and governed by international law, whether embodied in a single instrument or in two or more related instruments and whatever its particular designation'.[61] There are also regional treaties aimed at governing and regulating the energy sector at a regional level, as discussed below.

B. Role of Regional Energy Laws

(i) The Treaty Establishing the Economic Community of West African States (ECOWAS), 1975

ECOWAS is established under Article 2 of the ECOWAS Treaty of 28 May 1975. The main aim of the Community is stipulated in Article 3 which states that,

> The aims of the Community are to promote co-operation and integration, leading to the establishment of the economic union in West Africa in order to raise the living standards of its people … enhance economic stability …[62]

In 2003, ECOWAS adopted an Energy Protocol with the aim of promoting further cooperation in the energy sector among the member states.[63] Appendix II to this book outlines the main provisions of the ECOWAS Energy Protocol with respect to investment protection in the energy sector.

(ii) Treaty of the Southern Africa Development Community, 1992 (SADC Treaty)

SADC is established under Article 2 of the 1992 Treaty with its headquarters at Gaborone, Republic of Botswana. The objectives of SADC include, among others, achieving development, economic growth and poverty alleviation through regional integration.[64] The Treaty encourages member states to cooperate in areas such as infrastructure, natural resources and the environment.[65] The SADC Protocol on

[60] The IEC has been adopted and signed by over 80 countries and organisations including, among others, the United States, China, Burundi, Uganda, Chad the ECOWAS, EAC and the EU.
[61] Vienna Convention on the Law of Treaties, 23 May 1969, 1155 UNTS 331.
[62] Article 3(1) of the ECOWAS Revised Treaty.
[63] ECOWAS Energy Protocol, 2003.
[64] Article 5(1)(a) of the 1992 SADC Treaty.
[65] Article 21(3) of the 1992 SADC Treaty.

Energy was passed in 1996 with the main aim of ensuring regional cooperation in the energy sector.[66]

The next sub-section merely provides an introductory text on international and national instruments/ laws regulating the extractive industries. The relevant mining laws and regulations will be discussed briefly, drawing on examples from different African countries.

C. Snapshot of Mining Laws and Regulations in Africa

Legislation of the mining sector in Africa has been going through a transformative process and different mining codes have characterised a particular stage in this process. These codes are divided into different generations, including: the first generation which entails mining legislation of the 1980s; the second generation which entails mining legislation of the early and mid-1990s; and the third generation which refers to mining legislation of the late 1990s. The new wave of reforms in the current mining laws can arguably be referred to as the fourth generation of mining codes.[67]

(i) Mining Laws: The Case of Ghana

Ghana was the first country in SSA to gain independence, in 1957. The country is the second-fastest growing economy in Africa after Ethiopia.[68] The country is very rich in mineral resources including gold, manganese, bauxite, industrial diamonds, timber, rubber, silver, salt and limestone, just to mention a few. Gold and bauxite alone account for 64.4 per cent of Ghana's primary exports. Gold is one of the important minerals as it contributes to more than 90 per cent of the total value of the country's mineral wealth; this explains why in the past the country was called the Gold Coast. Ghana's gold production as of December 2018, was reported at 130 million kg, an increase from the 128 million kg reported in December 2017.[69] Additionally, the country's reserves averaged 8.73 tonnes from 2000 until 2019.[70]

Additionally, according to the Ghana Extractive Industries Transparency Initiative (GHEITI), the mining sector contributed GH¢1285 million to government revenue in 2015 as against GH¢1193 million in the year 2014. This represented an increase of 7.79 per cent over the previous year's figure.[71] Of the

[66] SADC Protocol on Energy, 1996.

[67] Nalule, VR, 'Regulation of mining in Africa' in Nalule, *Mining and the Law in Africa: Exploring the social and environmental impacts* (Palgrave Pivot 2020) pp 19–50.

[68] World Bank, 'Ghana Overview', can be accessed at, www.worldbank.org/en/country/ghana/overview, last visited on 6 August 2020.

[69] CEIC, 'Ghana Gold Production', can be accessed at, www.ceicdata.com/en/indicator/ghana/gold-production, last visited on 6 August 2020.

[70] Gold reserves are a country's gold assets held or controlled by the central bank.

[71] GHEITI, GHEITI Mining Sector Report for 2015 (2018), can be accessed at, https://eiti.org/sites/default/files/documents/2015_gheiti_mining_report.pdf.

total earnings from mineral exports in 2015 (US$3322.61 million), gold accounted for US$3212.59 million (96.68 per cent), bauxite exports were US$41.06 million (1.24 per cent),[72] while diamonds contributed US$4.22 million (0.31 per cent) and manganese brought in US$64.74 million (1.95 per cent).[73]

Drawing from the discussion above, it is clear that the mining sector greatly contributes to Ghana's economy. However, this has not always been the case, as for decades the country hardly benefited from the sector due to the unfavourable legal regime. Currently, the main laws governing the mining sector in Ghana include: The Mining and Minerals Act 2006 (Act 703); Minerals Commission Act, 1993 (Act 450); The 1992 Constitution of Ghana; Environmental Assessment Regulations 1999 (LI 1652); Mining Regulations including those for Health and Safety; Explosives and Crops compensations. All these laws are essential to the governance of the mining sector. For instance, the Minerals Commission Act, 1993 (Act 450) established the Minerals Commission as a corporate body to regulate and manage the utilisation of minerals and the coordination of policies related to them.

(ii) Mining Laws: Other Countries

In Uganda, there is the 2003 Mining Act. Besides their constitutions and mining acts, countries have in place other relevant regulations governing the mining sector. For instance, Rwanda has enacted a number of regulations for the mining sector, each touching or regulating in part ASM as elaborated below:

(a) Ministerial order on determining requirements for granted authorisations to import, manufacture, transport, trade in and use of dynamite in mining and quarry operations.[74]
(b) Regulations on determining the nature, amount and terms of the financial deposit that forms the rehabilitation guarantee:[75] These regulations aim at ensuring that mining or quarry licence-holders will rehabilitate the environment in respect of any degradation as a result of mining and quarrying operations.
(c) Regulations on determining the format and content of a mineral licence and the content of an agreement with mining or industrial quarry licence-holders:[76] This provides a sample format and content of small-scale mining licences and the contents of an agreement for mineral or industrial quarry exploitation licences for small-scale mining (contained in annexes I and V).

[72] Bauxite has been mined in Ghana since the 1940s. Currently, Chinese corporations are the most prominent in the industry through Bonsai Minerals Group's ownership of Ghana Bauxite Company. Ghana has large deposits of good quality bauxite in the western, eastern and Ashanti regions.
[73] GHEITI, GHEITI Mining Sector Report for 2015 (2018), can be accessed at, https://eiti.org/sites/default/files/documents/2015_gheiti_mining_report.pdf.
[74] Ministerial order No 013/MOJA/AG/19 of 16/07/2019.
[75] Regulations No 001/mines/RMB/2019 of 18/07/2019.
[76] Regulations No 004/mines/RMB/2019 of 18/07/2019.

(d) Regulations on determining the potential mining areas, criteria for the categorisation of mines, modalities and requirements for mineral licence applications and tenders.[77]

(e) Regulations on determining categories of quarries, requirements for acquisition of a quarry licence and reporting.[78]

D. Snapshot of Energy Laws and Regulations in Africa

With respect to energy laws, it is noted here that some countries have separate laws governing the oil and gas sector, the electricity sector, and the RE sector. In Uganda, for instance, the main laws relevant to the oil and gas sector include:

- The Constitution of the Republic of Uganda, 1995.
- The Petroleum (Exploration, Development and Production) Act 2013.
- The Petroleum (Refinery, Conversion, Transmission and Midstream Storage) Act 2013.
- The Public Finance Management Act 2015.

Additionally to the Constitution, there are specific RE laws and policies governing the deployment of renewable technologies. These have become important given the global move to transition to a low-carbon economy and also tackle climate change. These are highlighted in Table 1.1.

Table 1.1 Renewable Energy and Energy Efficiency Laws

Country	Sierra Leone	Uganda	Nigeria
Laws and policies	Energy Efficiency of 2016; Renewable Energy Policy 2016; National Energy Policy 2009; Medium-Term National Development Plan 2019–2023.	Biofuels Act 2018; Renewable Energy Policy 2007–2017; Atomic Energy Act 2008; Renewable Energy Policy, 2007; Energy Policy for Uganda, 2002.	National Renewable Energy and Energy Efficiency Policy, 2015; National Electric Power Policy 2001; Environmental Impact Assessment Act, 2004; Regulations on Feed-In-Tariffs for Renewable Energy Sourced Electricity in Nigeria; Nigeria Energy Efficiency Action Plan (2015–2030).

Source: Author.

[77] Regulations No 005/mines/RMB/2019 of 18/07/2019.
[78] Regulations No 007/mines/RMB/2019 of 18/07/2019.

As illustrated in Table 1.1, there are various laws and policies that support the deployment of RE and Energy Efficiency (EE) technologies in different countries. For instance, the 2016 Energy Efficiency Policy in Sierra Leone highlights different objectives including, among others: to ensure the development and prudent exploitation of the nation's energy resources, with diversified energy resource options, in order to enhance energy security and self-reliance, as well as to achieve an efficient energy delivery system with an optimal energy resource mix. The 2016 Renewable Energy Policy also highlights objectives that are in line with the global energy transition debate including, among others: to guarantee an adequate, reliable, affordable, equitable and sustainable supply of RE in a cost-reflective and environmentally-friendly manner.[79]

The issue of energy access has been cited among different SSA countries as being the springboard for the continued debate for these countries to utilise fossil fuels in the energy transition era.[80] Consequently, in the case study below, the energy profile of Swaziland is highlighted, specifically spotlighting the electricity situation and the relevant electricity laws in the country.

(i) Case of the Kingdom of Swaziland

Swaziland, officially known as the Kingdom of Swaziland, is a landlocked country with a Gross Domestic product (GDP) per capita of about US$3,000.[81] The country's economy primarily relies on agriculture as its main sector.[82] In energy terms, the country has no known oil or natural gas reserves, although it is rich in coal and renewable resources such as solar power.[83] Access to electricity is still a major challenge in the country as only 55 per cent of the 1 million inhabitants have access to electricity, mostly in urban areas. Swaziland Electricity Company (SEC) is engaged

[79] For more details, see Nalule, VR, 'How to Respond to Energy Transitions in Africa: Introducing the Energy Progression Dialogue' in Nalule, *Energy Transitions and the Future of the African Energy Sector* (Palgrave Macmillan 2021) pp 3–35.

[80] Nalule, VR, 'Transitioning to a Low Carbon Economy: Is Africa Ready to Bid Farewell to Fossil Fuels?' in Wood, G and Baker, K (eds), *The Palgrave Handbook of Managing Fossil Fuels and Energy Transitions* (Palgrave Macmillan 2020) pp 261–86.

[81] Swaziland is considered as a lower middle-income country and is closely linked to South Africa on which it depends for about 85% of its imports and about 60% of its exports. See the World Bank in Swaziland, www.worldbank.org/en/country/swaziland/overview. Last updated on 1 April, 2017. Last accessed on 18 March 2018.

[82] Swaziland's economy has been declining at a high rate, with growth projected to have declined to −0.06% in 2016 from 1.7% in 2015. This has been attributed to the decline in agricultural production as a result of the El Niño-induced drought. The drought negatively affected rain-fed crops such as maize and cotton, and irrigated crops including sugar cane. Additionally, Swaziland's economy was affected by the large decline in revenues from the Southern Africa Customs Union. See African Economic Outlook 2017, Swaziland Report, 2017 (OECD Publishing 2017). It can be accessed at, www.oecd-ilibrary.org/development/african-economic-outlook-2017_aeo-2017-en. Last visited on 10 March 2021.

[83] Coal reserves are estimated at 158.73 million short tons. See Swaziland Data Portal: Swaziland Coal Reserves, http://swaziland.opendataforafrica.org/wualcof/swaziland-coal-reserves. Last visited on 18 March 2018.

in the business of generation, transmission and distribution of electricity and the import and export of electricity to and from Swaziland.[84] The Electricity Act of 2007 governs the electricity sector and provides for the regulation of the electricity supply industry. The Act regulates the generation, transmission, distribution and supply of electricity in the country.[85] The Energy Regulatory Authority (ERA) was also established under the 2007 Electricity Act.[86]

Investments are needed to further develop the country's energy sector. The Swaziland Investment Promotion Act of 1998 regulates the investment sector and offers protection to investors and their property.[87] The Act also established the Swaziland Investment Promotion Authority (SIPA) to promote and facilitate foreign direct and local investment into the country, partly through providing a one-stop information and support facility to investors.[88]

There are various energy laws as will be discussed in Chapter 4. As mentioned previously, this section is only intended to provide an introductory text concerning the regulation of the energy and mining sectors in Africa. In the next section, the nexus between land access and extractives will be briefly discussed.

IV. Nexus between Land Access and Extractives

A. The African Extractives Industry: Highlighting the Land Issues

The extractives industry has been associated with economic development especially for resource-rich African countries since this sector contributes significantly to GDP. However, in some resource-rich countries, not much of this revenue has been reflected in infrastructural developments such as roads, schools, and hospitals.[89] In essence, this is what scholars have referred to as the resource curse.

[84] The Swaziland Electricity Company Act of 2007 transformed the Swaziland Electricity Board into a company called Swaziland Electricity Company.

[85] The Electricity Act of 1963 was repealed as a result of the promulgation of the Electricity Act of 2007 on 1 March 2007.

[86] The authority was established with powers and functions including: receiving and processing applications for licences; modifying and varying licences; and monitoring the performance and the efficiency of licensed operators among others.

[87] The Act stipulates that investors' property shall not be compulsorily acquired except in certain circumstances, namely: in accordance with applicable legal procedures; in the public interest; done without discrimination; and upon prompt payment of adequate and fair compensation. See Section 20 of the Swaziland Investment Promotion Act, 1998.

[88] The SIPA is established under Section 3 of the Swaziland Investment Promotion Act, 1998. There are also several incentives for investors including the repatriation of profits and fully-serviced industrial sites. Financial incentives for all investors also include tax allowances and deductions for new enterprises, exemption from withholding tax on dividends, and a low corporate tax.

[89] Nalule, VR, *Mining and the Law in Africa: Exploring the social and environmental impacts* (Palgrave Pivot 2020).

Simply defined, the resource curse or the paradox of plenty, refers to a situation where resource-rich countries are characterised by poverty, less economic growth and less democracy than countries with fewer natural resources. Indeed, it is worth briefly exploring the issue of the resource curse, as this is also an important aspect in understanding the land law reforms in different resource-rich African countries.

Basically, the negative correlation between economic growth and natural resources is puzzling. On the one hand, countries with little natural wealth have been some of the fastest growing economies over the last few decades including Hong Kong, Singapore, Korea and Taiwan.[90] On the other hand, countries endowed with massive natural resources are among the poorest. Examples of such countries include Sierra Leone, the Democratic Republic of Congo, and Angola.

(i) The Case of Sierra Leone

A cursory look at the case study of Sierra Leone reveals that the country is known for diamonds, rutile, bauxite, gold, iron ore, limonite, platinum, chromite, and coltan. These resources have, however, been associated with the instability and civil war that the country suffered in the past. The civil war, which began on 23 March 1991, lasted for 11 years and left over 50,000 people dead.[91]

The nexus between the resource curse and land access therefore can be understood in some of the negative impacts associated with it such as the relocation and displacement of people from their land due to civil war, as was the case in Sierra Leone. Consequently, in order to address issues associated with relocations, the country must embrace robust land reforms to ensure that people do settle peacefully following a civil war or other land-related disputes. Earlier studies that focused on post-war Sierra Leone highlighted various challenges that the country was experiencing in reconstruction and development. Some of the challenges highlighted included food insecurity and limited access to mining land by poor people.[92] In recent years, studies have shown that the communities in the mining areas of Sierra Leone (such as Bonthe district – Sierra Rutile Limited (SRL); Kono district – Octea Mining Company (OMC); and Port Loko district – Sierra Leone Mining Company (SLM)) are still faced with land issues that are a result of the negative environmental impacts associated with mining.[93] Additionally, the issue of 'blood diamonds' was also a marked feature of the civil war.[94] Although there

[90] Boschini, AD, Pettersson, J and Roine, J, 'Resource curse or not: A question of appropriability' (2007) 109(3) *Scandinavian Journal of Economics* 593–617.

[91] Isiani, MC and Ihediwa, NC, 'War and Gender: Socio-Economic Reflections on the Sierra Leonean Civil War' (2019) (3) *Cogito: Multidisciplinary Research Journal* 133–59.

[92] Unruh, JD and Turray, H, 'Land tenure, food security and investment in postwar Sierra Leone'. Food and Agriculture Organization of the UN, *LSP Working Paper 22* (2006).

[93] For more details, see Mabey, PT, Li, W, Sundufu, AJ and Lashari, AH, 'Environmental impacts: Local perspectives of selected mining edge communities in Sierra Leone' (2020) 12(14) *Sustainability* 5525.

[94] The term 'blood diamonds' refers to the diamonds mined or sold in conflict countries. For instance, during the civil wars in Sierra Leone, Ivory Coast, Liberia, Angola and Guinea Bissau.

have been initiatives to tackle the issue of the illegal diamond market in post-conflict Sierra Leone, some scholars do note that the illegal diamond economy has largely been peacefully integrated into the social and economic order of the post-conflict society, implying that it has been accepted as a moral economy of illegality.[95] Whereas not directly connected, all issues relating to mining do definitely raise environmental concerns – which in effect impact land use (such as farming and fishing). The issue of land access and mining will be illustrated further in Chapter three, but the key aim in this sub-section is to highlight the nexus between a resource curse and land access in resource-rich countries.

The above notwithstanding, it has been proved that if these resources are well managed, then countries can escape the resource curse, as was the case in Norway, Australia, Botswana and South Africa. With good governance and transparency, natural resources can be utilised for the inclusive social and economic development of a country's citizens.[96] Additionally, global initiatives such as the Extractive Industry Transparency Initiative (EITI) have contributed greatly to ensuring transparency and accountability in the management of natural resources.[97]

(ii) Other Cases Explored

Moving forward, in recent years, many African countries such as Ghana, Uganda and Kenya have attracted enormous investment in their respective energy and mining sectors. These countries are home to enormous mineral reserves including, among others, gold, copper, iron ore, steel, tin, tungsten, refined cobalt, salt, and refined lead. For instance, in Uganda, these minerals are geographically distributed across the country and are found in areas such as Kamwenge, Karamonja, Busia, Tororo, Kanungu, Mubende, Moroto, and Gulu to mention just a few.[98]

With respect to hydrocarbons, African countries including Nigeria, Algeria, South Sudan, Mozambique, and Angola are at the centre of oil and gas production in the African continent. New discoveries have also been made in countries such as Uganda, Ghana, Kenya, Chad and Niger. Uganda, for instance, discovered commercially viable quantities of petroleum in 2006, and is estimated to hold 6.5 billion barrels of which 1.2–1.7 billion barrels are estimated to be recoverable, and 500 billion cubic feet of proven reserves of natural gas.[99] Hydrocarbon discoveries and development have necessitated investments in energy infrastructure. For instance, on 10 September 2020, Uganda concluded and signed with Total, a Host

[95] For more details, see Engwicht, N, 'After blood diamonds: The moral economy of illegality in the Sierra Leonean diamond market' *MPIfG Discussion Paper, No 16/9* (2016).

[96] Elwerfelli, A and Benhin, JK, 'Oil a blessing or curse: A comparative assessment of Nigeria, Norway and the United Arab Emirates' (2018) 8(5) *Theoretical Economics Letters* 1136–60.

[97] Onditi, F, 'From resource curse to institutional incompatibility: a comparative study of Nigeria and Norway oil resource governance' (2019) 11(2) *Africa Review* 152–71.

[98] Nalule, VR and Ayebare, RT, 'Uganda: Mineral Policy' in Tiess, G, Majumder, T and Cameron, P (eds), *Encyclopedia of Mineral and Energy Policy* (Springer 2018).

[99] ibid.

Government Agreement (HGA) for the East Africa Crude Oil pipeline (EACOP) project.[100] Further, in high anticipation of the country benefitting from fossil fuels, Uganda and Tanzania, represented by the heads of state, finally signed the agreement to construct the 1,445 km (898 mile) EACOP. This US$3.5 billion project is intended to connect Uganda's oil fields to Tanzania's port of Tanga.[101] Gas infrastructure is evident in varied oil-rich countries. For instance, on 30 June 2020, President Muhammadu Buhari launched a US$2.6 billion gas pipeline project in Nigeria. The 614 km-long pipeline will run from Ajaokuta to Kano under the auspices of the Nigerian National Petroleum Corporation.[102]

As illustrated in the Ugandan and Nigerian examples above, energy projects are very expensive ventures, requiring significant amounts of (typically upfront) capital. Besides this, these projects also require massive areas of land to be effective. In the acquisition of the required land, however, social, environmental and economic issues do arise. Socially, many people are relocated to unfavourable places; economically, local communities are not given adequate compensation; and environmentally, extractive industries are associated with pollution which negatively impacts on the agricultural and fishing industries that the local communities inevitably depend on. This book will cover all these issues in detail. However, this section simply highlights the pertinent issues relating to land access and extractives, with a focus on relocation and environmental impacts. The main question to be addressed in this section is: What is the nexus between land and extractives? This question indeed forms the basis for this entire book, although it will be briefly addressed in the next sub-section.

B. Snapshot of the Impacts of Extractives on Land Use

A person is entitled to compensation if energy or mining projects are to be conducted on his/her land. Although people are often compensated for their land before energy projects are approved, there are various land uses such as agriculture and fishing that do directly have an impact on people's everyday lives. These activities are obviously affected by the large-scale acquisition of land for energy and mining projects. Additionally, the negative environmental impacts associated with the extractive industries make it impossible for people to fully utilise their land for economic benefit. Consequently, the negative

[100] Uganda New Vision: 'Uganda, Total sign key oil pipeline agreement'. Can be accessed at, www.newvision.co.ug/news/1526795/uganda-total-sign-key-oil-pipeline-agreement. Last accessed on 12 September 2020.

[101] BBC News: 'Uganda and Tanzania sign US$3.5bn oil pipeline deal'. Can be accessed at, www.bbc.co.uk/news/world-africa-54137090. Last accessed on 15 September 2020.

[102] *The Guardian*: 'Unlocking Nigeria's economic possibilities via gas infrastructure'. Can be accessed at, https://guardian.ng/energy/unlocking-nigerias-economic-possibilities-via-gas-infrastructure/. Last accessed on 10 September 2020.

impacts of extractives on land use have escalated poverty, especially for the rural communities that rely heavily on the land.

It is worth noting that a majority of the people in developing countries such as those in Africa do live in rural areas. These people heavily rely on land for survival, specifically through carrying out agricultural activities. There is indeed a significant connection between land access and the UN Sustainable Development Goal (SDG) 1 on poverty alleviation. It has been submitted that a great majority of rural folk, even in developed countries, are left poor because they are denied the means for self-improvement due to restricted access to their most basic need and resource – which is land.[103] This has necessitated various land reforms in different parts of the globe: these reforms are characterised by the need to ensure the redistribution of wealth and the promotion of economic development. This situation therefore points to the trilemma between the UN SDG 1 on poverty eradication, land access and extractives.

Eradicating poverty in all its forms is Goal 1 of the UN SDGs. Although there are global, regional and national initiatives to achieve this goal, these efforts will be greatly affected by the recent coronavirus pandemic. First detected in December 2019, in Wuhan City in the People's Republic of China, the disease has since spread to more than 114 countries affecting all sectors of the economies of these countries and indeed the entire world. The COVID-19 crisis has indeed tested the relevance of the energy sector especially in the economic sphere. Due to the several waves of lockdown, energy consumption in the transport and manufacturing industries has drastically reduced. With most factories shut globally, there have been supply-chain disruptions in key RE materials including solar panels, electricals and other materials needed in the energy sector, especially with this global move to transition to a low carbon economy.[104] These disruptions have also had an impact on RE projects in different countries, especially since many companies operating in these countries are foreign energy companies.[105]

Besides the impact on the energy sector, according to recent research, it is feared that the COVID-19 crisis will also negatively impact on the various efforts to eradicate poverty. Although there have been efforts to reduce poverty, with records showing that the number of people living in extreme poverty declined from 36 per cent in 1990 to 10 per cent in 2015,[106] this number has not been fully represented in developing resource-rich African nations. Additionally, with

[103] King, R, *Land reform: A world survey* (Routledge 2019).

[104] Nalule, VR, 'Energy Access Challenges in the COVID-19 crisis: Is there a future for Extractives in the Energy Transition Era'. *Extractives Hub Research Insight*, May 2020.

[105] Nalule, VR, 'Energy Access Challenges in the COVID-19 crisis: Is there a future for Extractives in the Energy Transition Era'. *Extractives Hub Research Insight*, May 2020.

[106] United Nations Sustainable Development Goals: Goal 1 on Poverty eradication. Can be accessed at, www.un.org/sustainabledevelopment/poverty/. Last visited 1 October 2020.

the current pandemic, experts are warning that poverty will escalate, affecting an estimated 8 per cent of the total human population.[107] Before the outbreak of the COVID-19 pandemic, many people were recorded to be living below the poverty line. Reliable data shows that already more than 700 million people, which is 10 per cent of the world population, still live in extreme poverty. The number is high in SSA, with the majority of people there relying on less than US$1.90 a day. This is despite the fact that some of these countries are endowed with massive energy and mineral resources.

Although there are some countries such as Botswana that have utilised the resources to pull people out of poverty, some countries have been marred with corruption and power governance. As such, resource extraction and production in many of the African countries has not fostered corresponding economic, social, and environmental development and growth for their citizens.[108] Mismanagement of extractives industry revenue has been evident in countries such as Nigeria, where it is estimated that at least US$400 billion of the country's oil revenue has been stolen or misspent since independence in 1960.[109] There are various cases of mismanagement which will not be dealt with exhaustively in this chapter. However, the focus is how extractive industries negatively impact on land, hence escalating poverty. So, what is the trilemma between extractives, land access and poverty? In addressing this nexus, this chapter will examine the case study of Nigeria's Niger Delta, specifically highlighting the environmental negative impacts of the extractive industries, which in turn have negatively impacted local communities both socially and economically.

(i) Case of the Niger Delta

What is the trilemma between extractives, poverty and land access? To sum up the answer, the nexus lies in the fact that extractives industry activities are characterised by various environmental impacts that affect the use of land, especially for farming and fishing. In Nigeria, the local communities in the Niger Delta region have suffered the impacts associated with gas flaring and oil spills, making it hard for them to utilise their land. An 'oil spill' is defined as the accidental release of a liquid petroleum hydrocarbon into the environment due to human activity. In Nigeria, there are several causes of oil spills, and it has been noted that approximately 50 per cent of the spills are attributable to pipeline vandalism and tanker

[107] United Nations Sustainable Development Goals: Goal 1 on Poverty eradication. Can be accessed at, www.un.org/sustainabledevelopment/poverty/. Last visited 1 October 2020.

[108] Olawuyi, DS, 'Introduction' in Olawuyi, *Extractives Industry Law in Africa* (Springer 2018) pp 3–17.

[109] Olawuyi, DS, 'Introduction' in Olawuyi, *Extractives Industry Law in Africa* (Springer 2018) pp 3–17, at p 6.

accidents; 28 per cent of spills are due to sabotage; production and operation account for 21 per cent; and the remaining 1 per cent is due to deficient equipment used in production. Additionally, the deliberate blowing up of pipelines by militant groups has also increased oil spillage in the Niger Delta region.[110] Oil spills are very prevalent in Nigeria and it is estimated that between 1 million and 13 million tons of hydrocarbons have been spilled in the region over the last 50 years. These have led to the destruction of rainforest habitat occupying land equating to 7,400 km^2, the loss of mangrove forests, the destruction of an equivalent of a year's supply of food, and causing strange diseases afflicting the local people, just to mention but a few.[111]

The issue of oil spills in the Niger Delta region gained a lot of international attention following the release of the Environmental Assessment of Ogoniland by the United Nations Environment Programme (UNEP) in 2011. The report, among other things, found that there was widespread oil contamination in Ogoniland and that the people have been living with this pollution for more than 40 years and continue to live with it. Additionally, the report found that the various institutions and ministries responsible for tackling oil spills lacked the necessary resources to do so. As such, this made the enforcement of environmental protection laws very hard. Nevertheless, the report identified eight issues which had to be tackled with emergency measures immediately, considering their serious negative impact on the people in the region. The emergency measures include the following:

- ensure that all drinking water wells where hydrocarbons have been detected are marked and that people are informed of the danger;
- provide adequate sources of drinking water to those households whose drinking water supply is impacted;
- people in Nsisioken Ogale who have been consuming water with levels of benzene pollution over 900 times the World Health Organization (WHO) guideline are to be recorded on a medical registry and their health status assessed and followed up;
- initiate a survey of all drinking water wells around those wells where hydrocarbons have been observed;
- post signs in areas where hydrocarbons have been observed in surface water, warning people not to fish, swim, or bathe in such locations;

[110] Allison, C, Oriabure, G, Ndimele, PE and Shittu, JA, 'Dealing with oil spill scenarios in the Niger Delta: Lessons from the past' in Ndimele, PE (ed), *The political ecology of oil and gas activities in the Nigerian aquatic ecosystem* (Academic Press, 2018) pp 351–68: Nalule, VR, *Energy Poverty and Access Challenges in Sub-Saharan Africa: The Role of Regionalism* (Springer 2018).

[111] Zabbey, N, Sam, K and Onyebuchi, AT, 'Remediation of contaminated lands in the Niger Delta, Nigeria: Prospects and challenges' (2017) 586 *Science of the Total Environment* 952–65. See Allison, C, Oriabure, G, Ndimele, PE and Shittu, JA, 'Dealing with oil spill scenarios in the Niger Delta: Lessons from the past' in Ndimele, PE (ed), *The political ecology of oil and gas activities in the Nigerian aquatic ecosystem* (Academic Press, 2018) pp 351–68; Nalule, VR, *Energy Poverty and Access Challenges in Sub-Saharan Africa: The Role of Regionalism* (Springer 2018).

- post signs around all the sites identified as having contamination exceeding intervention values; inform all families whose rainwater samples tested positive for hydrocarbons and advise them not to consume the water; and
- mount a public awareness campaign to warn individuals undertaking artisanal refining that such activities are damaging their health.[112]

Following the publication of the UNEP report, some developments have occurred in this respect including the introduction by the Federal Government of Nigeria of a clean-up and restoration of Ogoniland project on the shores of Bodo Creek on 2 June 2016. Besides this project, there are several other projects that were introduced in the past even before the release of the 2011 UNEP Ogoniland Report, not to mention the various national and international laws in place.[113]

The case study above is testimony to the negative impacts on land use associated with the extractives industry. As illustrated in the example above, if not well managed, fossil fuel activities can result in gas flaring and oil spillage which directly and negatively impact on land use, including activities such as fishing and farming. Besides Nigeria, other countries including South Sudan and Angola have also been at the centre of gas flaring. Nevertheless, there have been efforts to address gas flaring; in Angola, for instance, an effort to address gas flaring has led to the expansion in the production of Liquefied Natural Gas (LNG), which is used in cooking and general heating. Gas-fired power stations have also been established in countries such as Mozambique and South Africa.[114]

Environmental protection and land use cannot be separated. As such, any activities that negatively impact the environment also negatively impact land use. These impacts have been experienced in various African countries. In western Kenya, gold mining in the Migori Gold Belt has negatively impacted the environment, as this activity has resulted in concentrations of heavy metals above acceptable levels, mainly mercury (Hg), lead (Pb) and arsenic (As), from gold sites.[115]

Besides the issues discussed above, access to land, and having in place efficient land administration mechanisms, are key for the successful formalisation of ASM. The issue of ASM will be adequately addressed in Chapter three; however, what must be noted here is the fact that ASM miners who own land on which they work benefit more than those who do not own land. Additionally, the issues of land ownership have had a significant impact on efforts to address gender inequality in the mining sectors. For instance, in the fieldwork research I carried out in

[112] See UNEP, 'Environmental Assessment of Ogoniland' (Report, 2011). Can be accessed at, https://postconflict.unep.ch/publications/OEA/UNEP_OEA.pdf.

[113] For a full discussion, see Nalule, VR, *Energy Poverty and Access Challenges in Sub-Saharan Africa: The Role of Regionalism* (Springer 2018) p 104.

[114] Nalule, VR, *Energy Poverty and Access Challenges in Sub-Saharan Africa: The Role of Regionalism* (Springer 2018) p 104.

[115] Olawuyi, DS, 'Introduction' in Olawuyi, *Extractives Industry Law in Africa* (Springer 2018) pp 3–17, at p 6.

Uganda, I noticed that the ASM salt miners who owned land were at an advantage compared to those who did not.[116]

V. Structure of the Book

The book is organised into five chapters, this being the Introduction. Chapter two examines in detail the land reforms in Africa and their impact on the extractive industries. Chapter three examines the legal framework applicable to land access and administration in Africa from the perspective of the mining sector. Chapter four surveys the issue of land administration in Africa from the perspective of the energy sector. Chapter four further analyses the issue of climate change as it relates to land access and extractives. The book concludes in Chapter five, which offers reflections and recommendations. Prior to the recommendations, Chapter five further looks at the pertinent issues with respect to land access and extractives, including Social Licence to Operate (SLO), local content and regionalism.

VI. Conclusion

Access to land is key in the successful operation of energy and mining projects. Oil, gas and mining resources have long been exploited on the African continent, but little visible benefit accrues from these sectors, in some countries. This has necessitated concepts such as Corporate Social Responsibility (CSR) and SLO. However, few reforms have been made in the land administration systems to ensure that local people benefit from these resources. At the outset, it is obvious that access to land is key for these projects, and yet, many African countries still struggle to effectively address the issues associated with land and extractives. In the next chapter, the African extractives industry will be examined, taking note of the legal and institutional regimes, with a particular focus on how they relate to land access in Africa.

[116] Nalule, VR, 'Salt Mining in Uganda': www.youtube.com/watch?v=RKFP6DswMrM&t=564s.

2

Land Law Reforms in Africa and their Impact on the Extractive Industries

I. Introduction to Land Law

Land law, which is also referred to as 'the law of real property', is concerned with land, rights in and over land, and the processes whereby those rights and interests are created and transferred.[1] Understanding the law governing land reforms necessitates an understanding of the term 'land'. Some of the oldest legislation on land law endeavoured to define land. For instance, in England, land is defined in the Law of Property Act 1925, as follows:

> Land includes land of any tenure, and mines and minerals … buildings or parts of buildings and other corporeal hereditaments; also a manor, an advowson, and a rent and other incorporeal hereditaments, and an easement, right, privilege, or benefit in, over, or derived from land.[2]

Land includes not only the tangible physical property, but also intangible rights in the land such as easements. As such, land law is the study of the creation, transfer, operation and termination of these rights and the manner in which they affect the use and enjoyment of the physical asset.[3] Access to land is key in the successful operation of various projects across all the sectors of the economy. Consequently, the governance, management and administration of land matters have gone through various reforms on the African continent. These have specifically been influenced by dissatisfaction among the poor and less privileged people. With the various changes in the social, political and economic aspects of a country, it becomes important to review and reform the statutory land laws, so that they can effectively address these changes.

For instance, socially, we note that many countries in Africa will be at the centre of population growth and urbanisation. The International Energy Agency (IEA) data reveals that the African continent will become the world's most

[1] Dixon, M, *Modern Land Law*, 11th edn (Routledge 2018).
[2] Section 205(1)(ix) of the Law of Property Act 1925.
[3] Dixon, M, *Modern Land Law*, 11th edn (Routledge 2018) p 4.

populous region by 2023, as one-in-two people added to the world population between today and 2040 are set to be African (more than the combined growth of China and India).[4] Whereas the increase in population growth requires access to more land to support these people, unfortunately, land is finite and as such, does not increase or decrease depending on external factors. In essence, more people will be competing for the same land and this in return will result in friction and dissatisfaction, especially among the 'have-nots'. Additionally, the global boom in urbanisation is projected to increase, as almost 2 billion more people are likely to live in urban centres by 2040 and Africa is projected to contribute one-third of this increasing urbanisation.[5] One of the main features of urbanisation is infrastructural development, including structured facilities, employment centres, residential buildings, communication and transport networks, to mention but a few. All the construction facilities require large chunks of land, not to mention that urban centres are usually densely populated. In this respect therefore, land issues are not about to end.

In extractive terms, land is key in the establishment of various energy infrastructural projects. For instance, Nigeria is known for its massive oil and gas resources – the country holds the largest natural gas reserves on the continent and was the world's fifth-largest exporter of liquefied natural gas (LNG) in 2018. The country's economy is dependent on the fossil fuels sector; data shows that Nigeria's crude oil and natural gas exports earned US$55 billion in 2018, an increase of US$23 billion from 2016.[6] These massive resources have necessitated the establishment of oil and gas infrastructure. For instance, Mr Dangote, Africa's richest man, has undertaken a project of building the world's largest oil refinery, at an estimated cost of US$12 billion, on 6,180 acres of swampland. Upon completion, the refinery is projected to process 650,000 barrels of crude oil daily. There are various other oil and gas infrastructural projects in different African countries. What is important to note is that all such projects require large pieces of land to be effectively operational. In the acquisition of this land, several social and environmental issues do arise, as will be discussed in Chapters three and four of this book.

Moving on to the political aspects of land reforms on the African continent, it is crucial to understand the history behind the different land law reforms in each country. As briefly discussed in Chapter one of this book, before the reforms which commenced in the 1990s, countries were eager to reverse the colonial approach to land law. South African land reforms, for instance, are mainly driven by the desire to empower farm workers; empower previously unemployed Black people; redress the injustices the Black communities suffered during the apartheid regime, when Black people in urban centres were forcefully removed from their homes, that were

[4] IEA, *Africa Energy Outlook 2019* (IEA 2019): www.iea.org/reports/africa-energy-outlook-2019.

[5] BP, *BP Energy Outlook: 2018 Edition* (BP Plc 2018): www.bp.com/content/dam/bp/business-sites/en/global/corporate/pdfs/energy-economics/energy-outlook/bpenergy-outlook-2018.pdf.

[6] International Monetary Fund, 'Nigeria: 2019 Article IV Consultation, IMF Country Report no 19/92'.

subsequently declared white. In this respect, land reforms in South Africa can be described as an effort for 'land restitution', aimed at ensuring equality by empowering those who were farm workers under apartheid to own land and become farmers. Land restitution also relates to settling land claims, especially for the Black people who were forcefully removed from their homes as a result of the apartheid government's segregationist Group Areas Act.[7] The Act divided urban areas into 'group areas' in which ownership and residence was restricted to certain population groups. Many Black people were forced to leave their homes in urban areas which were considered white, including Sophiatown, Fietas, Cato Manor, District Six and Greyville.[8] Besides affecting the Black people in urban areas, apartheid land policies also led to the forceful eviction of Black people in rural areas. These brutal policies have had devastating negative impacts on the country, including the social-economic challenges the same people are facing today such as poverty, inequality and landlessness.

The South African example is proof that land reforms are triggered not only by social and economic changes, but also the political history of a country. In this respect, the land reform process in South Africa was mainly characterised by restitution, land tenure reform and land redistribution. These will be expounded on in the next sections. But briefly, under restitution, the government aims at compensating individuals forcefully removed from their land; redistribution occurs where land was bought from its owners (willing seller) by the government (willing buyer) and redistributed, in order to maintain public confidence in the land market. Land tenure systems basically recognised people's right to own land and therefore control the land.[9] For instance, in 1994, approximately 82 million hectares of agricultural land in South Africa was owned by the white minority. The country embraced various reforms aimed at addressing land injustices, and as a result approximately 4,813 farms were transferred to Black people and communities between 1994 and 2013.[10]

Scholars have identified two types of land reforms: transformation, and traditional land reforms.[11] The South African example mentioned above would definitely fall under the transformation type. It is also important to contrast

[7] The Group Areas Act, 1950 (re-enacted in 1957 and 1966).

[8] ibid.

[9] Binswanger-Mkhize, HP, 'From failure to success in South African land reform' (2014) 9(4) *African Journal of Agricultural and Resource Economics* 253–69.

[10] Various programmes were used in South Africa to address the land injustices. These include: (i) restitution of land to people who were displaced from their land under apartheid laws; (ii) the Settlement/Land Acquisition Grant (SLAG); (iii) Land Redistribution for Agricultural Development (LRAD) – this programme was initiated in 2001 to make it possible for beneficiaries to acquire larger areas of land for farming; (iv) the Comprehensive Agricultural Support Programme (CASP), created as a response to the growing crisis in post-settlement support; and (v) the Re-capitalisation and Agricultural Development Programme (RECAP), created to recapitalise failed or poorly performing land reform projects. For a detailed discussion on this, see Binswanger-Mkhize, HP, 'From failure to success in South African land reform' (2014) 9(4) *African Journal of Agricultural and Resource Economics* 253–69.

[11] McAuslan, P, *Land Law Reform in Eastern Africa: Traditional or Transformative?: A critical review of 50 years of land law reform in Eastern Africa 1961–2011* (Routledge 2013).

transformational and traditional developments: the former aims at change designed to ensure social justice in land laws, and the latter aims to continue the overall thrust of colonial approaches of land laws and land administration. The overall effect of the reforms has been traditional: it was colonial policy to move towards land markets, individualisation of land tenure and the demise of customary tenure, all of which have characterised the landscape of the post-1990 reforms.[12] Table 2.1 shows some of the land reforms in different African countries.

Table 2.1 Land Laws in the Era of Land Law Reform

Country	Date	Law
Kenya	1996	Physical Planning Act
	2012	National Land Commission Act Land Act Registered Land Act
	2016	Community Land Act
Mozambique	1997	Land Law
	2006	Regulation on Urban Soil
Rwanda	2004	Organic Land Law
Tanzania	1999	Land Act
	1999	Village Land Act
	2007 2007	Land Use Planning Act Urban Planning Act
Uganda	1924 1965 1998	The Registration of Titles Act (Cap 230) The Land Acquisition Act (Cap 226) The Land Act (Cap 227) as amended
	2010 2013	Physical Planning Act The Uganda National Land Policy, 2013

Table 2.1 is not exhaustive. It simply highlights some of the different land Acts and legislation implemented by different countries in different years. However, it is notable that every generation faces different economic, social and political challenges. In responding to these challenges, countries are often obliged to change their legal and fiscal regimes to effectively address the pertinent issues concerning land governance. As discussed previously, access to land is a key aspect not only socially but also economically and politically. In this respect, therefore, countries and politicians often put land matters at the forefront, hence necessitating various land reforms.

[12] McAuslan, P, *Land Law Reform in Eastern Africa: Traditional or Transformative?: A critical review of 50 years of land law reform in Eastern Africa 1961–2011* (Routledge 2013).

This book sets out to survey and assess efforts at the reform of land law made by African countries in recent years. The limits of what is being attempted in this book must be made clear at the outset. The book focuses on those parts of the laws that directly impact the extractives industry. In this respect, the book reviews those reforms relating to access to land, including issues relating to compensation, registration of title, and customary law, to mention a few. As such, the book will not consider the law of mortgages. This is not in any way to devalue or downplay the importance of this aspect. But a book can only be so long, and any attempt to review the law of mortgages will make it hard to discuss all the key issues relating to the extractives industry. Equally, the focus of the book is to illustrate the different land reforms with a specific emphasis on the statutory reforms. In this respect, this chapter will not dwell on land-related court cases but will rather consider land administration issues in the context of the extractive industries. This chapter is divided into four sections, this being the introduction. Section II analyses land law reforms in Uganda, Tanzania, Rwanda and South Africa, highlighting the land situation before and after independence. In this respect, the section reviews the land laws that were inherited during independence, and the various reforms that followed independence. Section III specifically draws from the Kenyan example, although it explores other case studies of relevance. Section IV gives concluding remarks. Prior to discussing section II of this chapter, the nature of land law is discussed, before setting out the conceptual framework of the book with a focus on land justice as a theory to be explored in the book.

A. The Nature of Land Law

While discussing land law reforms in Africa, it is worth noting that these were to some extent influenced by the laws of real property of the various countries that colonised Africa. As such, a brief understanding of some of these laws and practices is advantageous in understanding the history and current reforms of land laws on the African continent. This sub-section therefore draws on examples from English land practices and administration, as these in a way had an impact on the early land reforms in different African countries, specifically former British colonies.

In England, the history of land law is said to have its history in the feudal reforms imposed on England by William the Conqueror after 1066, which highly influenced the development of various concepts and principles of land law.[13] In England, it is clear that land law has been modernised following the various social, economic and political developments. Nevertheless, the substance of modern land law is still governed by the structure established by the Law of Property Act 1925 (LPA 1925). However, over several decades, judicial decisions influenced by the

[13] Dixon, M, *Modern Land Law*, 12th edn (Routledge 2021) p 2.

modern age and twenty-first-century challenges have all played a part in moulding the substantive law to the needs of modern society. Consequently, land law went through legislative progress, including the enactment of the Land Registration Act of 2002 (LRA 2002), which replaced the Land Registration Act 1925 (LRA 1925).[14] Although the LRA 2002 is seen as a legal framework addressing the challenges faced in the modern age, some of its provisions have been regarded as controversial, including the introduction of a system of paperless, electronic dealings with land (e-conveyancing) – which essentially represents a major contrast with the feudal past and the ancient origins of land law.[15]

The above developments in England have had an impact on all the African countries which were colonised by the British. This is because the former colonies often enacted laws which directly or indirectly imitated the practices of the former colonial master. A good example of the influence of English land law and practices in the former colonies is the aspect of legal and equitable rights. As will later be highlighted, a right in land can either be legal or equitable. In examining the history of the distinction between legal and equitable rights (these notions are recognised in some African countries), it is worth noting that these rights have their origin in the practices of the King's court (court of common law), and the Chancellor's court (Court of Chancery). In essence, the King's court would grant a remedy to a claimant who could establish a case 'at law', on proof of certain formalities and on pleading a specified 'form of action'. The strict reliance on formalities by the King's court led many claimants to suffer injustices. As a result, the harshness of the King's court was remedied by the Chancellor's court, which began to give an 'equitable' remedy to a deserving claimant, even in the absence of the proper formalities required for a remedy 'at law'. This therefore marked the genesis of the 'legal rules' which were dealt with by the common law courts, and the 'rules of equity' which were dealt with by the court of equity.[16] The 1875 Judicature Act, however, empowered all courts to apply both the rules of law and rules of equity.

The common law rules and rules of equity are embraced by different former colonies of the British, although not distinguished by the kind of court in question. In Uganda for instance, an equitable interest in land is understood to mean an interest held in land which has not been registered. These interests include, among others: an interest of a spouse in family land; tenants by occupancy; and an interest of a purchaser of land who has not yet been registered as the landowner. In Uganda, all interests which have not been registered under the Registration of Titles Act are equitable interests.[17] Legal interests in Uganda are defined under Section 54 of the Registration of Titles Act, as an interest held in land by a landowner who has registered under the Registration of Titles Act so as to give the

[14] The LRA 2002 was the result of extensive consultations by the Law Commission in conjunction with HM Land Registry. For further information about the reforms, see Law Commission Report No 271, titled, 'Land Registration for the Twenty-first Century: A Conveyancing Revolution'.

[15] Dixon, M, *Modern Land Law*, 12th edn (Routledge 2021) p 2.

[16] Dixon, M, *Modern Land Law*, 12th edn (Routledge 2021) p 2.

[17] Registration of Titles Act (Cap 230), 1924, Laws of Uganda.

world notice of his or her ownership, for instance owners of land in the mailo, freehold and leasehold tenures which have been registered.[18] Table 2.2 summarises the legal and equitable proprietary rights:

Table 2.2 Summary of the Legal and Equitable Proprietary Rights

Legal Proprietary Rights	Equitable Proprietary Rights
Defined in Section 1 of the LPA 1925. They include freehold; leasehold; easement; mortgage; right of re-entry.	An estate or interest not falling within Section 1 is equitable.
Right is legal if created with proper formality, eg by deed. Many legal rights must be substantively registered under the LRA 2002 in order to achieve legal status.	Created by a written contract or written instrument within Section 2 of the LP(MP)A 1989[19] or Section 53 of the LPA 1925.
Legal right would bind every transferee, owner or occupier of the land over which it existed.	Equitable right would bind every transferee or occupier of the land except a bona fide purchaser for value of a legal estate in the land who had no notice of the equitable right.

Source: Data partly drawn from Dixon, M, *Modern land law*, 12th edn (Routledge 2021) p 2.

The above principles in Table 2.2 are also important in matters of land law and the extractives industry; albeit that, in modern land law, these principles have been replaced by requirements of registration, or customary land ownership principles. At this juncture, it is worth exploring the issues relating to registered land and unregistered conveyancing.

(i) Registered and Unregistered Land

Registered land is land to which the title is substantively registered in a register.[20] The main advantage of registered title is that it guarantees ownership of the estate in question; as such, prospective purchasers may buy the land in the certainty that the title has been thoroughly investigated and approved before it was first registered.[21] In England, registered land is governed by the LPA 1925, common law and the LRA 2002. In registered land, the effect of a proprietary right on a transferee of the land is determined by its status under the LRA 2002. The concept of 'overreaching' may allow a purchaser of registered land to defeat certain equitable rights.[22]

[18] Section 54 of the Registration of Titles Act (Cap 230), 1924, Laws of Uganda.
[19] Law of Property (Miscellaneous Provisions) Act 1989.
[20] Every title is given a title number and the details of the current owners are registered against it.
[21] See *Habenec v Harris* (1998) unreported.
[22] For instance, a purchaser who pays the purchase price of land to the co-owners of a legal estate will 'overreach certain types of equitable interests'. See Dixon, M, *Modern Land Law*, 11th edn (Routledge 2018) p 23.

Unregistered land, on the other hand, is land to which the title is not registered (in most African countries, this falls under customary land).[23] The title is located in the old fashioned title deeds, and a prospective purchaser must investigate 'root of title' through examination of the title deeds in order to be confident of obtaining a secure right to the land. There are legal and equitable rights that can be enjoyed under unregistered land. The legal rights bind the whole world. Equitable rights in unregistered land fall into three distinct and separate categories including:

- Land charges within the Land Charges Act 1972: these are only binding if they are registered as a 'land charge' against the owner of the land over which they take effect.
- Other equitable rights are subject to the doctrine of notice. These are not land charges and they are not registrable under the Land Charges Act 1972.
- Rights that are overreachable. These are equitable rights of a special character, being rights capable of easy quantification in money.[24] They maybe 'overreached' so as not to bind a new purchaser of the land.[25]

Table 2.3 below summarises the distinction between registered land and unregistered land.

Table 2.3 Comparison between Registered and Unregistered Land

Registered land title	**Unregistered land title**
Officially recorded and guaranteed.	Not recorded. Purchaser must make his own investigation based on the title deeds.
Third-party rights are protected through registration or under the provisions relating to overreaching interests.	Legal rights are safe but equitable rights are protected by the doctrine of notice.
LRA 2002 expresses the effect of non-registration in terms of loss of priority, not voidness.[26]	The voidness rule is clear and strictly applied.
The register is conclusive not the search certificate.	The search is conclusive.

[23] Over 85% of all titles are registered and unregistered land is slowly disappearing. For more information, see Dixon, M, *Modern Land Law*, 11th edn (Routledge 2018) p 23.

[24] For instance, equitable ownership of a proportion of a house.

[25] Overreachable rights are those equitable rights that are excluded from the category of land charges because a properly overreaching transaction will sweep the interests off the land and cause them to take effect in the monies paid by a purchaser for that land. Overreaching will occur when: (1) the equitable right is capable of being overreached – these include equitable co-ownership rights existing behind a trust of land or a strict settlement; (2) the transaction is a 'conveyance to a purchaser of a legal estate in land' – this includes the sale of a freehold, the grant or assignment of a legal lease and the grant of a mortgage; and (3) the conveyance is made by those persons and in those circumstances that are capable of effecting an overreaching transaction. For further details, see Dixon, M, *Modern Land Law*, 12th edn (Routledge 2021) p 121.

[26] The 'voidness rule' is essential in determining the consequences of a failure to register a registrable land charge. The precise type of land charge in issue and the nature of the transferee of the burdened

(ii) Distinction between Land Law and Other Law Disciplines

As discussed in the previous sub-sections, land law involves not only physical rights but also intangible rights. Other legal disciplines essential in land law include the law of contract, since most transactions concerning land or intangible rights in land take place through the medium of a contract. Martin Dixon rightly summarises this relationship as follows:

> [L]and is sold through a contract and a mortgage is also a contract of debt between lender and landowner. Similarly the right to enjoy the exclusive possession of another's land for a defined period of time (a lease) may be given by a contract between the owner of the land (landlord) and the person who is to enjoy the right (tenant) … the conclusion of such a contract would bind the parties to it as a matter of simple contract law and the contract might require one of the parties to complete the transaction by executing a deed that formally grants the right to the other. In such cases, the contract is said to merge with the grant, and the contract ceases to have any separate existence as a legal concept. Whether the parties are bound by a mere contract, or by the more formal deed of grant, they may enforce the contract or deed against each other: in the former case, by action for damages or specific performance; in the latter, by relying on the covenants (promises) contained in the deed.[27]

Despite the strong nexus between land law and contract law, the distinguishing factor is worth noting. This basically relies on the proprietary rights conveyed by land law. Unlike an ordinary contract which establishes 'personal obligations', real property rights can affect other people, not simply the parties that created the right. In summary, any person who comes into ownership or possession of the land may be entitled to enjoy the benefits that now come with the land, or maybe subject to the burdens imposed on the land.[28] This, in essence, implies that the proprietary right is enforceable beyond the original parties to the contract. However, proprietary rights do not include all the rights merely connected with land. As far back as the 1960s, judges have endeavoured to identify what proprietary rights encompass. In this respect, in the case of *National Provincial Bank v Ainsworth*, Lord Wilberforce stated that:

> Before a right or an interest can be admitted into the category of property, or of a right affecting property, it must be definable, identifiable by third parties, capable in its nature of assumption by third parties, and have some degree of permanence or stability.

In that case, the essential point was whether a wife's right to live in the former matrimonial home could be regarded as a proprietary right, given that she did

land who is seeking to avoid enforcement of the land charge must be considered. It can be expressed in several ways including, 'a purchaser or transferee's knowledge of the existence of a registrable, but unregistered, land charge is generally irrelevant in determining whether it binds him when he becomes the new owner of the burdened land'. For more details, see Section 199 of the LPA; and Dixon, M, *Modern Land Law*, 11th edn (Routledge 2018) p 117.

[27] Dixon, M, *Modern Land Law*, 12th edn (Routledge 2021) p 4.

[28] Dixon, M, *Modern Land Law*, 12th edn (Routledge 2021) p 4.

not actually own a share of the property. If it could, the right might bind a third party such as the National Provincial Bank, which had a mortgage over the land and whose claim to possession might be defeated if a proprietary right existed. If, however, the right was purely personal – that is, enforceable by the wife only against the husband personally – it could never bind the land and the bank's mortgage would necessarily take priority. The bank could take the house. In this case the House of Lords decided that the wife's right to live in the property could only ever be personal if she had no actual share of ownership.[29]

Besides case law, as indicated in the case above, statutory law has also endeavoured to define proprietary rights. For instance, Sections 115 and 116 of the LRA 2002 confirm the proprietary status of previous disputed rights. Thus, rights of pre-emption, equities by estoppel and mere equities are confirmed as proprietary. In understanding proprietary rights, it is worth noting that they fall into two major categories including estates in land and interests in land. There are various examples of estates in land including: the freehold estate (the fee simple); the leasehold estate; the fee tail; and the life interest. It is imperative to note that a right to land might be legal or equitable.

In the extractive industries, families are usually affected by these activities, especially in instances where they are relocated or even in sharing the compensation in question. This is because some land is co-owned. Following this, it is important to briefly discuss the law of co-ownership in this chapter.

(iii) Co-ownership of Land

The law of co-ownership operates whenever two or more people enjoy the rights of ownership of land at the same time, whether that be freehold or leasehold land.[30] Co-ownership is expressly created where land is conveyed to two or more people. In instances where the legal title is only in one name, co-ownership can still be created where the legal owner expressly declares in writing that he/she holds the land on trust for another person. Additionally, a person may claim an equitable interest through the operation of a resulting or constructive trust or estoppel.[31]

Often, co-ownership is by way of either a joint tenancy or a tenancy in common. The key aspect of a joint tenancy is that each co-owner is treated as being entitled to the whole of the land and there are no distinct shares. However, a tenancy in common exists when two or more people own an undivided share in land, giving

[29] *National Provincial Bank v Ainsworth* [1965] AC 1175.

[30] The co-owners may be family members, married persons, friends, business partners. In England, the law of co-ownership is governed by both common law and statutory law.

[31] 'On the one hand, a resulting trust arises where the claimant has contributed to the purchase price of the property. On the other hand, a constructive trust arises either where the legal owner makes an express oral promise or agreement; or direct contribution to the purchase price'. For a detailed discussion on this, see Dixon, M, *Modern Land Law*, 11th edn (Routledge, 2018) p 178.

unity of possession, but where no other unities are necessary and where there is no right of survivorship.[32] With respect to possession and occupation, all the legal owners have a right to occupy the property unless there is something specific to the contrary in the document establishing the trust of land. It is possible to turn an equitable joint tenancy into a tenancy in common; this is referred to as 'severance'.[33] Other forms of tenancy are also worth exploring, as these apply in different jurisdictions. These include among others:

(a) Periodic Tenant

This refers to a person who enters an agreement with a landowner to occupy his or her land or property, enjoy exclusive possession and pay rent on a regular, periodic basis, for instance weekly, monthly, quarterly, bi-annually or annually. A periodic tenancy is renewable depending on the agreement between the parties. Reasonable notice should be given before this tenancy is terminated. Often, a weekly tenancy requires notice of one week, a monthly tenancy requires notice of one month, while a quarterly tenancy requires notice of three months.[34] An annual tenancy, however, requires notice of six months.

(b) Tenant at Will

This refers to a tenant who is in possession of the land with the consent or permission of the landowner before the tenancy contract is finalised or who continues to stay on the land after the tenancy has expired prior to its renewal.

(c) Tenant at Sufferance

This refers to a tenant who remains in possession of the land after the expiry of the tenancy without the consent or objection of the landowner. Although this tenant is not entitled to notice to leave the premises, case law has indicated that it would be prudent to give such tenants reasonable notice.[35]

[32] It is important to note that a joint tenancy is characterised by the right of survivorship and the four unities include: unity of possession; interest; title; and time. With respect to the equitable interest, it is worth noting that if the unities of interest, title or time are absent, a joint tenancy in equity cannot exist. Further, if 'words of severance' are used, then a tenancy in common will exist in equity.

[33] Severance occurs mainly to avoid the effect of the right of survivorship; however, a legal joint tenancy cannot be severed. Severance can occur either by statutory written notice or by the act of a co-owner operating on his own share or where the joint tenants decide to sever by mutual agreement; or where an intention to sever is manifested by the mutual conduct of the joint tenants or in cases of unlawful killing. See Dixon, M, *Modern Land Law*, 11th edn (Routledge 2018) p 189.

[34] *Musumba v Haji Kasaka* (1971) 1 ULR 222.

[35] *Christopher Sebuliba v Attorney General of Uganda*, Supreme Court Civil Appeal No 13 of 1991, [1992] UGSC 6.

B. Common Terms in Land Law

Table 2.4 below is an indication that there are various relevant terms which we cannot ignore when discussing land law. However, the list is not exhaustive. Nevertheless, some terms appearing in the table, such as leases, easements and mortgages, are worth briefly exploring first.

(i) Leasehold

A leasehold allows two or more people to enjoy the benefits of owning an estate in the land at the same time. Some of the characteristics of leases include: they contain covenants, whereby the landlord and tenant promise to do – or not to do – certain things in relation to the land; and the lease gives a person the right to exclusive possession of land for an agreed period of time and rent. It is possible to create either a legal or equitable lease. A legal lease is created by deed while an equitable lease derives from a written contract. However, an equitable lease can still be generated purely orally via the principle of proprietary estoppel. Leases may be terminated by effluxion of time, by forfeiture, by serving notice if the lease contains a break clause, by merger with the superior estate out of which it is carved, by frustration, or by surrender to the landlord. This list is not exhaustive.

(ii) Easements

Easements comprise certain limited rights that one landowner may enjoy over the land of a neighbour, such as right of way or right of light. One of the conditions for the existence of an easement is that there must be a dominant (the benefited land) and a servient tenement (the burdened land). Additionally, the creation and continued existence of an easement is dependent on the dominant and servient tenements being owned or occupied by different persons. An easement, once created, confers a benefit and burden on the land itself and as such, it may be enjoyed or suffered by any subsequent owner of the dominant or servient land.

(iii) Mortgage

A mortgage is security for a loan, which comprises a transfer (conveyance) of a legal or equitable interest in the borrower's land to the mortgagee, with a provision that the mortgagee's interest shall lapse upon repayment of the loan plus interest and costs. The creation of a mortgage can be legal or equitable. For a legal mortgage, the mortgagor may grant a legal mortgage of a registered title by means of a charge by deed, expressed to be by way of legal mortgage; equitable mortgages may exist when there is a mortgage of an equitable interest, when there is an informal mortgage of a legal interest under the rules for equitable charges, or via the operation of proprietary estoppel.[36]

On the one hand, the rights of the mortgagee under a legal mortgage include: an action on the contract for recovery of the debt; the power of sale; the right to possession; appointment of a receiver; and foreclosure. On the other hand, the rights of a mortgagee under an equitable mortgage include: the right to sue for the money due on the contract, where the equitable mortgage is made by deed; and the mortgagee has the power of sale, although no power to convey the legal estate to a purchaser.

Table 2.4 Key Terms in Land Law

Caution	A caution is a notice in the form of an entry on the register to the effect that no action of a specified nature in relation to the land in respect of which the notice has been entered may be taken without first informing the person who gave the notice.
Caveat	The lodging of a caveat over a property implies that someone else's interest over the said land already has priority.
Deed plan	This is a signed plan showing the precise particulars of a surveyed piece of land.
Estates in land	This is a right to use and control land as an owner for a specific period of time, subject to the relevant type of estate.
Easement	An easement is the right in another person's land. For instance, a right of way over someone else's land.
Mortgage	A debt secured on a debtor's land.
Restrictive covenant	The right to prevent an owner carrying out some specific activity on his/her own land.
Freehold estate (the fee simple)	The right to use and enjoy the land for the duration of the life of the grantee and that of his or her heirs and successors.[37] A freehold may either be legal or equitable.
Leases	A lease is an interest in land for a specific period of time and subject to payment of rent.
The fee tail	An interest in land permitting its owner the use of land for the duration of his life and that of his lineal descendants (not all heirs).[38] At the death of the last lineal descendant, the land will revert to the person entitled to the estate in fee simple or to the state/Crown.

(continued)

[36] A mortgagor has a contractual right to redeem the mortgage on the date specified in the mortgage contract. A mortgagor also enjoys the equity of redemption, which represents the sum total of the mortgagor's rights in the property, including his paramount title out of which the mortgage is granted.

[37] The freehold is freely transferable (alienable) during the life of the estate owner (by gift or sale), or on his or her death (by will or under the rules of intestate succession).

[38] A lineal descendant is a person who can show a parental, grandparental, or great-grandparental link to the person who was originally granted the fee tail.

Table 2.4 ***(Continued)***

Interest in land	Proprietary rights that one person enjoys in land/ estate of another. These may include easements, mortgages.[39]
Licence	Permission given by the owner of the land to another person, who may or may not own land themselves, to use the owner's land for some specific purpose.
Estoppel	A legal principle that prevents someone from arguing something or asserting a right that contradicts what they previously said or agreed to by law.
Proprietary estoppel	Defence to an action by a landowner who seeks to enforce his strict rights against someone who has been informally promised some right or liberty over the land. Certain conditions must be fulfilled including the existence of an assurance, reliance on the assurance, detriment, and circumstances in which it would be unconscionable to allow the landowner to escape from his promise.[40]
Adverse possession	The law of adverse possession offers an opportunity to a mere trespasser to acquire better title to land than the person who legally owns it and to whom it was once formally conveyed.[41]
Land transaction	These include selling, leasing, mortgaging or pledging, subdividing, creating rights and interests for other people in the land and creating trusts of the land.[42]
Family land	Refers to land (a) where the ordinary residence of a family is situated; (b) where the ordinary residence of the family is situated and from which the family derives sustenance; (c) which is treated as family land according to the norms, culture, customs, traditions or religion of the family.[43]
Land grabbing	This means the unlawful and illegal taking away of land belonging to an individual or a group of people.
Compensation	This is money paid to a person with an interest in land to make up for the loss suffered when the government takes their land through compulsory acquisition.

Table 2.4 above is not exhaustive. Rather, it highlights some of the key terms used with respect to land law, governance and management. The next sub-section briefly outlines the conceptual framework of this book.

[39] These rights may be transferred or sold to another person and may be binding against the new owner.

[40] See *Taylor Fashions Ltd v Liverpool Victoria Trustees Ltd* [1982] QB 133.

[41] This is based on the principle of limitation of actions which means that a person may be 'statute-barred' from bringing a claim against the adverse possessor to recover possession of the land after the period of limitation has expired.

[42] See for instance, Section 3(2) of the Land Act as amended in 2004, Laws of Uganda.

[43] See Section 38A of the Land Act as amended in 2004, Laws of Uganda.

C. Conceptual Framework

This sub-section discusses the conceptual framework to be relied on in this chapter with respect to the various land law reforms. The main key concept is that of justice, or more accurately, 'land justice'. The sub-section draws from the two recognised approaches of transformational versus traditional, the former aiming at change designed to ensure social justice in land laws, and the latter aiming to continue the overall thrust of the colonial approach to land laws and land administration. Scholars who have previously relied on the concept of justice to review the land reforms in different African countries, have made several conclusions including:[44]

- Land markets have been accepted and provided for everywhere.
- A corollary is that customary tenure is on the way out, although at varying speeds in different countries.
- All reforms write in a considerable degree of central government's continuing involvement in land administration.
- The reforms do not adequately address the urban land problem, nor do the reformed urban planning laws.
- Looked at in terms of a transformational versus traditional approach to land law reform, while most reforms have elements of the transformational in them, the overall effect of the reforms has been traditional: it was colonial policy to move towards land markets, the individualisation of land tenure and the demise of customary tenure. Implementation of the land law reforms leaves a good deal to be desired as there is a shortage of money and too much ambivalence on the part of implementers to move in a transformational direction.[45]

The summary above from McAuslan illustrates the pertinent issues with respect to land reforms in Africa. As has been illustrated throughout this book, land reforms in most African countries are driven by the need to address the land injustices (most emanating from the colonial period). Although there are various approaches that have been taken by different countries to address the vices of landlessness, land grabbing, land conflicts and other land-related matters, in this sub-section, the focus will be on the transformational approach and traditional approach to land reforms.

(i) Transformational Approach

Transformation has been defined to refer to changes in land law which have as their avowed and deliberate aim, the righting of past social and economic injustices. It also envisages the creation of a system of land law which is designed to ensure that those formerly maltreated or unfairly discriminated against by the land laws

[44] See McAuslan, P, *Land Law Reform in Eastern Africa: Traditional or Transformative?: A critical review of 50 years of land law reform in Eastern Africa 1961–2011* (Routledge; 2013) p 2.

[45] McAuslan, P, *Land Law Reform in Eastern Africa: Traditional or Transformative?: A critical review of 50 years of land law reform in Eastern Africa 1961–2011* (Routledge 2013) p 2.

are given at the least an equal opportunity, and preferably a favourable position, in a new land law regime, via the redistribution of rights and opportunities to enable them to better their life chances.[46] South Africa presents a good example of the inequalities created by colonial and apartheid land laws and policies, and as such, subsequent land reforms aimed at addressing these inequalities.

(ii) Traditional Approach

Scholars have described the traditional approach as accepting the colonial origins of the structure of land law in the country concerned. This approach also accedes to the colonial and post-colonial external analysis of the problems of land tenure and the solutions to those problems. In essence, with this approach, African countries inherited the colonial land regime and accepted all the injustices which characterised those regimes. Historically, colonial masters formulated land laws aimed at marginalising the indigenous inhabitants by denying them a right to own land.[47] McAuslan notes that:

> This was achieved by, on the one hand, the development of a land law modelled on the land law of the imperial power which applied to freehold and, on the other, the vesting of land governed by indigenous law in the colonial government – Crown land in British dependencies – which could be disposed of by the colonial government with minimal formality and less compensation, since the theory behind it was that the colonial government was merely succeeding to the radical title to land of the indigenous rulers and the subjects of those rulers had no security of tenure as they had no recognisable private rights in the land they occupied.[48]

The above clearly illustrates the various intentions of the former colonial masters with respect to land governance in Africa. A question to be asked now is, in the absence of colonial influences, what land reforms are suited to address the challenges faced by African countries? As discussed in Chapter one of this book, each country is faced with unique land challenges, most of which require tailored solutions. For instance, in countries that have been victims of civil wars (Rwanda, Sierra Leone), the land reforms will be driven by the need to resettle people, and also to resolve landlessness in the country. On the other hand, in countries that have suffered injustices due to the apartheid regimes (South Africa, Zimbabwe), the land reforms are driven by the need to ensure land justice (through, among other things, restitution).

In understanding the nexus between land access and extractives, it becomes imperative to identify and be guided by some set of principles, concepts, theories

[46] McAuslan, P, *Land Law Reform in Eastern Africa: Traditional or Transformative?: A critical review of 50 years of land law reform in Eastern Africa 1961–2011* (Routledge 2013).

[47] McAuslan, P, *Land Law Reform in Eastern Africa: Traditional or Transformative?: A critical review of 50 years of land law reform in Eastern Africa 1961–2011* (Routledge 2013) p 15.

[48] McAuslan, P, *Land Law Reform in Eastern Africa: Traditional or Transformative?: A critical review of 50 years of land law reform in Eastern Africa 1961–2011* (Routledge 2013) p 15.

or ideas by which to judge the impacts of extractives on land use. In this research, a reliance on the concept of justice becomes critical – specifically the land justice theory through the lens of energy justice. Although this concept was missing in earlier land publications,[49] it was recognised by some scholars who underlined the importance of including justice in land administration matters.[50]

(iii) Land Justice Theory through the Lens of Energy Justice

Land use and administration is prone to conflicts and disputes, characterised in most countries by human rights abuses, physical violence and death. In this respect, it is worth exploring the concept of justice as being key in land access in the extractive industries. Further, some countries in the SADC region, such as South Africa, have attracted more research focused on justice in land distributions, particularly since the end of apartheid in 1994.

The Oxford Dictionary defines 'just' to mean behaving according to what is morally right and fair.[51] Various developments with respect to the concept of justice have occurred as the concept was extended to other sectors. With respect to land administration, some scholars have focused on justice aimed at ensuring that the poor people are not negatively affected by the boom in urbanisation which is anticipated in the Global South. Effective land administration and governance are key in ensuring effective urban planning. At present, most towns and cities in developing countries, especially for poor people in peri-urban areas, lack access to shelter, infrastructure and services, and they are also faced with serious environmental issues.[52] As such, there is a clear need to ensure justice for the poor people in these cities, and one way of ensuring this is by putting in place effective land administration laws and institutions that can support efforts in urban planning. Similarly, scholars have emphasised justice in city planning. The theory of spatial justice has been expounded on by different scholars.[53] Spatial justice is summed up by Soja as follows:[54]

1. In the broadest sense, spatial (in)justice refers to an international and focused emphasis on the spatial or geographical aspects of justice and injustice. As a

[49] For instance, there was no mention of justice in the 2010 land policy publication: African Union, African Development Bank and Economic Commission for Africa, *Framework and Guidelines on Land Policy in Africa: Land Policy in Africa: A Framework to strengthen Land Rights, Enhance Productivity and Secure Livelihoods* (ECA 2010).

[50] McAuslan, P, *Land Law Reform in Eastern Africa: Traditional or Transformative?: A critical review of 50 years of land law reform in Eastern Africa 1961–2011* (Routledge 2013) p 3.

[51] Oxford Dictionary. (2019): https://en.oxforddictionaries.com/definition/just.

[52] Watson, V, '"The planned city sweeps the poor away …": Urban planning and 21st century urbanisation' (2009) 72(3) *Progress in Planning* 151–93.

[53] Soja, EW, 'The city and spatial justice' (2009) 1(1) *Justice Spatiale/Spatial Justice* 1–5.

[54] Soja, EW, 'The City and Spatial Justice', paper at a conference on Spatial Justice, Nanterre, 12–14 March 2008, pp 2–3: See also, McAuslan, P, *Land Law Reform in Eastern Africa: Traditional or Transformative?: A critical review of 50 years of land law reform in Eastern Africa 1961–2011* (Routledge 2013) p 5.

starting point, this involves the fair and equitable distribution in space of socially valued resources and the opportunities to use them.

2. Spatial justice as such is not a substitute or alternative to social, economic, or other forms of justice but rather a way of looking at justice from a critical spatial perspective.
3. Spatial (in)justice can be both outcome and process, as geographies or distributional patterns that are in themselves just/unjust and as the processes that produce these outcomes.
4. Locational discrimination, created through the biases imposed on certain populations because of their geographical locations, is fundamental in the production of spatial injustice and the creation of lasting spatial structures of privilege and advantage …
5. Combining the terms spatial and justice opens a range of new possibilities for social and political action, as well as for social theorization and empirical analysis, that would not be as clear if the two terms were not used together.

From this, we note an emphasis on a 'just city', which is the other term for spatial justice. The geography of land justice is also recognised, especially as it relates to locational discrimination, which Soja highlights above.

Other scholars have expounded on the debate on spatial justice/just cities.[55] The most recognised approaches to urban justice developed over the years include: (1) communicative rationality; and (2) recognition of diversity. Scholars have gone ahead to recognise that democracy, diversity, and equity are the three governing principles for urban justice.[56]

There is indeed a big connection between the theories of urban justice discussed above and the issue of land access. However, the focus in this sub-section is to establish a theory that encompasses both land justice and energy justice. Prior to this, it is worth exploring the literature on land justice. In using justice as a key concept for land reforms, some scholars have made reference to the affirmative and transformative approaches to reform.[57] Affirmative, in this sense, essentially means no reform at all but merely affirming the status quo – suggesting that the 'non-reformist' reform approach can lead to a more fundamental transformative approach. Scholars have also applied the transformative approach to property rights in South Africa. For instance, Van der Walt notes that:

> In short, the argument is that … the property regime, including the current system of property holdings and the rules and practices that entrench and protect them, tends to insulate itself against change (including social and political transformation) through the security and stability-seeking tendency of tradition and legal culture, including the

[55] Marcuse, P, Connolly, J, Novy, J, Olivo, I, Potter, C and Steil, J (eds), *Searching for the just city: debates in urban theory and practice* (Routledge 2009); Novy, J and Mayer, M, 'As "just" as it gets? The European City in the "Just City" discourse' in *Searching for the just city* (ibid) pp 123–39.

[56] Fainstein, SS, 'The just city' (2014) 18(1) *International Journal of Urban Sciences* 1–8.

[57] McAuslan, P, *Land Law Reform in Eastern Africa: Traditional or Transformative?: A critical review of 50 years of land law reform in Eastern Africa 1961–2011* (Routledge 2013) p 3.

> assumptions about security and stability embedded in the rights paradigm … the rights paradigm tends to stabilise the current distribution of property holdings by securing extant property holding on the assumption that they are lawfully acquired, socially important and politically and morally legitimate. This function of the rights paradigm tends to resist or minimise change, including change brought about by morally, politically and legally legitimate and authorised reform or transformative efforts.[58]

Van der Walt focuses here on applying justice in property rights, including examining the effectiveness of anti-eviction laws and policies and the limited interest in land enjoyed by squatters and other similar occupiers.

Returning to the theory of justice, it is notable that in the energy sector for instance, the concept of energy justice is commonly heard. In energy terms, some questions may arise, such as: How fair is it to have over 3 billion people lacking access to modern energy? Is it morally right to introduce strategies that will have an impact on investments in fossil fuels knowing that the number without access to modern energy is anticipated to escalate in developing countries? Data shows that, globally, 1.2 billion people have no access to modern energy such as electricity and nearly 3 billion people rely on traditional biomass (such as wood and charcoal) for cooking and heating. This number is high in SSA despite the region's richness in energy resources, with an estimated 65 billion barrels of proven oil reserves, equivalent to around five per cent of the world total.[59]

The above notwithstanding, recognising the differences in societies, discussion has flourished in the literature around terms such as energy justice, climate justice and just transition. Climate justice takes into account the need to share the benefits and burdens of climate change from a human rights perspective; energy justice refers to the application of human rights across the energy life cycle[60] and environmental justice aims to treat all citizens equally and to involve them in the development, implementation and enforcement of environmental laws, regulations and policies.[61] A concept that is relevant in the twenty-first century is that of a just transition, which aims to capture the just process for when societies move towards an economy free of CO_2 emissions. It has also been noted that justice is an important element to the transition, because often the rhetoric of governments, companies, institutions and researchers simply discusses 'a transition to

[58] Van der Walt, AJ, *Property in the Margins* (Bloomsbury Publishing 2009); See also McAuslan, P, *Land Law Reform in Eastern Africa: Traditional or Transformative?: A critical review of 50 years of land law reform in Eastern Africa 1961–2011* (Routledge 2013).

[59] Nalule, VR, 'How to Respond to Energy Transitions in Africa: Introducing the Energy Progression Dialogue' in Nalule (ed), *Energy Transitions and the Future of the African Energy Sector* (Palgrave Macmillan 2021) pp 3–35.

[60] Jenkins, K, McCauley, D, Heffron, R, Hannes, S, and Rehner, R, 'Energy justice: A conceptual review' (2016) 11 *Energy Research & Social Science* 174–82; Sovacool, BK and MH Dworkin, MH, 'Energy Justice: Conceptual Insights and Practical Applications' (2015) 142 *Applied Energy* 435–44.

[61] Heffron, R and McCauley, D, 'Just transition: integrating climate, energy and environmental justice' (2018) 119 *Energy Policy* 1–7.

low carbon economy' with no concomitant mention of 'just'.[62] Scholars have also expressed the need for a united justice, ie a concept that aims to unify all the other concepts of justice including climate, energy and environment.[63]

The above clearly illustrates the development of the 'justice theory' in the energy sector. Regarding land law, it is worth noting that the main feature of property rights is that they are not absolute. History has proved that property such as land has been subjected to restrictive regulations and reforms, sometimes triggered by public interest and issues of justice and morality. This implies that social justice affects and shapes the property regime; conversely, recognition of the need for social reform implies acceptance of the justification for reform of the property regime.[64] In this respect, therefore, land justice should govern the various land law reforms found across the African continent.

Land justice should encompass the need to rectify the historical wrongs, the need to cater for present land needs, and the ability to effectively plan for future generations. This, in essence, necessitates the sustainable use of land. For instance, with respect to mining operations, companies and governments should be able to enforce mining closure provisions and other legal provisions relating to land rehabilitation. In the oil and gas sector, companies and governments should be able to effectively enforce the legal requirements with respect to decommissioning. Additionally, given the negative environmental impacts associated with the extractive industries such as oil spills and gas flaring, which make it impossible for the local communities to utilise their land, companies and governments should make more effort in embracing practical initiatives to ensure that they do not interfere with communities' rights to use neighbouring land for fishing or agriculture. Land justice in the extractive industries also necessitates proper compensation and resettlement of the various people displaced due to the establishment of energy and mining projects. Guided by this principle of land justice, the next section therefore discusses the various land reforms in selected African countries.

II. Land Law Reforms and their Impact on the Extractive Industries: Case Studies

As discussed in the previous sections, land law in most African countries was influenced by the various colonial interests, which mostly focused on transferring property rights to Europeans at the expense of the indigenous people. After

[62] Heffron, R and McCauley, D, 'Just transition: integrating climate, energy and environmental justice' (2018) 119 *Energy Policy* 1–7.

[63] Heffron, R and McCauley, D, 'Just transition: integrating climate, energy and environmental justice' (2018) 119 *Energy Policy* 1–7.

[64] Van der Walt, AJ, *Property in the Margins* (Bloomsbury Publishing 2009); See also, McAuslan, P, *Land Law Reform in Eastern Africa: Traditional or Transformative?: A critical review of 50 years of land law reform in Eastern Africa 1961–2011* (Routledge 2013).

independence, some African countries adopted the land laws and policies relied on by the former colonial governments. In this respect, with the exception of private land, these countries became the allodial owners of the land on which African citizens lived and farmed. This became public land (Uganda, Tanganyika (known today as Tanzania)), trust land (Kenya) or vacant land (Rwanda, Mozambique) or some such term which had the effect of vesting such land in the state or the President or sometimes in 'the people' but with the usage administered on their behalf by the government.[65]

The privatisation of land was one of the marked features of land law reforms in Africa in the 1950s. Prior to the colonisation of Africa, land was held as communal property. The origin of privatisation is attributed to the desire by the colonial masters to individualise land tenures in the wake of the end of colonialism in the 1950s. For instance, in Kenya, the land policies of land adjudication and registration which commenced in the 1950s were influenced by the East Africa Royal Commission in 1955.[66] The report covered the then Tanganyika, Uganda and Kenya. The report had a profound influence on British colonial development policy generally; it was also influential in the World Bank policies concerning land.[67] In summary, the report recommended that:

> Policy concerning the tenure and disposition of land should aim at the individualisation of land ownership and mobility in the transfer of land which, without ignoring existing property rights, will enable access to land for economic use … exclusive individual ownership of land must be registered … individual rights of land ownership should be confirmed by a process of adjudication and registration …

The above, it is argued here, falls under the traditional approach of land reform, which as McAuslan explains,

> … adopts and continues the colonial approach of vesting land in the state, maintains a dual system of land tenure and at the same time adopts an overall policy perspective of moving towards a land market based on registered title to land which implies

[65] McAuslan, P, *Land Law Reform in Eastern Africa: Traditional or Transformative?: A critical review of 50 years of land law reform in Eastern Africa 1961–2011* (Routledge 2013) p 12.

[66] East Africa Royal Commission (Dow Commission) report (Cmd 9475, 1955–1956, XIII, 397, HMSO). The quotations are at pp 428–29, as cited by McAuslan, P, *Land Law Reform in Eastern Africa: Traditional or Transformative?: A critical review of 50 years of land law reform in Eastern Africa 1961–2011* (Routledge 2013) p 13.

[67] The two World Bank reports, 'The Economic Development of Tanganyika' (1961) and 'The Economic Development of Uganda' (1962), both referred approvingly to the report and recommended that individualisation of land tenure along the lines recommended in the report be adopted in both countries. Additionally, the World Bank Land Reform Policy Paper (1975) argued for the replacement of customary tenure with individualisation of land tenure on the basis of modern statute law. The 2003 World Bank policy document on land also stressed the importance of land markets and the formality of rights. See Deinninger, K, 'Land Policies for Growth and Poverty Reduction' (World Bank and Oxford University Press 2003). For more information, see McAuslan, P, *Land Law Reform in Eastern Africa: Traditional or Transformative?: A critical review of 50 years of land law reform in Eastern Africa 1961–2011* (Routledge 2013) p 15.

> or provides for the disappearance of customary tenure and, perhaps most important, makes no or little effort to address the inequalities and injustices of the land tenure system inherited at independence and indeed does equally little to prevent its continuance and worsening thereafter.[68]

The above notwithstanding, there have been various efforts to ensure land justice in the recent land reforms undertaken by different countries. In this respect, the next sub-sections explore the various land law reforms in selected countries. The discussion is not exhaustive, since most of the case studies have already been discussed or referred to in Chapter one.

A. Land Law Reforms in Tanzania

Tanzania is endowed with massive gas and mineral resources. In recent years, the country has attracted a lot of investments in the extractives industry. The historical events relating to land in Tanzania are important. With respect to general history, Tanzania has been considered as home to some of the oldest hominid settlements unearthed by archaeologists and is said to be home to 'The Cradle of Mankind', as prehistoric stone tools and hominid fossils have been found in and around Olduvai Gorge in northern Tanzania. Previously known as Tanganyika, the country was a colony and part of German East Africa from the 1880s to 1919 when, under the jurisdiction of the League of Nations, it became a British mandate. The British governed by proclamation until the constitutional basis under the League of Nations mandate was put in place in 1920.

With respect to the history of land tenure, it is important to note that upon independence, the country inherited the land policies and systems relied on by the former colonial master. As such, land administration was characterised by a dual system of land law; statutory rights of occupancy[69] for settlers; a very small amount of freehold land which was a hold-over from the German period of colonialism; and deemed rights of occupancy for African occupiers of land under customary tenure which were the only 'permissible' statutory interests in land. The country later abolished freehold tenures, and these were converted to 99-year government leases. The country later developed its *ujamaa* or villagisation policies, aimed at reaching out to peasants by providing better health, social and education facilities.

In order to enforce the villagisation policies, a Village Settlement Agency (VSA) was set up in 1963 to ensure the effective settlements for a villagisation programme. The first Five-Year Plan proposed to settle almost half a million people on 70 schemes, at a cost of over £12 million Sterling by 1969. *Ujamaa* villages also aimed to achieve the same objectives. These had their own legal framework via

[68] McAuslan, P, *Land Law Reform in Eastern Africa: Traditional or Transformative?: A critical review of 50 years of land law reform in Eastern Africa 1961–2011* (Routledge 2013) p 15.

[69] For the genesis of the rights of occupancy, see James, RW, *Land Tenure and Policy in Tanzania* (East Africa Literature Bureau 1971) 93–95, fn 3.

the Land Tenure (Village Settlements) Act 1965. The Act protected community interest in land.[70]

The rules and regulations for compulsory acquisition, which date back to 1967, are key concerns with respect to extractives and land access in Tanzania. They facilitate the acquisition of land for most extractive investment, although they provide limited protection for customary rights-holders. In terms of mining legislation, the first piece of law was the 1920 Mining Ordinance passed under British authority following the discovery of gold around Lake Victoria. Given the importance of access to land in the mining sector, the legislation laid the ground for who had priority over land rights/extractives in Tanzania. In this respect, the ordinance gave the holder of a prospecting licence the rights to search for minerals on any land in the territory except private land that had been granted or leased. Private land was mainly owned by European settlers, and as such they were entitled to compensation for mining activities carried out on their (private) land. For land occupied by the 'natives', however, the compensation would be paid to the District Political Officer, who could distribute the same to the affected natives.[71]

Besides the issue of compensation, it is worth noting that the 1929 Mining Ordinance vested all minerals in the Governor, who could then grant rights to individuals and companies. This control over natural resources by the colonial state was supplemented by the 1923 Land Ordinance, which declared all public land to be under the control of the Governor. With respect to petroleum, the 1958 Mining (Mineral Oil) Ordinance also had similar implications with respect to the ownership of petroleum resources in Tanzania.

Following independence, the government tried to remedy the injustices of the colonial era. Nevertheless, they retained some land policies which were introduced during colonialism, including the ownership and control of minerals, which were now vested in the government. Additionally, the various Acts that followed had the aim of protecting foreign investments (which were mostly owned by Europeans). As such, the 1963 Foreign Investment (Protection) Act guaranteed 'full and fair' compensation to landowners in case of nationalisation. This implied that it would become hard to remedy the past wrongs and ensure justice to the local Tanzanians.

Additionally, the colonial influence over the reforms in Tanzania can also be evidenced in an attempt by the British to pass a Bill of Rights, which would prioritise the rights of whites in the former colonised territories. In Tanzania, this was rejected by the party of liberation, the Tanganyika African National Union (TANU), and its leader, Julius Nyerere, on the grounds that the Bill would only favour the European and Asian minorities.[72]

[70] The discussion on Tanzanian land reforms will not include Zanzibar. Although part of a union with the Tanzanian mainland since 1964, Zanzibar has its own legislation when it comes to land.

[71] Pedersen, RH, Jacob, T, Maganga, F, Kweka, O, 'Rights to land and extractive resources in Tanzania (1/2): The history'. *DIIS Working paper 2016/11*.

[72] Pedersen, RH, Jacob, T, Maganga, F, Kweka, O, 'Rights to land and extractive resources in Tanzania (1/2): The history'. *DIIS Working paper 2016/11*.

In an effort to ensure that all Tanzanians benefited from the country's resources, in 1967 TANU proclaimed the Arusha Declaration, which spelled out a policy of socialism in Tanzania.[73] There were many implications for this declaration, including the nationalisation of various investments, but what is relevant with respect to land reforms is that it protected customary landowners and their rights to own the means of production. Additionally, the 1967 Land Acquisition Act provided the legal basis for acquiring land for any 'public purpose' in Tanzania. Although the Act provided for compensation, it can arguably be reviewed as a continuation of the colonial era land regime, mainly because land was vested in the government. The developments in the 1970s were marked by the insertion into the 1977 Constitution of a Bill of Rights in 1984. With respect to land reforms, this meant that natives had a right to own property and have their property protected. The influence of international organisations cannot be underestimated with respect to the liberalisation move that took place in Tanzania in the 1970s. However, a lack of capital, coupled with the poor performance of the parastatals (state-owned enterprises) also contributed to the government's focus and desire in attracting foreign investment.

In mining terms, although the state/government remained the owner of all the minerals, it was not mandatory for it to directly take part in the exploration of these minerals.[74] ASM mining was also encouraged in the 1970s.[75] In all these developments, the rights of landowners, including customary landowners, were protected.[76]

The above notwithstanding, the 1990s were characterised by widespread dissatisfaction amongst the rural population with villagisation and other land matters. This necessitated the establishment of the Presidential Commission of Inquiry into Land Matters. The Commission reported to President Mwinyi at the end of 1992.[77] Following the Commission's report, the National Land Policy (NLP) was adopted by the National Assembly in July 1995.[78] Consequently, the Land Act

[73] In 1967, President Nyerere published his paper 'Socialism and Rural Development', in which he recognised the essential role of land in economic development.

[74] The 1978 Mining Act of Tanzania and the 1980 Petroleum (Exploration and Production) Act both greatly encouraged the participation of foreign investors.

[75] For instance, the 1983 Small-Scale Mining Policy Paper encouraged people to supplement their incomes with mining activities.

[76] Pedersen, RH, Jacob, T, Maganga, F, Kweka, O, 'Rights to land and extractive resources in Tanzania (1/2): The history'. *DIIS Working paper 2016/11*.

[77] The Commission published its report in 1994. Various recommendations were made including divesting the ultimate land title from the state (although this was not implemented).

[78] Besides the National Land Policy, which dates back to 1995, each of the three land categories – general land, village land and reserved land – is governed by a number of different pieces of legislation. These include the Land Act of 1999, which governs general land, and the Village Land Act of 1999, governing village land. Reserved land is governed the Wildlife Conservation Act (WCA) of 2009 for wildlife resources and the Forest Act of 2002 for forestry.

and the Village Land Act were enacted.[79] Some of the key features of the NLP which were enshrined in land legislation included:

- The fundamental principle that all land is public land and as such is vested in the President as trustee for and on behalf of the citizens of Tanzania.
- The National Land Advisory Council was established by the Act, with representatives of civil society, to review and advise the Minister on the NLP and recommend changes where necessary.
- The operation and regulation of the land market.
- Village land administration to be administered by the village community.
- The Commissioner of Lands recognised as being central in land administration.

Whereas the early years following independence mirrored the influence of the colonial era on Tanzania's land policies, the 1999 Land Act disregarded reliance on English statutes. Consequently, Section 180(2) of the Land Act is to the effect that no more English statutes of general application could ever be held to apply to Tanzanian land law, after the Land Act came into force. Additionally, sub-section (3) directed the courts to develop a Tanzanian common law of land:

> On and after the commencement of this Act, it shall be the duty of all courts in interpreting and applying this Act and other laws relating to land in Tanzania to use their best endeavours to create a common law of Tanzania applicable in equal measure to all land and to this end the courts shall apply a purposive interpretation to this Act and shall at all times be guided by the fundamental principles of land policy set out in section 3.

In summary, the 1990s were characterised by three major pieces of legislation including: the Land Act of 1999 (as amended); the Mortgage Finance (Special Provisions) Act 2008; and the Village Land Act 1999.[80] The Tanzanian land reforms discussed above clearly indicate the nexus between land law and the extractive industries. The issue of ownership has clearly been a focal point since the time of colonialism, and it continued to play a central role even after independence. This is testimony that the success of any energy or mining projects clearly depends on effective access to the land in question. Consequently, the regulation and administration of land is essential in the extractive industries. Under the two 1999 Land Acts, land is owned either under a statutory individualised title – a granted right of occupancy – or under a certificate of customary right of occupancy (CCRO) approved by village authorities.[81] There are various issues addressed in the land laws

[79] The Land Act 1999 was brought into force in May 2001; the Village Land Act in 1999.

[80] The Village Land Act entrusts decision-making on land transfers of less than 250 ha to Village Councils, an elected body of village members, and approvals to Village Assemblies, a meeting of an entire village population. Additionally, land transfers of more than 250 ha require ministerial approval, under the advisement of the Village Assembly, Village Council, and District Council.

[81] A CCRO is to be issued according to local customary practices and confirmed by the village community in a participatory manner

and regulations in Tanzania. These include among others, the promotion of gender justice in access land. Accordingly, Section 60 of the Village Land Act mandates for more balanced gender representation in Village Land Councils.[82] Additionally, the Acts declare that where customary laws and gender equality come into conflict, the Land Acts (championing gender equality) should take precedence.

Although outside the extractive sector, it is worth noting the land conflicts in Tanzania that have been influenced by the move to a green economy. Notably, the Southern Agricultural Growth Corridor of Tanzania (SAGCOT) has attracted various land use conflicts.[83] Although there are various issues to be discussed with respect to SAGCOT, the issue that is of interest in this sub-section is that relating to land conflicts, which were caused due to the 2012 'Operation Save Kilombero' to remove livestock from the wetlands of the Kilombero floodplains.[84] This led to the pastoral eviction in Kilombero in 2012, consequently leading to the spill-over of pastoralists to other areas creating new farmer-herder conflicts as well as conservation conflicts. Often land conflicts in different countries are caused by many factors, including: increasing population pressure due to both natural population growth and mobility of people; dispossession of local people to pave way for large-scale investments; rent-seeking and speculation. In the Kilombero case, however, scholars identified that land use conflicts were to a large extent driven by narratives of environmental degradation, associated with livestock keeping in particular.[85] This, although not directly connected to the land conflicts in energy and mining, adds flavour to the discussion on community displacements due to land access for large-scale investments (including extractives industries).

B. Land Law Reforms in South Africa

In this South African case study, the focus will be on the current reforms aimed at ensuring land justice in the country. As such, this sub-section avoids discussing the historical land reforms during and immediately after apartheid (these have already been explored in the previous section). Rather, the focus is to highlight the different struggles of countries such as South Africa, which up to recently are focused on finding the best solution to ensure land justice. Previous land injustices, as manifested in the 1913 Natives Land Act, characterised the apartheid regime.[86] These in

[82] The Acts also emphasise the promotion of spousal co-registration of land certificates to provide legal protection for marital assets.

[83] Initiated first by President Kikwete at the World Economic Forum Africa Summit in 2010, SAGCOT is described as a public–private partnership that seeks to mobilise private investments across the agricultural value-chain and develop commercially successful and sustainable agriculture in the southern third of Tanzania. A central component is to integrate (some) smallholder farmers into agribusiness value-chains, in particular through various forms of contract farming.

[84] The Kilombero valley is centrally situated within SAGCOT and has become a national hotspot of land use conflicts.

[85] Bergius, M, Benjaminsen, TA, Maganga, F and Buhaug, H, 'Green economy, degradation narratives, and land-use conflicts in Tanzania' (2020) 129 *World Development* 104850.

[86] For a full discussion on this, refer to section I of this chapter.

turn influenced the current land reforms in South Africa including land redistribution. To date, many Black South Africans remain landless. This has influenced different approaches including a suggestion of expropriation without compensation. As far back as 2006, the African National Congress (ANC) mentioned its intentions to enforce expropriation of the various lands that were unjustly taken from the Black Africans. In this respect, in 2017, the ANC-led government made it clear that it would amend Section 25 of the South African Constitution regarding property rights to implement land Expropriation Without Compensation (EWC).[87] This was followed by the Parliamentary motion in February 2018 aimed at reviewing the property ownership clause of the Constitution, to allow for the expropriation of land in the public interest without compensation.[88] The motion laid the ground for more parliamentary discussions on constitutional land reforms.

Whilst this sub-section does not go into detail on all the various land reforms that have taken place in South Africa, it is clear that these have been influenced by the need for equality and ensuring land justice. The reforms aim to not only correct historical wrongs but also to confront present social and economic inequities and secure an equality-based future for all. This implies that the reforms are transformative in nature.

C. Land Law Reforms in Uganda

Pre-colonial Uganda was characterised by customary or traditional land ownership systems. Before 1888, what is now Uganda (the name didn't exist then) was divided into small kingdoms and a lot of different ethnic groups. Each ethnic group or tribe was ruled by a king or chief. These traditional leaders allocated land to members of their community according to customary law.[89] As in other parts of Africa, customary land tenure emphasised land justice; this was so because it ensured that every single person could access enough land for his own subsistence. Customary land tenure systems are still embraced in Uganda, although these exist alongside other tenure systems such as freehold, leasehold, and mailo tenure.[90]

[87] The announcement was made on 20 December 2017 at the 54th National Conference. At the conference, a resolution was passed to grant ownership of traditional land to the respective communities, about 13% of the country, usually registered in trust, like the Ingonyama Trust, under the name of traditional leaders to the respective communities.

[88] The reasoning behind this motion is based on the data that 72% of the nation's private farmland is owned by white people, who make up just 9% of the population. As such, in August 2018, the South African Government began the process of taking two white-owned farmland areas by filing papers seeking to acquire the farms via eminent domain for one tenth of their estimated value, which, in one case, is based on possible value when the farm is developed into an eco-estate.

[89] Although land justice was at the centre of customary land tenures in different African countries, it is worth noting that gender equality was never promoted in land ownership. This was so because most of the time land passed from father to son, since lineage is patrilineal in African countries such as Uganda.

[90] These three land tenure systems were introduced in Uganda by the British occupiers during the colonial period.

Land legislation in Uganda dates as far back as the early 1900s with the enactment of the Crown Lands Ordinance of 1903. Subsequent to the 1961 Constitutional Conference, the Crown Lands Ordinance was later repealed by the 1962 Public Lands Act (previously Public Lands Ordinance). With the new Act, Crown land was renamed public land and vested in the Uganda Lands Commission. Land Boards were established for every Federal State and every district, which had the same functions with respect to land in the State or district, such functions to be exercised for the benefit of the people of the area. There have been various land reforms since 1962, the notable ones being as follows. The 1975 Land Reform Decree declared all land in Uganda as public land. The freehold and mailo lands were converted into leases of 99 years for individuals and 199 years for public/religious bodies.[91] The 1975 reforms were ineffective and caused massive land conflicts. Consequently, the 1995 Constitution of Uganda recognised the existing land tenure systems and introduced other provisions aimed at addressing the land issues in Uganda. The Land Act was enacted in 1998.[92] The Act provides a legal framework governing land tenure, land administration and the settlement of land disputes. Both the Land Act and the 1995 Constitution have comprehensive provisions with respect to land governance in Uganda. Some of these provisions are highlighted in Table 2.5 below.

Table 2.5 Land Regulation and Governance in Uganda

1995 Constitution of Uganda	**Constitutional Provision**
Article 237 Land ownership	• Land in Uganda belongs to the citizens of Uganda and shall vest in them in accordance with the land tenure systems. • The Government or a local government may acquire land in the public interest. • Non-citizens may acquire leases in land. • Recognised land tenure systems in Uganda include: customary; freehold; mailo; and leasehold. • The Government or a local government is to hold in trust for the people and protect natural lakes, rivers, wetlands, forest reserves, game reserves, national parks and any land to be reserved for ecological and touristic purposes for the common good of all citizens. • Landowners under the customary tenure may acquire certificates of ownership. • Land under customary tenure may be converted to freehold land ownership by registration.

(continued)

[91] This happened in 1975 under the dictatorship of Idi Amin.
[92] The Land Act 1998 (No 16 of 1998), Laws of Uganda.

Table 2.5 ***(Continued)***

1995 Constitution of Uganda	**Constitutional Provision**
Article 238 Uganda Land Commission	• The Uganda Land Commission holds and manages any land in Uganda vested in or acquired by the Government of Uganda. • Consists of a chairperson and not less than four other members appointed by the President with the approval of Parliament.
Article 240 District land boards	• Functions include, among others, to hold and allocate land in the district which is not owned by any person or authority.
Article 243 Land tribunals	• The jurisdiction of a land tribunal includes: o the determination of disputes relating to the grant, lease, repossession, transfer or acquisition of land by individuals, the Uganda Land Commission or other authority with responsibility relating to land; o and the determination of any disputes relating to the amount of compensation to be paid for land acquired.
Article 244 Minerals	• Minerals and mineral ores shall be exploited taking into account the interests of the individual landowners, local governments and the Government.
Article 245 Protection of environment	• Parliament is to enact laws to protect and preserve the environment from abuse, pollution and degradation

As illustrated in Table 2.5 above, there are different land tenure systems, some of them being unique to Uganda. For instance, the mailo land tenure system is not available in other African countries.[93] This type of tenure is most common in central Uganda – specifically in the Buganda region. Mailo tenure refers to land holding by a landowner which has its roots from the 1900 Uganda Agreement and 1928 *Busullu Envujjo* Law.[94]

Although the mailo landowners have the same rights as freehold land owners, they must respect the rights of lawful and bona fide occupants and *Kibanja* holders to occupy and live on the land.[95] Section 29(2) of the Land Act defines a bona fide occupant as any person who, before the coming into force of the 1995 Constitution of Uganda, had either occupied and utilised or developed any land unchallenged by the registered owner or agent of the registered owner for 12 years or more;

[93] Mailo land is as a result of the 1900 Uganda Agreement between the British Government and the Kingdom of Buganda. Under this Agreement, the British granted some 8,000 square miles of land (hence known as 'mailo' land) to the Kabaka of Buganda and various other chiefs and notables.

[94] Article 237(3) of the 1995 Constitution of Uganda and Section 2 of the Land Act, 1998.

[95] Section 3(4) of the Land Act, 1998, Laws of Uganda.

or had been settled on land by the Government or an agent of the Government, which may include a local authority, for instance local council chairpersons.[96]

There are various land issues in Uganda which cannot be dealt with exhaustively in this section. Rather, the focus here relates to my 2019 experience as an energy and mining expert witness, before the Bamugemereire Commission of Inquiry into Land Matters in Uganda.[97] There were many concerns raised by the Commission with respect to land access for energy and mining projects. All these cannot be exhausted in this section, as such I will only address the issue concerning compensation with respect to land access for energy and mining projects. One of the questions raised by the Commission was how to adequately compensate the host communities for their land in the resource-rich areas in Uganda?

In Uganda, the ultimate ownership of land is vested in the country's citizens. The Constitution, under Article 237(1) and (3), vests the ownership of land in the citizens of Uganda.[98] The article further outlines the different tenure systems under which the land can be held.[99] As such, the owner of the land is entitled to compensation if oil, gas or mining activities are to be carried out on his/her land. The reasoning behind compensation is based on the fact that a mining title does not per se extinguish the rights of the landowner; rather it grants the owner of a mining licence a right to exploit the natural resources present in the subsoil, which definitely requires access to the surface.[100]

With respect to the nexus between land access and extractives, it is worth noting that in Uganda natural resources, including hydrocarbons and minerals, are held by the government on behalf of the people. In this respect, the state will intervene to ensure that the landowners are fully compensated. If no agreement can be reached, then the state may move to expropriate the land for mining purposes, in which case the landowner will still be entitled to compensation. A question then arises, what should be considered when compensating people in oil-, gas- and mineral-rich areas? Some of the key considerations are outlined below:

- Considering the fact that most land where mining is carried out is located in rural areas with communities who depend on agriculture, farming and

[96] A lawful occupant on the other hand, is defined under Section 29 of the Land Act to include persons occupying land by virtue of the repealed: (i) *Busuulu* and *Envujjo* Law of 1928; (ii) Toro Landlord and Tenant Law of 1937; and (iii) Ankole Landlord and Tenant Law of 1937.

[97] Videos when I appeared as an energy and expert witness before the Commission of Inquiry into Land matters in Uganda can be accessed at, 'Dr. Nalule as an Energy & Mining Expert Witness (A)' – *YouTube*; 'Dr. Nalule as an Oil, Gas & Mining Expert Witness (Part 3)' – *YouTube*; 'Dr. Nalule as an Oil & Gas Expert Witness (Part 2)' – *YouTube*. Last visited on 1 Jan 2021.

[98] The Constitution of Uganda, 1995, as amended.

[99] The Constitution of Uganda, 1995, as amended.

[100] Nalule, VR, *Mining and the Law in Africa: Exploring the social and environmental impacts* (Palgrave Pivot 2019).

fishing, it becomes imperative to calculate such compensation taking into consideration the livelihood of the local communities, and how they will be negatively impacted if they no longer have access to their land to carry out their daily activities.

- There is a need to ensure that women and children benefit from this compensation. In this respect policy-makers should ensure that the wife and older children of the landowner take part in the negotiations before the final compensation is agreed upon.
- There is also a need to have a resettlement plan so that the local people have better options for relocating.
- Compensation may also consider disruption caused to the landowner. In Uganda, this is well stipulated under Section 83 of the Mining Act, 2003.

Taking into account the above, it is notable that the land law reforms are focused on ensuring that local people are not unjustly treated in the acquisition of land for energy and mining projects. Although this section does not examine the various land laws in detail, it highlights the nexus between land and extractives.

D. Land Law Reforms in Rwanda

Rwanda is a landlocked country of Eastern Africa of 26,338 km^2. Just like in other African countries, access to land is essential in Rwanda since over 70 per cent of the population (especially in rural areas) relies on agriculture. After the 1994 genocide, land conflicts became rampant. As in other post-conflict communities (such as the Sierra Leon example I discussed in Chapter one of this book), access to land and ensuring land justice is often at the fore of government policies. Grievances over land ownership were common between residents and repatriated Rwandans after the 1994 genocide. These issues, among others, necessitated the various land reforms in the country.

The land law reforms in Rwanda have been influenced by not only the need to address the social injustices suffered during colonialism, but also the injustices caused by genocide. Colonisation introduced new elements into Rwandan society, including in the administration of land. Belgian colonisation introduced deep changes in the management of the country by encouraging the centralised administration of land. The 1926 reform abolished the traditional structures which focused on national unity, and instead divided the country into chieftainships and abolished the system by which a chief could own several land properties in different parts of the country, which hitherto characterised his importance in the country's hierarchy.

German colonisation (the predecessor to the Belgians) introduced the written law appearing in the codes and laws of Rwanda, particularly in order to guarantee land tenure security for settlers and other foreigners wishing to invest in land in Rwanda. The German colonial administration established the 1885 decree concerning land use. The following are the two main doctrines of this decree:

- Only the Colonial Public Officer could guarantee the right to use the land taken from indigenous Rwandans. Settlers or other foreigners intending to settle in the country had to apply to the colonial administration, follow its rules for obtaining land, and conclude settlement agreements.
- Land use had to be accompanied by a title deed. However, the natives were not to be dispossessed of their land. Vacant land was considered as state-owned land. This provision introduced the duality of systems in the country's land tenure system.

All occupied land remained subject to customary law, and only settlers and other foreigners could benefit from the new written law system that was protected by the colonial administration.

Post-colonialism, various land reforms were embraced in Rwanda. The 2003 Constitution of the Republic of Rwanda, as amended in 2015, recognises the need for effective land governance in the country. Article 35 of the Constitution provides that, 'private ownership of land and other rights related to land are granted by the State. A law determines modalities of concession, transfer, and use of land.' Besides the Constitution, there are other land legal reforms which took place in Rwanda, and these were evident in the 2000s, the notable one being the adoption of the 2004 National Land Policy.[101] The main objective of the NLP is stipulated in paragraph 4.1.1 and as such it reads as follows:

> In the perspective of the harmonious and sustainable development of our country, the overall objective of the national land policy is to establish a land tenure system that guarantees tenure security for all Rwandans and give guidance to the necessary land reforms with a view to good management and rational use of national land resources.

[101] The policy is governed by several principles as outlined in para 4.2. These include: 'Land is a common heritage for past, present and future generations'; 'according to the constitutional principle of equality of all citizens, all Rwandans enjoy the same rights of access to land without any discrimination whatsoever'; 'land administration should guarantee land tenure security'; 'the determination of the real purpose of land and information about land are a pre-requisite to the good management and rational use of land, which is the basic element of development and source of life'; 'methods of land management and land use differ according to whether they concern urban or rural land; existing fragile zones that are of national interest should be protected'; 'good land management should develop land use planning, including the organisation of human settlements and consolidation of small plots for a more economic and productive use of land'; 'land transactions and land taxation should be included in land administration as elements of land development'; and 'a well-defined legal and institutional framework is an indispensable tool for the establishment of a national land policy.'

Before the establishment of the 2004 policy, the country lacked proper law regulating land matters. Some of the obstacles which were created by this gap in land legislation include:

- Strong pressure on the already spatially limited land resources by a rapidly growing population.
- A land tenure system dominated by customary law which favours land fragmentation, a practice which incrementally reduces the size of family farms which are already below the threshold of the average surface area that is economically viable.
- A considerable number of landless persons who have to be resettled at all costs.
- The lack of a reliable land registration system guaranteeing the security of land tenure.
- Disorderly and fraudulent land transactions, necessitating the establishment of regulations that would enable the authorities to allocate to the land a recognised market value which brings considerable profit to the Government Treasury.[102]

Following the 2004 NLP, the Government of Rwanda enacted the Organic Land Law No 08/2005 of 14 July 2005. This law laid down in detail the legal, regulatory and institutional framework for land ownership, governance and management. Three years after the enactment of the 2005 Organic Land Law, the Government of Rwanda initiated the Land Tenure Regularization Program (LTRP) in 2008. The LTRP aimed at, among other things ensuring security of land tenures and enhancing efficient management and administration of land.[103] In 2006, the National Land Commission was established: the office of Registrar of Land Titles was also established around the same period. In June 2013, a new land law was enacted to replace Law No 22/99 of 12 November 1999. One of the key provisions of this law is the requirement for all landholders to formally register their land and transactions. In 2017, the National Land Center, currently known as the Rwanda Land Management and Use Authority (RMLUA), was established. In 2019, the new National Land Policy was adopted, replacing the 2004 NLP.

[102] The policy further illustrates the link between land and other aspects of life. As such para 5 states: 'Economic factors which highlight the value of the land and the economic stake of its control. – Legal factors which highlight the norms of land use, the legislative systems and the legal status of land and its underlying resources – Institutional aspects which highlight authorities responsible for arbitration, decision making, and land administration; – Technical aspects which promote techniques of development of space that improve the land's value and in some cases transform the status of the land; reliable methods of land allocation and rational land use. The land tenure system introduces the principle of land-use management and makes land management plan an essential and almost inevitable tool for land management'.

[103] The Land Administration and Information System (LAIS) is currently operational in Rwanda. Another thing to note about the land laws in Rwanda, is the emphasis on gender equality in land access.

The 2019 NLP recognises eight thematic areas, including:

- land use planning, surveying, and mapping;
- land utilisation by various sectors;
- efficient land use management;
- land for private sector investment;
- land registration;
- administration of land lease fees, real property taxes, and land markets;
- securing land rights and management of land disputes; and
- institutional and coordination framework of the land sub-sector.

There are several reasons that prompted the revision of the 2004 NLP. One of the reasons is that the 2004 NLP was mostly focused on land administration and less on land use management. In this respect the 2019 revised NLP, although it builds on the successes of the 2004 NLP, also takes into consideration the need to focus on land use planning and management while ensuring continuity and sustainability in land administration.[104]

The Rwanda case study above, although not extensive, is evidence of land reforms focused on tackling the social, political and economic challenges faced by citizens. The early post-colonial land laws, including the 2004 NLP, recognised the need for the land reforms not only to tackle the colonial land injustices but also the injustices suffered during and after the Rwandan genocide. However, with the current land developments at the national, regional and global levels, the current land laws, including the 2013 land law and the 2019 NLP, are more focused on addressing the land challenges faced in the twenty-first century. By so doing, the new land reforms emphasise the need for good governance and management of land use.

E. Other Case Studies Explored: Land Reforms in Kenya

Land in Kenya always had a very high profile during the colonial times, and this was reflected in the land laws and the clear division between African-occupied land and predominantly British-settler owned land. The colonial position is well summarised by Migot-Adholla[105] et al:

> Under colonial rule a dual system of tenure was instituted in which white settlers and private corporations were granted freehold titles or leaseholds in accordance with the

[104] The 2019 Revised National Land Policy of Rwanda. It can be accessed at Revised_National_Land_Policy_2019.pdf (rlma.rw).

[105] Migot-Adholla, SE, Place, F and Oluoch-Kosura, W, 'Security of tenure and land productivity in Kenya' in Bruce, JW and Migot-Adholla, SE (eds), *Searching for land tenure security in Africa* (Kendall/Hunt Publishing 1994) 119–40.

> provisions of the Land Titles Act 1908 later amended to provide for registration under the Torrens system (Registration of Titles Act 1919). During this period, most African areas were considered intact. As a strategy of political control, colonial administrators designated some local notables and 'chiefs' or installed certain marginal persons to the position, creating customary authorities with jurisdiction over almost all local matters except criminal justice …

The above notwithstanding, it is worth noting that, in Kenya, land was the major factor that drove the fight for independence from British colonial power. It is also important to note that various land reforms occurred both before and during independence.[106] Kenya secured independence from Britain in 1963.[107] The first Constitution was enacted in 1963; this was replaced in 1969 and again by the 2010 Constitution. This constitution widely departs from the two earlier constitutions, including on land and property. The 2010 Kenyan Constitution, under Chapter 5, lays out the basic principles for land governance in Kenya. These are briefly outlined in Table 2.6 below:

Table 2.6 Constitutional Land Provisions in Kenya

Provision	Basic principle
Article 60	Land to be managed in a sustainable, productive, efficient and equitable manner; elimination of gender discrimination in law; security of land rights.
Article 61	All land in Kenya belongs to the people of Kenya collectively as a nation. Land classified as public, community or private.
Article 67	Establishment of the National Land Commission. Some of the functions of the Commission include: • to manage public land on behalf of the national and county governments; • to advise the national government on a comprehensive programme for the registration of title in land throughout Kenya; • to manage public land on behalf of the national and county governments.
Article 64	Private land is held under any freehold or leasehold tenure.
Article 63	Community land is held by communities identified by ethnicity, culture or similar community interest.

[106] The main pre-independence law referred to is the Native Lands Trust Ordinance of 1938, especially as the post-independence Trust Land Act of 1968 was modelled on this colonial enactment. While amendments have been made since, the Trust Land Act was only repealed in 2016, to be replaced by the Community Land Act (CLA). Another early law post-independence referred to is the Land (Group Representatives) Act 1968, also repealed by the CLA in 2016.

[107] Prior to independence, however, the late 1950s saw a major policy initiative – the Swynnerton Plan – to begin the process of creating individual registered titles for Africans out of customary tenure in Kenya; this necessitated the passing of a plethora of laws which culminated in the 1962 Registered

As illustrated in Table 2.6 above, land in Kenya is classified into public, community and private land. The 2010 Kenyan Constitution emphasises the need for equitable access to land and effective land administration. Gender justice and environmental protection are also echoed in the Constitution as two of the main principles of land administration. Given the role of communal land in most parts of Kenya, the Constitution, under Article 60(1)(g), encourages communities to settle land disputes through recognised local community initiatives.

Whereas the National Land Commission, established under Article 67, is empowered to oversee public land management and allocation, corruption and mismanagement have surrounded the administration of public land. For instance, prior to the enactment of the 2010 Kenyan Constitution, in 2003, Kenya established the Commission of Inquiry into the Illegal/Irregular Allocation of Public Land. The Commission was chaired by Paul Ndungu and it was, among other things, responsible for inquiring into the extra-legal allocation of public lands reserved for public purposes to private individuals and corporate entities, and charged with providing recommendations to the Government for the restoration of those lands to their original purpose or other appropriate solutions.[108] Prior to the 2003 Commission, however, the Njonjo Commission of Inquiry into Land Law systems was established in 1999, with the main objective of formulating the principles of a National Land Policy framework.[109]

The land reforms in Kenya were focused on not only ensuring land justice and protection of basic human rights, but also 'getting the incentives right'. Besides the independent National Land Commission, other actors such as urban planners are key in ensuring effective land reforms. With the boom in urbanisation and population growth, some of the key concerns in land governance in Kenya have hinged around the need to ensure the construction of habitable cities across the country. With the boom in urbanisation and population growth, many cities in SSA have suffered from poor infrastructural development (roads, healthcare services and schools), congestion and pollution. These issues have been partly attributed to lack of finance and poor urban planning.[110]

Most of the land principles contained in the 2010 Constitution are influenced by the recommendations in the 2009 National Land Policy Sessional Paper, which

Land Ordinance which has, since that date, been the foundation of statutory land law in Kenya. See McAuslan, P, *Land Law Reform in Eastern Africa: Traditional or Transformative?: A critical review of 50 years of land law reform in Eastern Africa 1961–2011* (Routledge 2013) p 20.

[108] Prior to the 2003 Ndungu Commission of Inquiry, the reports from the 1998 Commission of Inquiry into repeated tribal clashes had indicated that the clashes were politically motivated and linked to land grievances and ethnicity. Basically, the 1998 Commission of Inquiry was established by President Moi. It was tasked with the main duty of investigating ethnic conflict in Kenya, including those which occurred in the Rift Valley in 1992 and 1997, the Coast province in 1997, and the areas of Molo and Laikipia in 1998.

[109] The Commission was chaired by the former Attorney-General Charles Njonjo.

[110] There is also a challenge of ineffective and under-financed government institutions.

basically sets the framework for constitutional changes.[111] The Policy aimed at the following:

- promoting positive land reforms for the improvement of the livelihoods of Kenyans through the establishment of accountable and transparent laws, institutions and systems dealing with land;
- securing rights over land and providing for sustainable growth, investment and the reduction of poverty in line with the Government's overall development objectives.

The main objectives of the Policy are stipulated in Chapter 1.4 and they include:

> The overall objective of the National Land Policy is to secure rights over land and provide for sustainable growth, investment and the reduction of poverty in line with the Government's overall development objectives. Specifically the policy shall offer a framework of policies and laws designed to ensure the maintenance of a system of land administration and management that will provide: (a) All citizens with the opportunity to access and beneficially occupy and use land; (b) Economically viable, socially equitable and environmentally sustainable allocation and use of land; (c) Efficient, effective and economical operation of land markets; (d) Efficient and effective utilisation of land and land-based resources; and (e) Efficient and transparent land dispute resolution mechanisms.[112]

Most of the provisions in the National Land Policy were reflected in the 2010 Constitution and the supporting land laws and regulations.[113] Besides the Statutory Laws, Case law addressing issues of land administration in Kenya, is worth noting. Notable cases include the 2013 High Court of Kenya case *Amoni Thomas Amfry and another v The Minister for Lands and another.*[114]

In summary, this sub-section has mostly focused on the land reforms that characterised the 2000s. Given the central role of land, the 2010 Kenyan Constitution

[111] National Land Policy (Sessional Paper No 3 of 2009), Kenya.

[112] See Chapter 1.4, para 5 of the National Land Policy (Sessional Paper No 3 of 2009), Kenya.

[113] Some of the relevant laws include: The 2012 National Land Commission Act, which established the NLC pursuant to the 2010 Kenyan Constitution; the 2012 Land Act, which replaces former categories of government and trust land; vests land in county and national government; the 2012 Land Registration Act, establishing detailed procedures for land registration; the 2016 Community Land Act, which replaced former trust land held in trust for communities by County Councils; and the Land Laws (Amendment) Act, 2016, which was assented to by the President on 31 August, 2016 and came into effect on 21 September, 2016.

[114] *Thomas Amfry and another v The Minister for Lands & another*, Petition 6 of 2013, [2013] eKLR. The main issue for consideration in this case was whether the Court should issue an order directed at the President to 'Gazette' the Chairperson and Members of the National Land Commission established under Article 67 of the Constitution in accordance with the provisions of the National Land Commission Act, 2012 (Act No 5 of 2012). Another case is the Supreme Court of Kenya *Reference No 2 of 2014, In the Matter of the National Land Commission* [2015] eKLR, which concerned an application by the National Land Commission for an Advisory Opinion under Article 163(6) of the Constitution of Kenya. First hearing of the NLC and MoL dispute over various land acts, 2012 National Land Commission Act, 2011 Urban Areas and Cities Act, National Land Policy, etc.

requires that all laws relating to land are revised, consolidated and rationalised. Consequently, besides the NLP – which was adopted in 2009 – in 2012, the Kenyan Parliament enacted the Land Act; the Land Registration Act; and the National Land Commission Act. A National Land Commission was formed in 2013 to act as the lead agency in land matters, working with the Ministry of Lands, Housing and Urban Development and county-level institutions.

There are various issues with respect to land administration in Kenya. However, this sub-section will focus on community land, specifically referring to the Community Land Act 2016.[115]

Basically, community land is provided for under Article 63, which defines it as land vested and held by communities identified based on ethnicity, culture or similar community of interest. The article further outlines the various types of community land, including:

- land lawfully registered in the name of group representatives under the provisions of any law;
- land lawfully transferred to a specific community by any process of law;
- any other land declared to be community land by an Act of Parliament;
- land that is lawfully held, managed or used by specific communities as community forests, grazing areas or shrines;
- ancestral lands and lands traditionally occupied by hunter-gatherer communities;
- land lawfully held as trust land by the county governments, but not including any public land held in trust by the county government under Article 62(2).

Article 63(3) of the 2010 Kenyan Constitution further stipulates that, 'any unregistered community land shall be held in trust by county governments on behalf of the communities for which it is held'.

The management of community land is essential and as such, in Kenya, there is a register of all community land. Communities can be registered as corporate bodies and a register maintained. Registration is also to be done in the name of the community.

According to Section 14 of the CLA, community members own the land jointly. As such, the section stipulates that individuals, families, and other customary groups or new groups formed by community members, such as a cooperative or association, can be acknowledged as the owners of rights to particular parts of the community's domain. However, under Section 27 of CLA, individual members, families and groups may register (lesser) title to specific areas, most usually for house and farm plots.

[115] Appendix I of this book highlights Part III of the Community Land Act, No 27 of 2016, which relates to the management and governance of community land in Kenya

All the aspects of community land cannot be exhausted in this chapter. However, what is clear from the Kenyan example is the willingness of African Governments to embrace customary law relating to land ownership. The enactment of the 2016 Kenyan CLA is a clear indication that African countries are embracing transformational land reforms which are centred on empowering the local communities.

III. Environmental Impacts Associated with Extractives and Land Access

The negative environmental impacts associated with extractive industries directly affect land use. Petroleum and mining activities, although they are a main source of revenue for the resource-rich countries in Africa, are also a source of pollution and human rights abuses. These sectors are characterised by oil spillages, gas flaring, discharge of heavy metals from mining, chemical pollution, and mine dumps such as tailings and slag material. All these negatively impact on land use, especially farming, fishing and hunting.

Throughout this book, the environmental impacts associated with the extractive industries are discussed (in Chapters one, three and four). As such, this section will be brief.

As noted in Chapter one, with respect to the petroleum industry and the related environmental and land use issues, Nigeria provides a good example, especially with respect to gas flaring and oil spillage. The local communities in the Niger Delta region have suffered the impacts associated with gas flaring and oil spills, making it hard for them to utilise their land. An 'oil spill' is defined as the accidental release of a liquid petroleum hydrocarbon into the environment due to human activity. In Nigeria, there are several causes of oil spills, and it has been noted that approximately 50 per cent of the spills are attributable to pipeline vandalism and tanker accidents; 28 per cent of spills are due to sabotage; production and operation account for 21 per cent; and the remaining 1 per cent is due to deficient equipment used in production. Additionally, the deliberate blowing up of pipelines by militant groups has also increased oil spillage in the Niger Delta region.[116] Oil spills are very prevalent in Nigeria and it is estimated that between 1 million and 13 million tons of hydrocarbons have been spilled in the region over the last 50 years. These have led to the destruction of rainforest habitat occupying land equating to 7,400km^2, the loss of mangrove forests, the destruction of

[116] Allison, C, Oriabure, G, Ndimele, PE and Shittu, JA, 'Dealing with oil spill scenarios in the Niger Delta: Lessons from the past' in Ndimele, PE (ed), *The political ecology of oil and gas activities in the Nigerian aquatic ecosystem* (Academic Press 2018) pp 351–68; Nalule, VR, *Energy Poverty and Access Challenges in Sub-Saharan Africa: The Role of Regionalism* (Palgrave Macmillan 2018).

an equivalent of a year's supply of food, and causing diseases afflicting the local people, just to mention but a few.[117]

With respect to the mining industry, the waste generated contains high concentrations of metals and metalloids which have resulted in contamination of ground and surface water. For instance, the mining of gold in the Witwaterstrand Basin of South Africa has resulted in environmental degradation. It has been observed that the concentrations of heavy toxic metals – mainly arsenic (As), cadmium (Cd), cobalt (Co), copper (Cu), lead (Pb), uranium (U), and mercury (Hg) – from gold sites are above acceptable levels in South Africa.[118] Other African countries including South Sudan; the DRC and Uganda are also victims of the negative environmental impacts associated with the mining industry.

The table below summarises the negative environmental impacts associated with mining and petroleum activities. The table also highlights the key international environmental agreements. As noted earlier, these issues have been fully examined in the various chapters of this book (Chapters one, three and four).

Table 2.7 Environmental Impacts Associated with the Extractive Industries

Mining	**Petroleum (Oil & Gas)**	**International Instruments**
Soil contamination and surface destruction	Oil spills	The United Nations Convention to Combat Desertification (UNCCD), 1994
Deforestation and desertification	Gas flaring	The Stockholm Declaration on the Human Environment, 1972
Noise pollution and vibration	Air pollution	The Stockholm Convention on Persistent Organic Pollutions (POPs), 2004
Air pollution	Water pollution	The Basel Convention on the Control of Transboundary Movements of Hazardous Wastes and their Disposal, 1989
Tailings/ Discharge or dumping of mine wastes into the environment	Displacements and forced relocations	The United Nations Framework Convention on Climate Change (UNFCC)

(continued)

[117] Zabbey, N, Sam, K and Onyebuchi, AT, 'Remediation of contaminated lands in the Niger Delta, Nigeria: Prospects and challenges' (2017) 586 *Science of the Total Environment* 952–65. See Allison, C, Oriabure, G, Ndimele, PE and Shittu, JA, 'Dealing with oil spill scenarios in the Niger Delta: Lessons from the past' in Ndimele, PE (ed), *The political ecology of oil and gas activities in the Nigerian aquatic ecosystem* (Academic Press 2018) pp 351–68; Nalule, VR, *Energy Poverty and Access Challenges in Sub-Saharan Africa: The Role of Regionalism* (Palgrave Macmillan 2018).

[118] For a detailed discussion, see, Olawuyi, DS, *Extractives Industry Law in Africa* (Springer International Publishing 2018) p 270.

Table 2.7 ***(Continued)***

Mining	**Petroleum (Oil & Gas)**	**International Instruments**
Acid rock drainage/ Acid mine drainage	Loss of subsistence rights and business profits	The International Convention for the Prevention of Pollution from Ships 1973/78 (MARPOL)
Health risks	Health risks	The Stockholm Convention on Persistent Organic Pollutants (POPs), 2004

As illustrated in Table 2.7 above, the negative environmental impacts associated with the extractive industries do directly impact land use, including agriculture and farming. For instance, land degradation as a result of petroleum and mining activities not only causes soil erosion, but it also negatively impacts on farming activities. There are various environmental laws in different countries aimed at tackling these challenges. At an international level, several conventions are also dedicated at resolving the environmental issues. For instance, as outlined in the Table 2.7 above, the United Nations Convention to Combat Desertification (UNCCD) directly links the environment and development to sustainable land management. The Convention addresses specifically the arid, semi-arid and dry sub-humid areas, known as the drylands, where some of the most vulnerable ecosystems and peoples can be found.[119] Additionally, the main objective of the 1989 Basel Convention is to protect human health and the environment against the adverse effects of hazardous wastes.[120] With respect to climate change, the 2015 Paris Agreement, which entered into force in 2016, provides a legally binding international treaty on climate change.[121] Other international instruments also require states to take all measures to reduce pollution from their activities.[122] All these indicate a willingness to tackle the environmental impacts associated with energy and mining activities. However, implementation of both the international and national environmental laws is key in addressing these vices.

[119] The new UNCCD 2018-2030 Strategic Framework includes the global commitment to achieve Land Degradation Neutrality (LDN).

[120] The provisions of the Convention centre around the following principal aims: the reduction of hazardous waste generation and the promotion of environmentally sound management of hazardous wastes, wherever the place of disposal; the restriction of transboundary movements of hazardous wastes except where they are perceived to be in accordance with the principles of environmentally sound management; and a regulatory system applying to cases where transboundary movements are permissible.

[121] It was adopted by 196 Parties at COP 21 in Paris, on 12 December 2015 and entered into force on 4 November 2016.

[122] See Article 194(2) of the UNCLOS Convention, United Nations Convention on the Law of the Sea (1982) 21 ILM 1261 (adopted on 10 December 1982, and entered into force on November 16 1994).

IV. Conclusion

Access to land is crucial for the economic development of African countries, where over 70 per cent of the population rely on land for agriculture and other economic activities, albeit many poor people remain landless. Land management and governance present a topical problem due to various factors including political instabilities; the ever-increasing population growth; the move towards industrialisation and urbanisation in different African countries; and corruption and mismanagement surrounding the relevant land institutions.

As illustrated in this chapter, the different land reforms in African countries have had an impact on the management of energy and mining resources. This is, in one part, influenced by the principle of ownership of both land and the natural resources. The historical events during and after colonialism have also influenced to a great extent the land reforms in Africa. Considering the discussion above, it can be concluded that most of the land reforms in Africa are transformational – that is, they are driven by the need to ensure justice for the countries' citizens and to ensure that people benefit from the resources.

3

Land Access from the Perspective of the African Mining Sector

I. Introduction to Mining in Africa

A. Snapshot of the Mining Industry

In simple terms, mining basically refers to the extraction of coal and other substances from the earth. A mineral refers to a naturally occurring metallic or non-metallic substance formed through biogeochemical process.[1] There is no agreed universal definition of the term 'mineral', as different legislation confers slightly different meanings, depending on the jurisdiction concerned. In this respect, the legal connotation of the term can include all solid, gaseous or liquid natural resources, or in some jurisdictions, be limited solely to solid metals. For instance, the Kenyan Mining Act 2016, defines 'mineral' to mean:

> … a geological substance whether in solid, liquid or gaseous form occurring naturally in or on the earth, in or under water, in mine waste or tailing and includes the minerals specified in the First Schedule but does not include petroleum, hydrocarbon gases or groundwater.[2]

One issue that has raised a lot of concern with respect to the definition of 'mineral' is the aspect of sand and gravel. Previously, most mining legislations throughout the world did not recognise sand as a mineral. For instance, Article 244 (3) of the Ugandan constitution states that:

> For the purpose of this article, 'mineral' does not include clay, murram, sand or any stone commonly used for building or similar purposes.[3]

Other jurisdictions also exclude sand and gravel in their definition of a mineral, albeit this exclusion is subject to ownership. A case in point is the Alberta Mines and Minerals Act Chapter M-17, in Alberta, Canada. Section 1 of the Act defines

[1] Nalule, VR, *Mining and the Law in Africa: Exploring the social and environmental impacts* (Palgrave Pivot 2020).
[2] Section 4 of the Kenyan Mining Act, 2016.
[3] Article 244(3) of the Constitution of Uganda, 1995 as amended.

'mineral' as illustrated below. The summary below also provides definitions from South Africa and Nigeria.

Legislative Definitions of a Mineral

Alberta definition[4]

'minerals' means all naturally occurring minerals, and without restricting the generality of the foregoing, includes

(i) gold, silver, uranium, platinum, pitchblende, radium, precious stones, copper, iron, tin, zinc, asbestos, salts, sulphur, petroleum, oil, asphalt, bituminous sands, oil sands, natural gas, coal, anhydrite, barite, bauxite, bentonite, diatomite, dolomite, epsomite, granite, gypsum, limestone, marble, mica, mirabilite, potash, quartz rock, rock phosphate, sandstone, serpentine, shale, slate, talc, thenardite, trona, volcanic ash, sand, gravel, clay and marl, but

(ii) does not include

 (A) sand and gravel that belong to the owner of the surface of land under section 58 of the *Law of Property Act*,

 (B) clay and marl that belong to the owner of the surface of land under section 57 of the *Law of Property Act*, or

 (C) peat on the surface of land and peat obtained by stripping off the overburden, excavating from the surface, or otherwise recovered by surface operations;

South African definition[5]

'Mineral' means any substance, whether in solid, liquid or gaseous form, occurring naturally in or on the earth or in or under water and which was formed by or subjected to a geological process, and includes sand, stone, rock, gravel, clay, soil and any mineral occurring in residue stockpiles or in residue deposits, but excludes –

(a) water, other than water taken from land or sea for the extraction of any mineral from such water,

(b) petroleum, or

(c) peat;

Nigerian definition[6]

'*Minerals*' or '*Mineral resources*' means any substance whether in solid, liquid or gaseous form occurring in or on the earth, formed by or subjected to geological processes including occurrences or deposits of rocks, coal, coal bed gases, bituminous shales, tar sands, any substances that may be extracted from coal, shale or tar sands, mineral water, and mineral components in tailings and waste piles, but with the exclusion of petroleum and waters without mineral content.

[4] The Alberta Mines and Minerals Act Chapter M-17, s 1(1)(p).

[5] South African Mineral and Petroleum Resources Development Act No 28 of 2002, s 1.

[6] Nigerian Minerals and Mining Act No 20 of 2007, s 164.

The above definitions are elaborative and include all the various types of minerals including precious minerals, critical minerals[7] and construction minerals. As illustrated above, the ownership of construction minerals is an issue of concern in different countries. In Kenya, unlike other minerals which are expressly vested in the ownership of the state, Section 7 of the Mining Act makes an exception for sand and other construction minerals. As such, these can still be owned or mined by the local communities, as part of their customary practices. The section states that:

> (1) Nothing in this Act shall prevent any person from taking, subject to such conditions as may be prescribed from time to time by the Cabinet Secretary, soil, clay iron, salt or soda from any land, except land within the area of a mineral right, from which it has been the custom of the member[s] of the community to which that person belongs to take the same.
> (2) The Cabinet Secretary may, by notice in the Gazette, and with the advice of the Mineral Rights Board, prescribe materials of customary usage.[8]

The above provision considers the customary practices and attachments with respect to construction minerals. However, with the increasing role of sand in the twenty-first century, countries have been persuaded to legislate for sand mining, hence amending mining laws to reflect sand as a mineral. In Uganda, for instance, just like in many African countries, previous mining legislation did not consider the regulation and governance of construction minerals such as sand. However, this is being rectified by new mining laws. In this respect, Part V of the Mining and Mineral Bill, 2019 provides for the exploitation of construction minerals. Under clause 100, the Bill requires mining companies seeking to mine construction minerals for commercial purposes to acquire a licence. The Bill also provides for large-scale mining and ASM of construction minerals.[9] Although the Bill recognises that the government has ownership of these minerals,[10] the issue that arises is whether there are strong institutions to ensure that the government governs sand extraction across the whole country. With the increased role of sand, it might be necessary for the government to establish an independent institution focused on managing sand mining activities in the country.[11]

Additionally, it is important to note that construction minerals are different from precious minerals, and as such the technical and financial requirements to

[7] Critical minerals are minerals that are considered vital for the economic well-being of the world's major and emerging economies, yet whose supply may be at risk due to geological scarcity, geopolitical issues, trade policy or other factors.

[8] Section 7 of the Mining Act of Kenya, 2016.

[9] Large-scale mining is provided for under Clauses 103–106; small-scale mining is provided for under Clauses 107–109; and artisanal mining is provided for under Clauses 110–112. The Mining and Mineral Bill, 2019.

[10] Clause 99 of the Mining and Mineral Bill, 2019.

[11] Nalule, VR, *Mining and the Law in Africa: Exploring the social and environmental impacts* (Palgrave Pivot 2020).

develop these resources may differ greatly. Are these differences taken into consideration by the policy-makers when including provisions relating to construction minerals in the mining laws? What about the rehabilitation and mining closure requirements? Are the concerned companies able to offer financial guarantees to ensure that the land is rehabilitated at the end of their operations?

The above notwithstanding, the main characteristics of the mining industry are that mining activities are capital-intensive, and mineral deposits are location-bound and exhaustible. The main unique feature about the mining sector is its dependence on geological surveys to map the exact location of minerals. In this respect, then, the geological potential for the target mineral is a key factor to consider before investing in the prospection, exploration and exploitation of mineral raw materials. Other relevant factors include: the security of land tenure; the measure of profitability; the legal and regulatory framework; investment protection; and the taxation regime, to mention but a few.[12]

For countries endowed with mineral resources, the mining sector significantly contributes to these countries' economic development as it has the potential to finance infrastructural development. In Botswana, for instance, approximately 70–80 per cent of export earnings are attributed to diamond mining. Indeed, if well managed, revenues from the mining sector can be used to tackle the poverty challenges facing the continent. However, some countries have fallen prey to the resource curse, due to poor governance, corruption and mismanagement. Nevertheless, countries such as Botswana and Norway are testimony to the fact that if these resources are well managed, they can contribute significantly to the country's economic development. Additionally, there are national, regional and international initiatives such as the Extractive Industries Transparency Initiative (EITI), aimed at ensuring transparency and accountability in the extractives industry.

The importance of the mining sector to the economy cannot be ignored. This is because various minerals are used as raw materials in different sectors including construction and transport. Most importantly, mineral materials also play an important role in industrialisation and urbanisation which are now rapidly escalating on the African continent.[13] Additionally, the increasingly crucial role of critical minerals in the twenty-first century cannot be ignored. The issue of critical minerals will be extensively examined in the next sections.

B. Mining in Africa

Africa is home to 30 per cent of global mineral reserves and these contribute significantly to exports and tax revenues for most countries on the continent.

[12] Nalule, VR, *Mining and the Law in Africa: Exploring the social and environmental impacts* (Palgrave Pivot 2020).

[13] Nalule, VR, 'Introduction to Mining in Africa' in Nalule, *Mining and the Law in Africa: Exploring the social and environmental impacts* (Palgrave Pivot 2020) pp 1–17.

Besides agriculture, mining is one of the oldest industries to be found on the African continent, and the region is endowed with various minerals including gold, diamonds, vermiculite, manganese, cobalt, zirconium, salt, and phosphate rock. These minerals are also geographically distributed across the continent, with Namibia, Zimbabwe, South Africa, Botswana and the Democratic Republic of the Congo (DRC) representing some of the African historical giants in the mining industry. Namibia, for instance, is historically known for diamond mining. The country is also the world's fourth-largest producer of uranium oxide. Mining is considered the country's leading economic sector, accounting for roughly 10 per cent of Namibia's annual GDP. In Ghana, the mining sector accounts for about 5 per cent of the national GDP, with gold accounting for over 90 per cent of total mineral exports. Countries like Mozambique are known for minerals such as aluminium; Zambia is a major producer of copper; Niger is responsible for around 44 per cent of Africa's uranium supply; and Guinea is responsible for more than 95 per cent of Africa's bauxite production. These are just a few examples of the different African countries that possess mineral wealth.[14] Table 3.1 briefly highlights some of the minerals found in different African countries.

Table 3.1 Minerals in Africa

Country	Minerals
South Africa	diamonds, gold, iron ore, platinum, manganese, chromium, copper, uranium, silver, beryllium, and titanium
Botswana	diamonds, silver, copper, nickel, coal, soda ash, potash, and iron ore
Namibia	diamonds, silver, tungsten, lead, zinc, tin, uranium, and copper
DRC	cobalt, copper, zinc, diamonds, gold, tin and manganese
Nigeria	gold, iron, lead, zinc, rare metals (selenium (Sn), niobium (Nb), tantalum (Ta)), coal and gemstones
Ghana	gold, diamonds, bauxite and manganese
Tanzania	gold, diamonds, gemstones, Iron and Base metals, platinum group metals
Uganda	cobalt, gold, copper, iron ore, tungsten, steel, tin
Sierra Leone	diamonds, rutile, bauxite, gold, iron and limonite
Rwanda	tin ore, gold, methane and tungsten ore
Zimbabwe	coal, chromium ore, nickel, copper, iron ore, vanadium, tin, platinum group metals

Source: Compiled by the author.

[14] The list of African countries and their mineral wealth are discussed in more detail elsewhere; see Nalule, VR, *Mining and the Law in Africa: Exploring the social and environmental impacts* (Palgrave Pivot 2020).

The table above is not exhaustive. As illustrated, different African countries possess different types and amounts of mineral reserves. Further, although these minerals have been exploited for decades in these countries, the benefits have not been particularly visible, necessitating various reforms in the sector, including the nationalisation of mining activities in the distant past, and the current legal and regulatory reforms. Most African countries are also in the process of reviewing fiscal regimes, especially taxation laws to ensure that the sector benefits local people.[15]

C. Brief about Mineral Reserves and Production

(i) Gold

Gold is one of the rarest elements in the world, making up roughly 0.003 parts per million of the earth's crust. With respect to global gold production, China has been a top producing country, accounting for 11 per cent of total global production. In 2019 China produced 383.2 tonnes, Russia 329.5 tons, Australia 325.1 tons, the United States 200.2 tons, Canada 182.9 tons, Peru 143.3 tons, Ghana 142.4 tons, South Africa 118.2 tons, Mexico 111.4 tons, and Brazil 106.9 tons.[16]

With respect to African countries, in 2019 Ghana was the continent's largest producer of gold, overtaking South Africa.[17] In consequence, companies such as AngloGold Ashanti and Gold Field shifted their focus from South Africa to Ghana, where deposits are cheaper and easier to mine. Nevertheless, South Africa is still home to the world's deepest gold mine, the Mponeng mine, extending 2.5 miles underground. Other African countries with significant gold reserves include Eritrea, Liberia, Sudan, Tanzania, Mali, Morocco, Nigeria, Uganda, Zimbabwe, Namibia, Ethiopia, Equatorial Guinea, Rwanda, Sierra Leone and Mozambique.[18]

(ii) Bauxite

A sedimentary rock with a high content of aluminium,[19] bauxite is used in the production of various products like cement, chemicals, face makeup, soda cans,

[15] Nalule, VR, *Mining and the Law in Africa: Exploring the social and environmental impacts* (Palgrave Pivot 2020).

[16] World Gold Council, US Global investors.

[17] South Africa, however, remains a leading country in the gold mining sector. The country's mineral wealth is typically found in geological formations and settings, such as the Witwatersrand Basin, which yields some 93% of South Africa's total gold output.

[18] Gold has been mined for a very long time – more than 6,000 years. Gold has been discovered in around 95 countries globally, with South Africa historically taking the position of the world's dominant gold producer. For more information, see Olawuyi, DS, *Extractives Industry Law in Africa* (Springer 2018).

[19] Globally, bauxite reserves amounted to 30 billion dry metric tons. In 2019, Guinea held the largest portion of world reserves of bauxite, which amounted to about 7.4 billion metric dry tons (almost a quarter of total global reserves).

dishwashers, siding (cladding) for houses, and other aluminium products. In 2019, global bauxite production amounted to 370 million metric tons, a slight increase from 2018 which saw 320 million metric tons produced worldwide. In Africa, Guinea is the biggest producer of bauxite. The resource is also predominantly mined in Ghana and Mozambique. Other notable aluminium-producing countries include Egypt, Cameroon, and South Africa.[20]

(iii) Diamond

Diamond crystals are found across the world, including Canada, Russia, Botswana, Namibia, South Africa, Australia, Sierra Leone, the Ivory Coast, Venezuela and Brazil. Russia, the DRC and Botswana hold the world's largest diamond reserves. Russia holds 650 million diamond carats, representing around 52 per cent of global capacity, the DRC holds 150 million carats or 13 per cent of the world's total, and Botswana holds 90 million carats. Africa accounts for 65 per cent of the world's diamond production. Besides Botswana and the DRC, other African countries ranking amongst the top diamond-producing countries in the world include Zimbabwe and Angola.[21]

(iv) Copper

Copper is an essential mineral. For example, it is used in making electrical wires, telecommunication cables and electronics.[22] It is also used in home roofing, painting and plumbing. Copper ranks as the third-most-consumed industrial metal in the world, after iron and aluminium. On the African continent, Zambia is the top producer of copper, accounting for 3.57 per cent of total world copper production. Other copper-producing countries in Africa include Morocco, the DRC, Botswana, South Africa, Namibia and Zimbabwe. The world's largest copper region is found in Africa – a 480-km-long belt extending from the northern part of Zambia and stretching northwest across the Katanga province of the DRC.[23]

[20] In 2019, Australia produced the largest amount of bauxite worldwide. In that year, the country produced 100 million metric tons of bauxite.

[21] The African continent is home to massive diamond reserves. World Diamond Council records show that approximately US$8.5 billion worth of diamonds come from African countries every year. For instance, in 2013, Botswana produced 23.2 million carats with a stated value of US$3.63 billion. In Namibia, the industry generates over 40% of the country's annual export earnings. Other African countries including the DRC, Sierra Leone, and Liberia have also heavily benefited from the diamond industry.

[22] Historically, humans have been relying on copper for centuries, having learned how to smelt the metal by approximately 4500 BCE. With technological advancements, humans started creating copper alloys by adding tin to copper, thus creating a harder metal than its individual parts: bronze. Most copper occurs in ores and must be smelted, or extracted from its ore, for purity before it can be used.

[23] See Olawuyi, DS, *Extractives Industry Law in Africa* (Springer 2018).

(v) Cobalt

Cobalt is a highly crucial mineral given its important role in the energy transition. It is used in the technology industry, with close to 50 per cent of exported cobalt used for electric vehicles and cell phone batteries. The DRC is the world's biggest supplier of cobalt.[24]

(vi) Soda Ash

Soda Ash (sodium carbonate) is used for making paper, industrial chemicals and glassware. In Africa, Kenya is the best-known exporter of soda ash, mined from Lake Magadi, the southernmost lake in the Kenyan Rift Valley.

(vii) Platinum Group Metals (PGM)

PGM metals are known for their purity, high melting points and unique catalytic properties. They include palladium, rhodium, iridium, osmium, and ruthenium. South Africa is the top producer of PGM in the African continent.

(viii) Iron ore

Iron ores consist of rocks and minerals from which metallic iron can be economically extracted. In Africa, Guinea has one of the world's largest untapped iron ore reserves, at Simandou, a 110 km range of hills deep in the hinterland. Following aluminium, iron ore is the most explored for and widely utilised metal. Iron ore production in Africa is dominated by South Africa, Mauritania and Algeria. Other African countries also endowed with iron ore include Libya, Uganda, Tunisia, Liberia, Ghana, Gabon, Cameroon, Zimbabwe, and Senegal.

D. Influence of History on the African Mining Sector

Mining in most African countries is carried out on both large-scale and small/artisanal scale bases. While large-scale mining involves companies employing advanced technology and enormous capital to extract minerals, ASM involves the

[24] Cobalt is also used in jet engines and gas turbines, magnetic steels and stainless steels. Like nickel, cobalt is found in the Earth's crust only in a chemically combined form, save for small deposits found in alloys of natural meteoric iron. There are several social and environmental negative impacts associated with cobalt mining, especially in this energy transition and climate change era. Child labour, lung disease and heart failure have been linked to cobalt, as countries like the DRC, Zambia and Cuba are discovering. Environmental issues – including devastated landscapes, water pollution, contaminated crops and a loss of soil fertility – are also associated with cobalt mining.

use of rudimentary methods by individuals who are not officially employed by a mining company.[25] There are various issues associated with each type of mining.[26]

Mining, just like agriculture, is one of the earliest humankind activities with a rich history on the African continent. Besides being 'the birthplace of humanity', Africa is also the birthplace of mining activity. Identified as the oldest and most enduring landmass in the world with 97 per cent of what lies beneath the African soil in place for more than 300 million years, Africa is home to the oldest mine in the world, the hematite mine at Bomvu Ridge in Swaziland. This mine is believed to be 45,000 years old. To put this into context, copper metallurgy was developed in Mesopotamia 9,000 years before the Christian era, and around 1500 BCE, iron was produced in Asia Minor.[27]

Historically, mining on the African continent was carried out on a small scale and, as such, artisanal mining was rampant. The miners basically used hand tools and other rudimentary methods to extract resources, employing crude methods of ground control, ventilation, haulage, hoisting, lighting and rock breakage. For instance, before discovering metal smelting, the miners initially used metals in their native form as they obtained these by washing river gravel in placer deposits.[28] With respect to rock breaking, early miners still relied on native methods and tools made of bone, wood and stone. These methods indeed made the work of the miners hard until the invention of dynamite by Alfred Noble in 1867.[29] Prior to the use of dynamite, miners had discovered another method called fire-setting, where the rock was heated first before dousing it with cold water to contract and break it. As society progressed, so did the methods of mining as various technologies and machinery were introduced, and these are most common in large-scale mining.

When discussing the history of mining, it is important to note that many important cultural eras are associated with and identified by various minerals or their derivatives. These include the Stone Age (prior to 4000 BCE), the Bronze Age (4000–3000 BCE), the Iron Age (1500 BCE–1780 CE), the Steel Age (1780–1945) and the Nuclear Age (1945–the present).[30]

Indeed, in discussions about mining in Africa, it is worth exploring the connection between Africa's mineral wealth and colonialism. The demarcation of the African states was agreed upon at the Berlin Conference of 1884–85, directly

[25] Hilson, G, Goumandakoye, H and Diallo, P, 'Formalizing Artisanal Mining "Spaces" in Rural Sub-Saharan Africa: The Case of Niger' (2019) 80 *Land Use Policy* 259–68.

[26] Nalule, VR, *Mining and the Law in Africa: Exploring the social and environmental impacts* (Palgrave Pivot 2020).

[27] Nalule, VR, *Mining and the Law in Africa: Exploring the social and environmental impacts* (Palgrave Pivot 2020).

[28] In geology, a 'placer deposit' or 'placer' is an accumulation of valuable minerals formed by gravity separation from a specific source rock during sedimentary processes. The name is from the Spanish word placer, meaning 'alluvial sandbank'.

[29] Nalule, VR, 'Introduction to Mining in Africa' in Nalule, *Mining and the Law in Africa: Exploring the social and environmental impacts* (Palgrave Pivot 2020) pp 1–17.

[30] Nalule, VR, *Mining and the Law in Africa: Exploring the social and environmental impacts* (Palgrave Pivot 2020) p 12.

leading to the continent being split into colonies and ruled by various European countries. Colonisation was characterised not only by the stealing of natural resources but also forced labour, heavy taxation and the exploitation of tribal and cultural differences by Europeans. The mineral wealth of African states is one of the reasons why colonisation escalated in the nineteenth and twentieth centuries. The diamond rush in Southern Africa, for instance, was the basis for the prolongation of European rule in Africa. In 1869, an 83.5-carat rough diamond was discovered by a Griqua herdsman in Hopetown in South Africa. The first diamond rush was followed by the second one in 1870 when diamonds were found in river diggings at Klip Drift (now Barkly West); diamonds were also found in 1870 at Bultfontein farm on the edge of modern-day Kimberley, and in December of that year, diamonds were found in the adjacent Du Toit's Pan, triggering the third diamond rush. The diamond rush in Southern Africa attracted a host of prospectors, smugglers and speculators who were supported by British Imperialism.[31] Indeed, some well-known mining companies were established during this period. For instance, both the De Beers Mine and Kimberly Mine (originally 'New Rush') were discovered in 1871. Consequently, De Beers Consolidated Mines Limited was established on 12 March 1888, and Cecil Rhodes was named founding chairman. Besides De Beers, other prominent companies including Rio Tinto and Consolidated Gold Fields were also established.[32]

These mining companies also played a significant role in the escalated colonisation of African countries. The companies made huge profits and, given their close ties with British and European financial centres, gained power and prestige. A case in point is the British South Africa Company (BSA) which played a significant role in the colonisation of central Africa. BSA was founded by Rhodes, and its role in colonisation is evidenced via its rule over the territories of Zimbabwe and Zambia (then Southern and Northern Rhodesia) – until the mid-1920s when the British administration took over. BSA was also involved in the distribution of mining rights and the grant of concessions. As such it granted an exclusive prospecting licence to two mining enterprises owned by British, American and South African interests. Zambia only gained control over its own mining sector following independence in 1964, and in this regard, the concessions rights were transferred to the Zambian government against 'compensation' of £2 million.[33]

The above illustrates the role of private companies in not only exploiting the natural resources in Africa but also in the colonisation of Africa. These companies were always supported by their imperial states, as evidenced further in the Belgian Congo, where the Katanga Mining Company ruled the territory in exchange for an exclusive mining concession granted by the Belgian state, which derived its 'rights'

[31] Nalule, VR, 'Introduction to Mining in Africa' in Nalule, *Mining and the Law in Africa: Exploring the social and environmental impacts* (Palgrave Pivot 2020) pp 1–17.

[32] For a full history of African Mining, see Nalule, VR, *Mining and the Law in Africa: Exploring the social and environmental impacts* (Palgrave Pivot 2020).

[33] ibid.

in the Congo from the Berlin Conference of 1885. Although the search for minerals played a major role in the colonisation of various African countries, it is worth noting that other factors including food production and land occupation were also essential in the colonisation process.

Taking stock of the above, it is clear that the challenges experienced in the African mining sector have their root in the colonial era. As such, when enacting laws governing the mining sector, it is essential to appreciate the historical events and devise ways of tackling the injustices that have followed from the exploitation of minerals on the African continent.

E. Importance of Minerals: The Rising Role of Critical Minerals

The importance of various minerals including metallic, industrial and construction minerals in today's economy cannot be underestimated in both developed and developing countries. Industrialisation and urbanisation are escalating in developing countries such as those in Africa and Asia, making minerals essential for the economic growth of these countries. According to the 2018 *BP Energy Outlook*, the global boom in urbanisation is projected to increase, as almost 2 billion people are likely to live in urban centres by 2040 and Africa is projected to contribute one-third of this increase in urbanisation. Productivity levels are also expected to increase and it is estimated that 2.5 billion people will be lifted from the low income bracket.

All of the above developments will necessitate an increase in different minerals across the African continent. Additionally, the developed world is heavily industrialised and as such it relies heavily on minerals in the form of raw materials, which are an essential primary input for industry. Taking metallic minerals as an example, these are essential in the automobile, aerospace technology and electrical engineering sectors. For instance, more than 40 different minerals are required in the production of a car, including iron, aluminium, platinum, copper and zinc; gold is used in jewellery production and iron ore in steel production.[34]

(i) Role of Minerals in the Value-Chain

A minerals industry value-chain essentially refers to the various stages a minerals project undergoes to produce the final product. Each stage adds value to the product and in economic terms, presents opportunities. Most minerals are used as raw materials in various sectors of the economy and as such they have a significant

[34] For a detailed discussion, see Tiess, G, *General and International Mineral Policy: Focus: Europe* (Springer Wien 2011) p 40.

role to play at the beginning of a value-chain. For instance, the engineering and electrical industries are dependent on metals. The electricity sector is a significant consumer and processor of non-ferrous metals, particularly lead, copper, tin and aluminium. Currently, critical minerals play an essential role in the transition to a low-carbon economy. The next sub-section briefly discusses critical minerals.

(ii) A Panoramic Overview of Critical Minerals

Minerals considered as critical or strategic are those scarce metals and non-metals that are crucial for the economy. They are characterised by geological scarcity, hence limiting their supply. Geography and availability of domestic supply often defines which minerals are deemed 'critical' for any particular region or country. As mentioned, the importance of critical minerals has increased in recent years given the global move to transition to a low-carbon economy.

As discussed in Chapter four of this book, energy transitions are characterised by the deployment of renewable energy and energy efficiency technologies. Among the minerals that are considered to be critical are those metals and semimetals used in the manufacture of wind turbines, electric cars, solar panels, and other high-tech applications which are crucial for shifting to a low-carbon economy. For instance, copper is essential for the use of electricity throughout the energy system, and platinum is a key material in many clean energy technologies and emissions control devices. Lithium, cobalt and nickel provide batteries with greater charging performance and higher energy density. Some rare earth elements such as neodymium make powerful magnets that are vital for wind turbines and electric vehicles.[35]

The above highlights the vital role of critical/strategic minerals in this era of energy transition. Additionally, pandemic-related disruptions have proved the importance of reliable supply for critical minerals. Due to their scarcity, any disruptions in the supply of these minerals can disrupt global efforts to shift to a low-carbon economy. For instance, during the COVID-19 pandemic, some countries were forced to halt mining operations during the early stages of lockdown, including Peru and South Africa. Peru is responsible for 12 per cent of global copper production whilst South Africa is responsible for 75 per cent of global platinum production. The lockdown measures which were temporarily imposed on the mining sector in these two countries significantly disrupted the supply of critical minerals, hence highlighting the need for global initiatives to ensure security of supply for these minerals, even during a pandemic. This is because low-carbon technologies require more minerals than fossil fuel technologies. For instance, an

[35] International Energy Agency, 'Clean energy progress after the Covid-19 crisis will need reliable supplies of critical minerals' (IEA 2020): www.iea.org/articles/clean-energy-progress-after-the-covid-19-crisis-will-need-reliable-supplies-of-critical-minerals.

electric car uses five times as much minerals as a conventional car and an onshore wind plant requires eight times as much minerals as a gas-fired plant of the same capacity.[36] Consequently, electric transport and grid storage are currently the largest consumers of lithium, together accounting for 35 per cent of total demand.[37]

Table 3.2 Key Issues with Respect to Critical Minerals

Production of critical minerals is concentrated in a few countries[38]
Critical minerals are vital for renewable energy technologies
Supply of these minerals may be affected by not only local geological and market parameters, but also by regulatory change
Geopolitics plays a vital role in the supply of critical minerals

The table above highlights the vital role of critical minerals in this energy transition era. With respect to land access, the increasing demand for critical minerals has not only escalated hazardous conditions for extracting these minerals, but also increased pollution. As noted in Chapter two, the use of harmful chemicals negatively impacts the environment; hence affecting agricultural land relied on by many local communities.[39]

II. Land Access from the Perspective of Large-Scale Mining

Large-scale Mining (LSM) involves a large company that employs workers to extract minerals. LSM is capital intensive and, unlike ASM, it is characterised by advanced technology and mechanisation. Africa is home to massive deposits of profuse minerals including bauxite, cobalt, gold, diamonds, manganese, phosphate rock, platinum group metals and soda ash, to mention but a few. These minerals have attracted various foreign companies which are involved in LSM on the African continent. LSM has its roots in the colonial period, when numerous European investors established a host of productive, large-scale mines in remote

[36] IEA, 'Clean energy progress after the Covid-19 crisis will need reliable supplies of critical minerals' (IEA 2020): www.iea.org/articles/clean-energy-progress-after-the-covid-19-crisis-will-need-reliable-supplies-of-critical-minerals.

[37] IEA, 'Clean energy progress after the Covid-19 crisis will need reliable supplies of critical minerals' (IEA 2020): www.iea.org/articles/clean-energy-progress-after-the-covid-19-crisis-will-need-reliable-supplies-of-critical-minerals.

[38] Close to two-thirds of the global supply of rare earth elements are produced in China. The DRC produces over 70% of global cobalt supplies.

[39] Some of the minerals that are considered to be critical in the 21st century include: aluminium, fluorspar, manganese, tellurium, cobalt, antimony, gallium, niobium, tin, arsenic, germanium, titanium, baryte, uranium, and vanadium.

sections of SSA. Most of the mining communities lacked developmental infrastructure, but this partly changed for some communities where foreign investors, in an endeavour to establish a township, established necessary infrastructure such as roads and healthcare services and trained thousands of unskilled and semi-skilled workers. In essence, mining created backward and forward linkages, as will be explained in this section. Prior to that discussion, the next sub-section discusses the key stages in mineral extraction.

A. Key Stages of Mineral Extraction

(i) Prospecting and Exploration

Prospecting is the first stage in mining. It involves the field search for mineral deposits which can lead to the location of mineral deposits either on or underneath the surface. Prospecting is a branch of geological science which involves digging by hand, physical observation, rock sampling, geological surface analysis, remote sensing techniques, laboratory testing and assays, or other surveys or studies of surface geology. Prospecting or reconnaissance is usually carried out with the ultimate objective of economic development by mining operations. The process involves specialised techniques, and once successful in terms of identifying potential presence of valuable minerals, exploration studies are conducted.

(ii) Mineral Exploration

Mineral exploration involves searching for evidence with respect to the existence, quality, quantity and economic value of minerals hosted in the surrounding rocks. The process involves extracting pieces of geological information for purposes of chemical or other analysis aimed at defining the quality, characteristics and economic value of a mineral discovery. Exploration is an expensive process that can last around 3–10 years before feasibility decisions are made. The process can also cost around US$20 million to US$150 million.[40] In simple terms, the process involves defining the type of mineral the company is interested in. This guides the work of geologists and other professionals involved in the study and analysis of rocks and minerals. This then follows the selection of the geographical region to be explored, which mainly involves the determination of 'geological fertility'. Other key indicators in exploration include the competitiveness and stability of future mines, tax and labour legislation, operational safety, logistics availability, and environmental and social factors.

[40] Olawuyi, DS, *Extractives Industry Law in Africa* (Springer 2018) pp 3–17.

(iii) Discovery and Development

After the minerals have been located, the next stage is discovery and development, which involves the planning and construction of the mining project. Not all discovered minerals become producing mines, and it may take 10–15 years or more for a mine to be developed. The development stage involves the construction of the mine. It also necessitates the establishment of key infrastructure such as roads, processing plants, railways, sewer and waterlines, and housing to support the operation.

(iv) Operation and Production

This stage involves the actual mining and processing of minerals. It is at this stage that host governments consider beneficiation, processing and contract mining. Mining operations involve ore breaking, loading and hauling to a mill for treatment. This stage can be carried out in different ways including surface, underground, dredging and artisanal mining. The time frame for this mining phase varies, dependent as it is on the amount and quality of the mineral in question.

(v) Decommissioning and Mining Closure

After the minerals have been exhausted, or where a company wishes to abandon its mining activities, the next stage involves decommissioning and closure. Mining closure represents the shutting down of mining operations on a temporary or permanent basis. The closure follows decommissioning, where operators take apart the mining processing facilities and equipment. All equipment and machinery used in the mining process must be repurposed, demolished or recovered, and the waste disposed of. This follows post-closure monitoring and reclamation: here the company must ensure proper reclamation of the land and water courses to an acceptable standard of productive use.

Decommissioning a mine site involves a process where the site's infrastructure and plant including processing facilities and equipment are safely demolished. The process also requires cleaning of the area, draining of pipelines and disposal of any waste. The aim of decommissioning and closure is to ensure that the mine site is at an acceptable standard of productive use by others.

Due to the finite nature of the extractive industry, companies must prepare for mine closures at the end of the life span of mining operations or upon abandonment or renunciation of mining rights. Often, mining companies prior to the granting of licences must share their mining closure plans. However, in some cases, the closure may happen unexpectedly due to any of the following reasons: lack of financial support; market fluctuations; and political climate. In addition to mining planning, there is also closure planning which continues during the life of a mine, starting with the conceptual closure plans prior to production, periodic updates throughout the life of the mine and the final decommissioning plan.

Some common ways of mine closure include capping of mine shafts, which involves placing a large concrete plug around the shaft to cover it. The plug can be a metallic grill; however, in some remote areas where ASM is carried out, these can also be in the form of wooden beams.

(a) What to Consider in the Mining Closure Plan?

The closure of a mine will affect the societies that have become heavily dependent on the mining activities. In this respect, various considerations must be addressed in a mining closure plan. Some of the key considerations are highlighted below, especially with respect to the social transition of the society concerned.

What other activities can the miners be engaged in? Do they have the necessary skills or financial means? This will require stakeholder consultations during the design of the closure plan. The consultations should provide an opportunity to all people to be represented including indigenous people, representatives of the miners, women and youth. Such consultations are necessary to estimate the cost of the social transition, which can differ depending on the communities concerned and based on the environmental and economic impact the mine has had on the land.

Financial issues: The mining company must prove that it has the necessary money and finances required to ensure a successful mining closure. Prior to the granting of mining licences, financial assurance from mining companies is mostly requested by African governments. This may take the form of a rehabilitation fund, security deposit or payment of a provision by a mining company. Financial assurances can be provided through, among others: irrevocable letters of credit, trust funds, corporate guarantees and cash deposits.

There is also the need to include a schedule for post-closure monitoring. This is essential to ensure that environmental and social conditions have been adhered to, for example, ensuring good quality of the groundwater, physical site and surface water.

(b) Mine Rehabilitation

Mine rehabilitation is the process whereby the post-mined landscape is restored to enable the use of land for other activities. Rehabilitation work can consist of reforestation, the removal of all installations and ensuring the safety of perimeters. Whereas it is the duty of the mining company to establish and present a mine rehabilitation plan and to finance the process, it is the duty of the state to supervise and ensure that the company complies with the plan.

Various mining legislation contains provisions that require companies to enforce rehabilitation plans. Many mining communities in countries such as Tanzania and South Africa have been faced with fatal accidents, health and safety issues and environmental degradation resulting from unclosed mines. Additionally, local communities are mostly dependent on agriculture; as such, they run the risk of being unable to reuse the land following the mine cycle if the open mine is left unattended. All these have necessitated the existence of rehabilitation provisions in mining laws.

B. Linkages in the Mining Sector

The presence of LSM companies in different mining communities is prima facie associated with increased public investment in social and economic infrastructure including transport systems, healthcare and educational facilities. In this respect, investments in the extractives sector do create economically viable linkages. To ensure that the host communities benefit from such investments, governments have embraced various strategies and policies, including local content policies, corporate social responsibility (CSR), and local processing standards. Nevertheless, most mining communities remain under-developed with poor infrastructure networks. Table 3.3 outlines the different types of linkages in the extractive industries.

Table 3.3 Linkages in the Extractive Industries

Economic Linkages	Details
Fiscal linkages	These deal with payments and taxes. In the extractive industries, these are intended to enable the state to maximise economic returns. They include, among others, cost recovery provisions; mining royalties; oil production sharing; fiscal pricing; service contracts and bonus payments.
Production linkages	These include: Backward (or upstream) linkages and Forward (or downstream) linkages.

Some of the linkages stated in Table 3.3 positively and directly impact host communities. For instance, backward linkages involve not only employment opportunities but also the supply of goods, services and security. On the one hand, the enforcement of local content policies in different countries is, in principle, aimed at achieving the backward/upstream linkages. On the other hand, forward/downstream linkages are focused on adding value to the commodities extracted. The establishment of infrastructure such as refineries is key in achieving forward linkages. Nevertheless, although the African continent is home to massive oil and mining resources, it has the fewest refineries; hence limiting the benefits that accrue from forward linkages including job creation. Forward linkages are therefore focused on beneficiation or value addition which can lead to tax and export earnings. Some resource-rich African countries such as Botswana have benefited from both the forward and backward linkages. Specifically, the establishment of Debswana Diamond Company enabled De Beers' sales and sorting operations to move from London to Botswana.

Besides the production linkages, other benefits that accrue from the extractive industries' activities include the establishment of developmental infrastructure such as roads, healthcare services, and water facilities. These are sometimes referred to as Side-stream linkages. Additionally to technology transfer, extractive industries' activities also are associated with skills development which can easily be transferred to other non-extractive industries sectors. Furthermore, with increased earnings, consumption linkages are realised. The presence of many LSM companies is associated with the realisation of various economic linkages. Table 3.4 highlights some of the LSM companies operating in different African countries.

Table 3.4 Large-scale Mining Companies Operating in African Countries

Mineral	Company	Country
Gold	AngloGold Ashanti Limited;[41] Gold Fields Limited	South Africa
	Kefi Gold and Copper; Newmont	Ethiopia
	Acacia Mining Tanzania	Tanzania
	Orca Gold Inc	Sudan
Diamonds	De Beers	Namibia; South Africa
	Namdeb – a partnership between De Beers and the Republic of Namibia.	Namibia
	Debswana Diamond Mining Company – a partnership between the Botswana government and De Beers.	Botswana
	Lucapa Diamond Company	Angola
Aluminium	Chalco; Hongqiao, and Xinfa	China
	Rusal	Russia

Some of the companies listed in Table 3.4 above have been in existence since the colonial era. For instance, Gold Fields Limited is one of the oldest gold mining companies with an operation history dating as far back as 1887, when Cecil John Rhodes and Charles Rudd founded Gold Fields of South Africa. The company's modern incarnation came to be with the 1998 Gold Fields of South Africa/Gencor merger. Briefly known as Goldco, this new entity was subsequently renamed Gold Fields Limited. In 1888, De Beers established the first diamond mine in South Africa. In 1905, the world's largest diamond, the 3,016.75 carat Cullinan, was discovered in South Africa.[42]

[41] AngloGold Ashanti has been involved in the gold mining industry in South Africa since 1998, and has been a leading player in South Africa's gold mining industry. AngloGold is the end product of the century-old Anglo-American Company consolidating its uranium and gold mining enterprises. The current form of AngloGold Ashanti came to be through the 2004 merger of AngloGold Ltd and Ashanti Goldfields Company Ltd.

[42] The Venetia, Finsch and Kimberley mines are some of the top diamond mines in South Africa.

Whereas mining started in South Africa during the colonial era, diamond mining in Botswana started in 1967 after the country gained independence from Britain. Botswana is home to some well-established mines including Jwaneng, Karowe and Letlhakane. Ownership and control of minerals dictates the licensing regime and operation of LSM. In this regard, the next section discusses the licensing regime for LSM.

C. Licensing for LSM Companies

As discussed in Chapter one, in most African jurisdictions, the natural resources are vested under the ownership and control of the state on behalf of its citizens. The supreme law of the land, which is usually the Constitution, empowers the national parliament to enact laws aimed at regulating the mining sector. For instance, Article 244 of the Ugandan Constitution states that:

(1) Subject to clause (2) of this article, Parliament shall make laws regulating—

- (a) the exploitation of minerals;
- (b) the sharing of royalties arising from mineral exploitation;
- (c) the conditions for payment of indemnities arising out of exploitation of minerals; and
- (d) the conditions regarding the restoration of derelict lands.

(2) Minerals and mineral ores shall be exploited taking into account the interests of the individual landowners, local governments and the Government.

As stipulated in the provisions above, Parliament must enact the necessary mining laws which, among other things, regulate the mining licensing regime. In this respect, for any company to acquire the rights to exploit these resources, in addition to getting the necessary licences, they must also fulfill the legal and regulatory requirements. For instance, Section 32 of the Kenyan Mining Act provides for the different mineral rights. The section states that:

(1) The Cabinet Secretary, on the recommendation of the Mineral Rights Board, may grant, deny or revoke a mineral right.

(2) A mineral right may be granted in respect of a large-scale operation or small-scale operation.

(3) The following licences and permits may be granted for a mineral right under this Act to authorize a mineral right holder to engage in—

- (a) large scale operations which shall include—
  - (i) a reconnaissance licence;
  - (ii) a prospecting licence;
  - (iii) a retention licence;
  - (iv) a mining licence; or
- (b) small scale operations, which shall include—
  - (i) a prospecting permit; or
  - (ii) a mining permit.

(4) The Cabinet Secretary may on the recommendation of the Mineral Rights Board, by notice in the Gazette, designate any other mineral right which may be granted under this Act.[43]

Subsequent to an application for a mineral right, the relevant authority can either approve or reject the application.[44] After acquiring the necessary licences, a company can then rightly own the resources in question. For instance, with respect to diamond mining in Namibia, NamDeb – a 50:50 joint venture between the Namibian government and De Beers – is the primary land-based diamond mining company. Debmarine Namibia handles offshore diamond mining and is also a 50:50 joint venture between the Namibian government and De Beers.[45] Prior to discussing the licensing regime, it is worth discussing the relevant mining policies and laws.

(i) Mining Policies

A mining policy is essential in the regulation of the sector as it is a benchmark for all other relevant laws. Generally, a minerals policy highlights the key issues to be considered in the governance of the mining sector. In simple terms, a policy refers to a system of principles agreed to by a group/organisation or government to guide decision-making. In this respect, a national minerals policy is defined as the entirety of actions of a state for influencing the supply of and demand for mineral resources on its territory and beyond that.[46]

Different policies serve different purposes. For instance, a foreign policy is essential as it sets the objectives of trade and development through diplomatic dialogue with other countries; trade policy secures access to minerals through multilateral contracts; and economic policy covers issues relating to

[43] Section 32 of the Mining Act of Kenya, 2016.

[44] For instance, Section 33 of the Kenyan Mining Act states that: '(1) A person shall make an application for a mineral right in the prescribed manner to the Cabinet Secretary. (2) The Cabinet Secretary shall, on the recommendation of the Mineral Rights Board, approve or reject an application – (a) within ninety days in the case of an application for prospecting licence or reconnaissance licence; or (b) within one hundred and twenty days in the case of an application for a mining licence. (3) Subject to sub-section (2), the Cabinet Secretary shall notify the Mineral Rights Board of the decision to approve or reject an application before notifying the applicant. (4) Subject to subsection (2), the Cabinet Secretary shall notify the applicant in writing whether the application has been accepted or rejected. (5) Where the application is approved, the applicant shall by notice in writing accept or reject the offer for grant of the mineral right within twenty-one days from the date of receipt of notification of the approval. (6) Where the applicant does not notify the Cabinet Secretary of the acceptance of the offer, the approval of the application shall lapse after twenty-one days. (7) An applicant who is aggrieved by the decision of the Cabinet Secretary may appeal to the High Court within thirty days'.

[45] Chamber of Mines of Namibia. Link, https://chamberofmines.org.na/portfolio/diamonds/. Last accessed on 2 October 2020.

[46] Nalule, VR, 'Regulation of Mining in Africa' in Nalule, *Mining and the Law in Africa: Exploring the social and environmental impacts* (Palgrave Pivot 2020) pp 19–50.

government budgets, taxation and the labour market, whilst also greatly influencing state politics. There is a strong connection between a minerals policy and an economic policy. As such, a minerals policy should indeed bring into consideration the social, economic, political and environmental objectives of the country. Given the important role of mining policies, these have been adopted in several different African countries. For instance, in 2001 Uganda passed its mining policy and this was subsequently replaced by the 2018 policy – the main goal of which is, 'to develop the mining industry through increased investment, value addition, national participation and revenue generation to contribute significantly to socioeconomic transformation and poverty eradication'.[47]

The 2018 Ugandan Mining Policy lists various objectives which take into consideration new challenges in the mining sector which were not anticipated when drafting the previous 2001 Mining Policy. In this respect, the 2018 Mining Policy has several objectives including:

- To strengthen the legal and regulatory framework for the development of the mineral sector;
- To ensure efficient, equitable, accountable and transparent management of mineral revenues;
- To establish, manage and promote the country's mineral potential;
- To enhance and strengthen the institutional capacity for effective governance of the mineral sector; and
- To organise and legislate for ASM in Uganda.

As highlighted above, Uganda is committed to addressing the current challenges in its mining sector. This necessitates the amendment of existing mining laws and regulations. There are, however, certain objectives of mining policies which are common to most of the African countries. These are outlined briefly below:

- To regulate and improve artisanal mining;
- To strengthen local capacity for mineral development;
- To promote private sector participation;
- To develop and strengthen local capacity for mineral development;
- To address child labour in the mining sector;
- To promote gender equality in the mining sector;
- Value addition and revenue generation.

[47] Mining and Mineral Policy for Uganda, 2018.

African countries face common challenges in the mining sector including: the informalities in ASM; gender inequality; lack of infrastructure for value addition; and many others. In this respect, the mining policies of most of these countries have similar objectives which are rooted in the need to tackle the various challenges faced by the mining sectors.

Most developing countries such as those in Africa are exporting countries and, as such, the key focus for these countries' mining policies is to contribute to the economic development and consequently alleviate poverty. For instance, the mineral policies of Tanzania and Uganda clearly state that the mining sector must contribute to national GDP, increase foreign earnings and increase employment opportunities.[48] Emphasis on social and economic development follows numerous complaints raised, especially from communities adjacent to mineral resources which carry the burden of the negative environmental and social costs and yet gain little or no benefits from the actual mining.[49] Issues relating to land acquisition and the resettlement of affected communities cannot be ignored, particularly as in most cases the local people are not given fair and timely compensation.[50]

Whereas *exporting* countries are concerned with utilising the resources for their economic development, the focus for *importing* industrialised countries is to ensure guaranteed supplies of minerals at low prices. Importing countries therefore consider various aspects, including foreign trade issues and domestic economic issues.[51] Importing countries are also more concerned with minerals supply policies whereby they ensure the security of supply of the necessary raw materials with fewer disruptions. In contrast, exporting countries, especially from Africa, are generally more concerned with utilising the resources to eradicate poverty.

Moving forward, for a minerals policy to be effective, there is a need for the establishment of clear laws and regulations. These laws should not only ensure sustainable exploitation of the resources but also create state mineral rights and a favourable fiscal policy for the investors. Additionally, a minerals policy must stipulate the role of the state and the private sector, the institutions responsible for the mining sector and their role, and the interrelation of different policies (interactions). The next sub-section explores the laws and regulations governing the mining sector in Africa.

[48] The Tanzanian Mineral Policy of 2009 replaced that of 1997.

[49] Magai, PS and Márquez-Velázquez, A, 'Tanzania's Mining Sector and Its Implications for the Country's Development' *Working Paper No 4/2011* (Berlin Working Papers on Money, Finance, Trade and Development) (DAAD Partnership 2011) retrieved 21 January 2018.

[50] Lugoe, F, 'Governance in Mining Areas in Tanzania with Special Reference to Land Issues', *ESRF Discussion Paper No 41* (Economic and Social Research Foundation 2012).

[51] With foreign trade aspects, importing countries guarantee the supply of minerals through international mining investments and participation in foreign mining projects. Domestic economic aspects are intended to ensure independence from imports and as such importing countries try to strengthen, improve and coordinate their domestic raw materials.

(ii) Laws and Regulations Governing the Mining Sector

The mining sector is governed by various legislation, the key pieces being mining laws and regulations. Besides mining laws, other laws are relevant in the governance of the mining sector including environmental laws, taxation laws, land laws and employment laws. In Botswana, for instance, there are various laws governing the mining sector. These are outlined below:

- The Mines and Minerals Act (Cap 66:01);
- The Mineral Rights in Tribal Territories Act (Cap 66:02);[52]
- The Mines and Minerals (Health, Mortality and Labour Returns) Regulations;
- The Precious and Semi-Precious Stones (Protection) Act (Cap 66:03);
- The Mines and Minerals (Prospecting and Leasing Charges) Regulations;
- The Unwrought Precious Metals Act (Cap 20:03);
- The Mines and Minerals (Demarcation of Mining Lease Areas) Regulations;
- The Mines and Minerals (Restriction of Prospecting Activity for Coal) Order;
- The Mines, Quarries, Works and Machinery Act (Cap 44:02);
- The Mines, Quarries, Works and Machinery Regulations;
- The Diamond Cutting Act (Cap 66:04); and
- The Export and Import of Rough Diamonds Regulations.

Each law/Act outlined above tackles a specific aspect of the mining sector. In this sub-section, the focus will be on mining laws and regulations, specifically discussing the key provisions of these laws, including mining rights and the granting of licences and concessions.

Regulation of the mining sectors in Africa has been going through a transformative process and different mining codes have characterised particular stages in this process. These codes are divided into different generations, including the first generation which comprises the mining legislation of the 1980s, the second generation which comprises mining legislation from the early to mid-1990s, and the third generation which refers to the mining legislation of the late 1990s. The new wave of reforms in the current mining laws can arguably be referred to as the fourth generation of mining codes.[53]

The first generation of mining laws was characterised by the withdrawal of the state from actively being involved in the mining sector, as a way of attracting investors. Ghana is a good example of this generation of laws. Generally, liberalisation

[52] This Act transfers mining rights from specified tribes and tribal authorities to the state of Botswana in the manner and under such conditions as are specified in agreements for this purpose.

[53] Nalule, VR, 'Regulation of mining in Africa' in Nalule, *Mining and the Law in Africa: Exploring the social and environmental impacts* (Palgrave Pivot 2020) pp 19–50.

of the mining sector took off in the 1980s, resulting in the reduction of state involvement in mining activities. Although it was against the interest of states, international monetary organisations such as the World Bank encouraged African countries to completely withdraw from the sector as a prerequisite for attracting the much-needed investments.[54]

The second generation was characterised by the regulation of the mining sector, including putting into consideration environmental and health protection, which, contrary to present practice, were left to be a responsibility of the private sector, ie non-state actors. Guinea provides a good example of this second-generation mining legislation. The need to ensure the observance of social and environmental rules by multinational companies was the cornerstone of the second generation of mining codes which were enacted in the early 1990s, albeit, due to the limited powers and influence of the state in mining activities, they could hardly enforce such rules against multinational companies.

The late 1990s witnessed the emergence of the third generation of mining codes. Unlike the first generation, the third generation recognised and encouraged the role of the state in the facilitation and regulation of the mining sector, with the caveat that the reforms reduced the state's role and ownership in the mining sector. Mali, Madagascar and Tanzania provide good examples of the third-generation laws. In Mali, for instance, the 1999 Mining Code emphasised the need to attract foreign investors to the country and as such many incentives were provided by the government to foreign mining corporations. The same objective was shared by the 1999 Madagascar Mining Code, which aimed to reduce state engagement in mining operations and increase foreign investments in the sector.

There have been various reforms in the mining sector, and these have necessitated the adoption of new mining laws which arguably form the fourth generation of mining codes that have come about in the 2000s. For instance, in 2015 Burkina Faso passed its new mining law;[55] in 2016, Kenya also adopted its new Mining Act; and in 2017 Tanzania adopted new laws relating to the mining sector.[56] The new laws essentially deal with the attraction of foreign investment and most importantly ensuring local participation in and economic development from the mining activities. Given the global efforts to tackle climate change, the fourth generation of mining codes also emphasises the need for environmental protection. In this respect, environmental protection is now a key aspect of most mining legislation in Africa.

[54] Nalule, VR, 'Regulation of mining in Africa' in Nalule, *Mining and the Law in Africa: Exploring the social and environmental impacts* (Palgrave Pivot 2020) pp 19–50.

[55] In Burkina Faso, the Mining Code was adopted by the National Transition Council on 26 June 2015.

[56] Several pieces of legislation were enacted in Tanzania, including the Natural Wealth and Resources (Review and Re-negotiation of Unconscionable Terms) Act, 2017 and the Natural Wealth and Resources (Permanent Sovereignty) Act, 2017.

(iii) Mining Rights

Mining rights grant an individual or company permission to extract minerals from a piece of land. Such rights should not be confused with property rights, which stipulate the rights of property owners. In this respect, besides mining laws and regulations, other laws must be taken into consideration, including land laws which stipulate the rights of landowners and tenants.

A question may arise as to whether the owner of a piece of land also owns the minerals and resources underneath? In most jurisdictions, ownership of minerals is vested in the state on behalf of the people. The state becomes the custodian of mineral resources on behalf of its people. In this respect, the state holds responsibility for transforming the revenue from the minerals into tangible infrastructure such as roads, hospitals, schools which can improve the citizens' standard of living.

In summary, the state has sovereignty over its natural resources, and any person or company can only acquire mineral rights through the acquisition of the necessary mining licences and leases. However, not everyone can acquire such mining rights. Some jurisdictions in Africa have restrictions regarding eligibility to acquire mineral rights. In most cases, these restrictions consider the age, financial capability and nationality/citizenship of the person concerned. Under the law, a person can be an individual or a registered company. In Uganda, mineral rights are restricted to Ugandan citizens above the age of 18 and/or companies registered in Uganda or incorporated under the Companies Act of Uganda. Additionally, it is essential for interested individuals or companies to have a good financial record. In this respect Section 5 of the Ugandan Mining Act is to the effect that individual applicants should not be bankrupt or, in the case of a corporation, undergoing liquidation.[57]

(iv) Mining Licences

As discussed above, the ownership of minerals in most African countries is vested in the government on behalf of the people. In this respect, an individual or company will require a mining licence or lease to acquire mineral rights. A mining licence basically gives a person/company the rights to mine the specified minerals on a defined area for an agreed period of time. Mining licences include a prospecting licence, an exploration licence, a retention licence and a mining lease or location licence. The different types of licences are highlighted in Table 3.5, with a focus on examples from Ugandan laws.

[57] Section 5 of the Mining Act of Uganda, 2003, Laws of Uganda.

Table 3.5 Types of Mining Licences

Prospecting licence	Exploration licence	Retention licence	Mining lease	Location licence
Prospecting is the first stage of the geological analysis; Allows the holder to prospect for minerals; Involves the physical search for minerals; It is mineral- or area-specific; In some jurisdictions it is valid for one year.	Grants a holder exclusive rights to carry out exploration operations on the land in question; In some jurisdictions, it does not exceed three years.	Gives the holder more time for planning and obtaining financing; It is a holding title for a mineral resource which has been identified but cannot be mined or explored immediately.	Grants the holder the right to develop, mine and produce the mineral deposits in the land in question.	Applies to small-scale miners (see for instance Section 54 of the Mining Act of Uganda); Grants them a right for prospecting and mining in the areas where the licence applies.

As illustrated in Table 3.5, different licences grant the holder different rights. The prospecting licence grants the holder prospecting rights, while an exploration licence grants exclusive rights to carry out exploration operations in the relevant land. There are steps which the holder must take in order to acquire these licences and these are well stipulated in the relevant laws and regulations. These steps may differ depending on the country in question.

Taking the example of Uganda, the Mining Regulations, under Parts II, III, IV, V, VI and VII, provide detailed steps that applicants should consider when applying for the prospecting licence, exploration licence, retention licence, location and mining leases, respectively.[58]

There are various institutions relevant in the granting of mining licences and in the general governance of the mining sectors. In Uganda for instance, the key institutions responsible for the mineral sector include the Ministry of Energy and Mineral Development, the Directorate of Energy and Mineral Development, and the Geological Survey and Mines Department. Key officials include the Minister, the Commissioner and other senior officials. The Commissioner for the Geological Survey and Mines Department has several duties regarding mining licences and leases, and as such has the powers to grant, transfer, cancel, suspend and renew

[58] Uganda Mining Regulations, 2004.

mining licences/leases or export and import permits, and powers of inspection and information gathering. These powers can also be exercised by the Minister or delegated to other senior officials in the Ministry of Energy and Mines.

Besides national laws and regulations, regional initiatives to govern the mining sector on the African continent must be considered, such as the African Mining Vision (AMV). AMV is a policy framework created by the African Union (AU) in 2009 to ensure that Africa utilises its mineral resources strategically for broad-based inclusive development. It has been more than a decade since the AMV came into existence, and the question that arises and which needs to be addressed is what chance the AMV has of being implemented. How can African leaders embrace the AMV and how can this instrument tackle pertinent challenges in the African mining sectors? In addressing these questions, it is important to note that African countries must have the political will to implement the provisions of the AMV.

III. Land Access from the Perspective of Artisanal and Small-Scale Mining

While large-scale mining involves companies who employ advanced technology and enormous capital to extract minerals, ASM involves the use of rudimentary methods by individuals who are not officially employed by a mining company.[59]

ASM is associated with various social, economic and political impacts. Economically, ASM employs a significant number of local people in different African countries. For instance, it is estimated that over 500,000 people are directly involved in ASM in Uganda, 1,500,000 in Tanzania, and many others elsewhere in Africa. Besides the people directly employed in ASM, there are also millions of poor dependents who rely on ASM miners. This means that ASM is a very crucial and important sector in developing countries as it has a significant role to play in the eradication of poverty. In addition to employment, ASM also contributes to national revenue, and to the overall mineral output. However, there are also various social and environmental negative impacts associated with ASM including child labour, gender inequalities, violence, and health and safety concerns.

The negative impacts associated with ASM are escalated with the illegality and informality that characterises the sector. Additionally, these illegalities in ASM have escalated gender inequalities in the sector.

[59] Nalule, VR, *Mining and the Law in Africa: Exploring the social and environmental impacts* (Palgrave Pivot 2020).

ASM in most developing countries is characterised by informality. As such, the majority of ASM miners operate without legal title.[60] Mining rights are acquired through the issuance of licences and leases: for informal ASM therefore, miners carry out their activities without the required mining licences. Informality in ASM has escalated human rights abuses and environmental degradation.[61] It is for these reasons that several African countries are embracing the formalisation of ASM.

Formalisation entails the enactment and adaptation of mining laws and policies which recognise and regulate ASM.[62] The essence of formalisation is to control illegal activities in ASM by ensuring that miners acquire legal title. Several African countries have amended their mining laws and policies to reflect the formalisation of ASM.

Table 3.6 Key Issues in Artisanal and Small-scale Mining

Gender inequalities	Child labour	Use of rudimentary methods	Environmental degradation	Land issues	Health issues
Women lack sufficient finances and capital to adequately benefit from ASM	Children work alongside their parents; they are exposed to dangerous chemicals; they miss schools	Lack of machinery and advanced technology has led to a reliance on hand tools in ASM	Use of dangerous chemicals such as mercury endangers the environment and public health; deforestation	Pollution associated with ASM interferes with land use	Miners work without basic protective equipment; exposure to dangerous chemicals

Table 3.6 highlights some of the key issues with respect to ASM. Concerning child labour, it is worth noting that mining and quarrying are among the most dangerous and unhealthy occupations; the working conditions in these sectors are not good for adults, let alone for children. An estimated one million plus children between the ages of five and seven are believed to work in the small-scale mining and quarrying sectors and these children are lured into these activities due to the poverty in their homes.[63] These children are also engaged in all aspects of mining

[60] Hilson, G, Hilson, A, Maconachie, R, McQuilken, J and Goumandakoye, H, 'Artisanal and small-scale mining (ASM) in sub-Saharan Africa: Re-conceptualizing formalization and "illegal" activity' (2017) 83 *Geoforum* 80–90.

[61] Nalule, VR, *Mining and the Law in Africa: Exploring the social and environmental impacts* (Palgrave Pivot 2020).

[62] Echavarria, C, '"What is legal?" Formalising artisanal and small-scale mining in Colombia' (IIED and ARM 2014) p 79.

[63] Nalule, VR, 'Social and Environmental Impacts of Mining' in Nalule, *Mining and the Law in Africa: Exploring the social and environmental impacts* (Palgrave Pivot 2020) pp 51–81.

including rock breaking, mineral transportation and crushing and pounding. Child miners run the risk not only of mercury poisoning, but also of being exposed to severe injury, diseases and risks of death, be it in the mining or quarrying sectors. Another effect of child labour is the loss of an opportunity to acquire an education. My fieldwork in the salt mines in Uganda spotlighted various issues associated with child labour in ASM, including an exposure to dangerous chemicals.[64]

Concerning health issues, there has been an increasing number of health and safety issues in various mining communities. Taking the example of ASM, most miners operate without basic protective equipment such as gloves, boots and goggles. Further, ASM is associated with the use of dangerous chemicals such as mercury, poorly constructed shafts/tunnels, and poor waste management leading to contamination and diseases – all of which pose health and safety risks including death.[65] For instance, in February 2019 over 20 miners drowned in Kadoma, Zimbabwe, following the heavy rains which flooded two mines including Silver Moon Mine and Cricket Mine. The Cricket Mine is owned by Rio Zimbabwe and the company alleged that miners had illegally gained access to sealed shafts at the mine which was not in operation.[66]

Whereas various pieces of mining legislation have elaborative health and safety provisions, a question arises as to how can these provisions be effectively enforced to ensure that the health of miners is protected? Unlike ASM, LSM companies are required to prove that they have the capacity to adhere to health and safety laws before they are granted mining licences. This requirement is reflected in certain mining legislation such as the Mining Code of Mali under Sections 31 and 39.[67] Failure to comply with health and safety requirements can lead to the withdrawal of a mining licence as is the case in Rwanda and Ethiopia.[68]

Companies have indeed been involved in health and safety measures, including displaying relevant safety rules in their areas of operation, training workers and the establishment of personnel equipment rules. These are well stipulated in some mining laws, such as in the Mining Code of the DRC with respect to displaying safety rules;[69] in Malawi with respect to establishment of personnel equipment rules;[70] and in Rwanda with respect to training workers.[71] In addition to relevant

[64] See field work video by Dr Victoria Nalule in the salt mines of Uganda, Link to the video: www.youtube.com/watch?v=RKFP6DswMrM&t=532s.

[65] Nalule, VR, 'Social and Environmental Impacts of Mining' in Nalule, *Mining and the Law in Africa: Exploring the social and environmental impacts* (Palgrave Pivot 2020) pp 51–81.

[66] BBC News, 'Zimbabwe Gold Miners Feared Dead in Kadoma Flood', www.bbc.co.uk/news/world-africa-47238271, last updated on 14 February 2020.

[67] Sections 31 and 39 of Law No 2012-015 of 27 February 2012 Enacting the Mining Code, Laws of Mali.

[68] For Ethiopia, Article 44 of Proclamation No 678/2010 Promoting Sustainable Development of Mineral Resources; for Rwanda, Article 25 of Law No 13-2014 of 20 May 2014 on the Exploitation of Mines and Quarries.

[69] Article 210 of Law No 007-2002 of 11 July 2002 Relating to the Mining Code. Democratic Republic of Congo.

[70] See Articles 13 and 14 of the Mining (Safety) Regulations of Malawi.

[71] See Article 33 of Law No 13-2014 of 20 May 2014 on the Exploitation of Mines and Quarries, Laws of Rwanda.

mining Acts there are also specific laws that apply to health and safety and these in effect supplement the provisions contained in mining legislation. For instance, in Uganda there is an occupational Safety and Health Act;[72] the same Act is available in Kenya and other African countries.[73] There is, however, a need to ensure *enforcement* of health and safety requirements in ASM and this can only happen if governments and relevant bodies are able to monitor these activities in the first place.

Besides the health issues discussed above, ASM is also associated with violence and conflicts, especially in instances where foreign companies attempt to take over the mining areas where ASM miners operate. For instance, in 2013 ASM in Ghana attracted Chinese illegal miners who got into conflict with local miners.[74] An estimated 50,000 Chinese illegal miners, mostly exclusively from Shanglin County in Guangxi province, were involved in AGM in Ghana. Consequently, over 4,000 Chinese citizens involved in ASM were deported. There was also an escalation of armed robbery in AGM, often blamed on the guns brought in by the Chinese to protect themselves. Additionally, violence is escalated by the trafficking and use of narcotics, as some miners use cocaine and other drugs to get the courage to work in such dire conditions.[75]

ASM, especially gold mining, has also been associated with gang battles. In 2015, gang battles associated with illegal gold mining were reported in South Africa, as criminal gangs took control over disused and abandoned tunnels. Nevertheless, criminal activity in South Africa is also attributed to poverty, the decline in gold mining, unemployment and illegal migration.[76]

Taking stock of the above, it is clear that the nexus between land access and ASM mostly lies in the fact that the environmental impacts associated with ASM affect land use. This is true especially for rural communities that rely on land use for agriculture, fishing and farming. The other key issue is that lack of access to land titles has left many ASM miners as squatters on land, thus reducing the profits from ASM activities. Often, owners of land where ASM activities are carried out are entitled to rent and other royalties from the miners. As such, miners who cannot afford to pay these specified fees are left without work. The disparities in land ownership, especially between men and women, have escalated gender inequalities in ASM. This is common in communal or customary landownership systems, where women often own little or no land at all, thus limiting their ability to participate in, and effectively benefit from, ASM.

[72] The 2006 Occupational Safety and Health Act, Laws of Uganda.

[73] The 2007 Occupational Safety and Health Act, Laws of Kenya.

[74] Burrows, E and Bird, L, 'Ghana: Gold, Guns and China-Ghana's fight to end galamsey', *AllAfrica*, 30 May 2017. Can be accessed at, https://allafrica.com/stories/201706050394.html.

[75] ibid.

[76] BBC News, 'Illegal gold fuelling gang battles in South Africa', by Nomisa Maseko, *BBC News*, can be accessed at, www.bbc.co.uk/news/av/world-africa-34589143/the-illegal-gold-fuelling-gangbattles-in-south-africa, last visited on 14 February 2020.

IV. Gender Justice in the Mining Sector

Achieving gender equality is a recognised goal at the national, regional and international level as stipulated in Sustainable Development Goal 5.[77] From an economic perspective, gender equality entails access to equal opportunities and equal pay among men and women; socially and politically, it entails women having equal roles and responsibilities.[78]

Mining and farming, as some of the earliest areas of human enterprise, traditionally involved both men and women actively engaging in these activities. However, compared to men, women do not have access to the same benefits that accrue from the mining sector, and yet they still suffer the negative impacts associated with mining. The situation is exacerbated in the ASM sector in most African countries. Some of the key questions to be asked in an attempt to address gender inequalities in ASM include:

- Does the law mandate equal pay for males and females in ASM?
- Do married men and women have equal rights to property and land in ASM?
- Does the law mandate paid or unpaid maternity leave in ASM?

Answering the above questions is indeed necessary, but how do we incorporate these in the mining sector? Most mining legislation does not explicitly mention the need for equality among men and women in the sector. Additionally, most mining communities are occupied by miners who, in most cases, lack advanced training or education. In this respect, therefore, in addition to ensuring that international and national legislation is taken into consideration, local and community laws should adequately address gender inequality in the mining sectors. These laws should also ensure that women have access to alternative agricultural and farming land in the event they have to relocate due to mining activities.[79]

Unlike LSM, ASM attracts a significant number of women to the sector. The challenges women face in ASM can be grouped into three categories: economic challenges; social challenges; and political challenges.[80]

Economically, women have no access to finance, limiting them in acquiring the land, machinery and equipment needed in ASM activities. Additionally, lack

[77] Internationally, there are various instruments including: the Convention on Elimination of all forms of Discrimination Against Women (CEDAW); the Beijing Platform for Action; the United Nations Declaration on the Rights of Indigenous Peoples; and the Protocol on the Rights of Women in Africa (Maputo Protocol).

[78] Inglehart, RF, Norris, P and Welzel, C, 'Gender Equality and Democracy' (2002) 1(3/4) *Comparative Sociology* 235–64.

[79] Nalule, VR, 'Achieve Gender Equality and Empower All Women and Girls' in Parra, C, Lewis, B and Ali, SH (eds), *Mining, Materials, and the Sustainable Development Goals (SDGs): 2030 and Beyond* (CRC Press 2020) pp 39–50.

[80] Nalule, VR, 'Achieve Gender Equality and Empower All Women and Girls' in Parra, C, Lewis, B and Ali, SH (eds), *Mining, Materials, and the Sustainable Development Goals (SDGs): 2030 and Beyond* (CRC Press 2020) pp 39–50.

of finance has forced many women to work without the necessary protective gear and this has exposed them to dangerous diseases and health risks. A case in point is salt mining and gold mining.[81]

Socially, the cultural and traditional expectations from women hinder their active participation in the mining sector. For instance, in some cultures in Africa, women are not allowed to get involved in certain stages of mining including the digging of ores, and sale of minerals. In some cultures, it is believed that it is bad luck for a woman to be involved in the first and last stage of mining. Additionally, such activities have often been labelled as 'men's work'.[82] This only serves to undermine the role of women in ASM despite women playing a significant role in the sector.

The above notwithstanding, there is a need to advocate for the strong participation of women in the whole cycle of mining and related activities from exploration to consumption. It is also worth noting the valuable domestic roles of women including cooking, raising children, and looking after the household, to mention but a few. These domestic roles, besides making it hard for women to be actively involved in ASM, also make it difficult for some women to acquire the necessary education and training that are essential to take up some formal jobs in the mining sector.[83]

Politically, women have often been victims of rape in war-torn, resource-rich areas where rape is sometimes used as a weapon of war. The mining sector is generally characterised by gender-based violence, especially in conflict-intense countries such as the DRC. Moreover, rape is often used as a tool to oppress the local communities.

V. Mining Disputes and Land Access

Disputes in the mining sector can be grouped into two categories: economic disputes; and environmental disputes. Whereas environmental disputes are triggered by the negative impacts associated with mining, economic disputes are triggered by monetary concerns. Economic disputes can involve ASM versus LSM (where artisanal miners clash with LSM companies with respect to mining rights in a specified area); host government versus ASM (in instances of continued illegality and informalities in ASM); host government versus LSM (usually concerning the

[81] For an overview of the impact of salt mining to women in Uganda, watch the video by Dr Victoria Nalule recorded from the field. Link: www.youtube.com/watch?v=RKFP6DswMrM&t=491s.

[82] Nalule, VR, 'Achieve Gender Equality and Empower All Women and Girls' in Parra, C, Lewis, B and Ali, SH (eds), *Mining, Materials, and the Sustainable Development Goals (SDGs): 2030 and Beyond* (CRC Press 2020) pp 39–50.

[83] Nalule, VR, 'Achieve Gender Equality and Empower All Women and Girls' in Parra, C, Lewis, B and Ali, SH (eds), *Mining, Materials, and the Sustainable Development Goals (SDGs): 2030 and Beyond* (CRC Press 2020) pp 39–50.

fiscal regime); and host communities versus LSM (community dissatisfaction with mining operations).

In LSM, the increase in mechanisation and digitalisation has resulted in increased unemployment from the sector, fuelling conflicts and disputes, even though there are economic and social benefits from LSM. For instance, in November 2018, miners in South Africa went on strike and were also accused of arson at the Gold Fields-owned South Deep Mine in South Africa. This strike was organised by the National Union of Mineworkers in response to Gold Fields' plans to cut a further 1,500 jobs at the mine after the loss of 1,100 jobs the previous month. The strike not only affected the workers but also the mining company, resulting in a loss of around 2,800 oz of gold, equivalent to R50 million.[84]

With respect to conflicts or disputes between host governments and LSM, these have their genesis in the unfavourable fiscal regimes relied upon by most African countries. In this respect, countries such as Tanzania have not only introduced new legislation but also set up committees to investigate the taxing system for mining companies. For instance, in July 2017, Tanzanian authorities demanded that gold miner Acacia pay US$190 billion in unpaid taxes following the Committee findings that the firm was operating illegally and had understated its gold exports.[85] Acacia Mining, a company majority owned by Barrick Gold Corp, owns and operates Tanzania's three major mines – Bulyanhulu, Buzwagi and North Mara. In October 2018, some of the company's staff and former employees were detained by the country's anti-corruption authority for money laundering and tax evasion. The above are just a few examples of mining disputes. In the next sub-section, mining conflicts relating to land use will be discussed.

A. Mining Disputes and Conflicts Related to Land Use

As discussed in this chapter, the mining sector greatly contributes to the economic development of resource-rich countries. In Canada, mining accounts for approximately 15 per cent of national exports and 4–5 per cent of national GDP. In Zambia, mining activities contribute 20 per cent to GDP, and account for 90 per cent of export earnings. Whereas there are several benefits associated with mining activities, these have also been the source of conflicts, specifically concerning land use.

Mining operations often take place in villages. In addition to the migration of labourers from various villages to the mining community, backward and forward linkages also typically characterise the sector. Nevertheless, there has been an increasing number of land use conflicts between LSM companies and

[84] Mining Technology, 'Gold Fields reports arson and violence at South Deep mine protests' (November 2018), can be accessed at, www.mining-technology.com/mining-safety/goldfields-reports-arson-violence-south-deep-mine-protests, last visited on 14 February 2020.

[85] BBC News, 'Acacia Mining rejects US$190bn Tanzanian tax bill', can be accessed at, www.bbc.co.uk/news/business 40714086, last visited on 14 February 2020.

local communities on the one hand; and LSM and ASM on the other hand. As noted previously, mining projects require a significant amount of land to operate. In the acquisition of the land, and the development of mining projects, conflicts and disputes can and do erupt between mining companies and indigenous peoples. In some countries, this has in effect made it hard for mining companies to co-exist with the local communities. With respect to land use, the conflicts are mostly related to the environmental impacts associated with mining projects, including pollution, vegetation removal, erosion and sedimentation. Additionally, mining activities on land make it impossible for local communities to utilise the land for other activities including small businesses, farming, fishing, forestry and many others.

If these conflicts are to be avoided or even resolved, then all relevant stakeholders, including governments, host communities and mining companies, should communicate effectively and find ways of resolving land use conflicts as soon as they arise. Local or regional governments have a key role to play in coordinating the efforts of international agencies and ensuring that appropriate compensation packages are provided to impacted communities. However, there are various limiting factors, including ineffective regulatory frameworks, minimal government intervention and little or no support schemes for community and industrial groups.

Land use conflicts impact the development and utilisation of natural resources, hence leading to violence, and they also undermine livelihoods. With respect to environmental protection, forest and vegetation are often cleared to ensure that the mining companies have access to underlying ore bodies, and a vast quantity of often productive topsoil – through continuous exposure to weathering agents – erodes and collects in nearby water bodies. The resultant impacts of mining activities often lead to land conflicts.

The other negative impacts associated with mining include loss of agricultural opportunities, displacements and relocation of local peoples, fundamental disrespect to traditions and cultures, chemical spillage, collapses of tailings dams and heavy metals leaching. Additionally, major population influxes – namely, the migration of thousands of foreign and non-local employees to the area occupied by a mine – can upset the social balance of local communities, and impact local water supplies, resource availability and regional hunting. Below is a summary of land conflicts related to the mining sector.

(i) Land Use Conflicts between LSM and ASM

ASM employs a large number of local people. In this respect, many countries have attempted to legalise and formalise the sector by granting licences to small-scale miners. In some cases, these licences apply to nearby areas where LSM activities are carried out. In turn this has escalated land use disputes between LSM and ASM miners. For instance, land use conflicts related to gold mining in Ghana have been evidenced in the Tarkwa and Ashanti (near Oda) Regions of the country, as a result of ASM operations in areas where LSM companies legally operate. In 1990, seven cooperative groups of small-scale miners were registered in an area of 155 acres within the same concession awarded to the Ghanaian mining company Abosso Goldfields Ltd. ASM miners are often reluctant to leave due to the ancestral ties to the land and because most of them depend on ASM for their livelihood.

(ii) Land Use Conflicts between Mining and Other Industries

Mining projects present pressure on land use. As previously stated, most of these projects are carried out in villages where the majority of people rely on fishing and farming. In this respect, mining companies often infringe on the agricultural land relied on by local communities. The negative impacts associated with mining also present difficulties for the local communities to continue using their land for agricultural or forestry purposes during or post mining projects. Brazil is a good example of this, as conflicts between gold miners and small-scale cattle herders have been documented, especially the impacts of mercury use in some regions of the Brazilian Amazon.[86]

(iii) Mines, Communities, and Land Use Conflicts

In addition to the issues outlined above with respect to the conflicts between LSM and ASM, conflicts may emerge between mining companies and local communities. On the one hand, mining companies often feel that their efforts are not appreciated by the local communities and that the demands placed on them by these communities are often changing. On the other hand, local communities feel like they are not effectively involved, and that they do not have access to all the relevant information relating to the mining operations in their areas.

The cultural impacts of mining activities on Aboriginal and indigenous peoples are often the causes of these conflicts. Additionally, the local communities often rely on land for agriculture and, as mentioned previously, the negative impacts associated with mining such as pollution do interfere with land use, leading to dissatisfaction and conflicts. However, these local conflicts are minimised through achievement of the Social Licence to Operate (SLO) and Corporate Social Responsibility (CSR). Key concerns for the indigenous communities therefore include:

- Self-determination, including demands related to property rights over land and resources;
- Prior informed consent in relation to the protection of traditional knowledge and plant medicines;

[86] Hilson, G, 'An overview of land use conflicts in mining communities' (2002) 19(1) *Land Use Policy* 65–73.

- Cultural rights that include the right to express and maintain different cultures, the right to religion, language, and access to sacred sites and religious practices;
- Rights to communal property in lands and territories; and
- The right to control the traditional knowledge of property.

Although most conflicts between mining companies and local communities have been resolved amicably, there are instances where violence has erupted. The case of the Ok Tedi Mine in Papua New Guinea provides an effective illustration of the way in which irresponsible mining activities can cause major disputes between local villagers and mine personnel.

In this case, the Australian mining company BHP Minerals began prospecting at the Ok Tedi site in the 1970s, with excavation work commencing during the mid-1980s. BHP Mineral's activities left one of the biggest open-cut copper and gold mines in the world. Consequently, the mine has destroyed over 1,000 km^2 of virgin rainforest and wetlands. It has also gouged an enormous crater in the mountain; each day this crater discharges some 80,000 tonnes of limestone sludge containing copper and toxic chemical residues into the upper regions of the Ok Tedi River, causing it to rise between 4 and 5 metres in some places. Furthermore, in June 1984, a barge carrying containers of sodium cyanide and hydrogen peroxide lost its cargo, setting free 180 drums into the Ok Tedi River, and although many were recovered, others, for a number of economic reasons, were not. The pollution in the river caused mass fish, prawn, turtle and crocodile deaths. Most significantly, intensive mining at Ok Tedi has led to the displacement of a number of native *Wopkaimin* communities. Following several disputes, in 1996, an out-of-court settlement was finally reached, under which BHP would: stop dispensing tailings into the Ok Tedi/Fly River system; offer US$56 million in compensation to villagers; and provide an additional US$20 million to downstream villagers most affected by waste effluent. This case is an indication that, in order to minimise community-related land use disputes with mining companies, both parties should effectively communicate with each other. Close supervision of mining activities is also key in following up the resultant impact of mining activities on land use.[87]

B. Other Mining Disputes: Arbitration Cases Explored

Besides land use-based conflicts, the mining sector is prone to various disputes between host governments and mining companies. Key issues of concern often relate to the nature of the mining sector generally, including the fact that it is capital intensive. Additionally, these are long-term ventures which are easily affected by price volatility, hence necessitating security of tenure which is in most cases

[87] Hilson, G, 'An overview of land use conflicts in mining communities' (2002) 19(1) *Land Use Policy* 65–73.

provided through stabilisation clauses. Additionally, outdated mining codes/laws have often led to misunderstanding between host governments and the mining companies. Extractive disputes, including mining-related ones, are often resolved through arbitration. For instance, Africa-related ICC cases increased from 72 to 208 in 2017 (with 153 from SSA). Nevertheless, local courts have also played a role in resolving these disputes. Table 3.7 provides a few examples of mining disputes that have taken place in Africa.

Table 3.7 Mining Disputes in Africa

Dispute	**Brief description**
Zambia: *Vedanta v Government*	This case concerns the takeover of a mine and liquidation for Konkola Copper Mines (KCM). Parties include India-based Vedanta and Zambia's state mining company, ZCCM-IH, which owns 20 per cent of the operation. Dispute has been ongoing since May 2019, when Lusaka appointed a liquidator for the mine.
Sierra Leone: *Gerald International Limited v Republic of Sierra Leone*	This is the International Centre for Settlement of Investment Disputes (ICSID) Case No ARB/19/31. It involves criminal investigations of SL Mining Limited by the Sierra Leone Government. On 19 May 2020, SL Mining Limited filed a request for provisional measures against the Government of Sierra Leone at the ICSID in a bid to obtain the immediate release from detention of employees of SL Mining
Tanzania disputes: Acacia Mining; Montero Mining and Exploration	The Acacia Mining disputes concern a claim by Tanzania over a US$190 billion tax bill handed to Acacia in 2017 for allegedly under-reporting output. Following new legislation and a dispute with Barrick/Acacia, several claims are moving to the ICSID. These include claims by Canadian company Winshear Gold Corporation and Indiana Resources Limited, a mining company linked to the UK and Northern Ireland.
Zimbabwe: Amari dispute	Amari formed platinum and nickel ventures with Zimbabwe Mining Development Corp (ZMDC) that were 50 per cent and 45 per cent owned, respectively, by the state company. These were cancelled by Zimbabwe, arguing that the deals had not been appropriately approved by ZMDC officials and the nation's Minister of Mines. In a ruling by the International Court of Arbitration, made after a hearing in Lusaka, Zambia, Amari Holdings won the right to seize assets worth US$65.9 million in compensation for ZMDCs cancellation of nickel and platinum ventures formed in 2007 and 2008.

(continued)

Table 3.7 ***(Continued)***

Dispute	Brief description
Ghana: AngloGold Ashanti dispute	On 11 April 2016, the ICSID received a request for arbitration from AngloGold Ashanti (Ghana) Limited against the Republic of Ghana. The request was filed on the basis of the Mining Lease entered into on 5 March 1994 by the Government of Ghana and AngloGold, as amended in March 2007 with retroactive effect to 18 February 2004. The case was discontinued in 2018.
Rwanda: BayView and Spalena dispute	ICSID 2019: Alleged expropriation of five mining projects for tantalum, tin and tungsten.
Mali: Randgold dispute	2016 ICSID case concerning a breach of stabilisation by Mali. This was a win for Randgold. However, Mali then claimed the investor owed back taxes and a settlement was subsequently reached.

Table 3.7 spotlights some of the mining disputes between mining companies and host governments. These mostly relate to changes in the legal and fiscal regimes. Additionally, failure to comply with the requirements in mining licences has often led to mining conflicts.

Mining conflicts are typically caused due to a clash of interests, mistrust, and/or different objectives of the key stakeholders. Additionally, poverty and divergence of opinions in mining communities are also causes of mining conflicts. These are exacerbated by the negative environmental impacts associated with mining and land use. Additionally, poor governance on the part of the government, including a lack of transparency and accountability in resource allocation and weak institutions, has also led to conflicts.

Discontent amongst stakeholders has often led to prolonged disruptions of mining activities, criminal acts, costly litigation, fatalities and death. When faced with such evidence of discontent among stakeholders, it is advisable to immediately resolve the issues before a conflict erupts. In essence, this is the prevention principle of international law which recognises the importance of preventing environmental and social challenges that trigger conflicts. This principle is founded on the notion that *prevention is better than the cure.*[88]

Given the human rights abuses associated with mining, there is a need to ensure good governance in the sector. Besides transparency and accountability, good governance in summary requires the application of the PANEL Principles – **P**ublic participation, **A**ccountability and access to information, **N**on-discrimination and equality, **E**mpowerment and public awareness, **L**egality and access to justice.

[88] Olawuyi, DS (ed), *Local Content and Sustainable Development in Global Energy Markets* (Cambridge University Press 2021).

There are several instruments that are useful with respect to preventing or addressing mining disputes. These include among others:

- African Union's Action Plan for Implementing the African Mining Vision (December 2011);
- United Nations Guiding Principles on Business and Human Rights: Implementing the United Nations 'Protect, Respect and Remedy' Framework;
- African Commission on Human and Peoples' Rights Resolution 367: Resolution on the Niamey Declaration on Ensuring the Upholding of the African Charter in the Extractive Industries Sector;
- The ECOWAS Conflict Prevention Framework enacted on 1 January 2008 by the Mediation and Security Council of ECOWAS; and
- Report of the African Union Panel of the Wise on Improving the Mediation and Resolution of Natural Resource-Related Conflicts Across Africa.

The above instruments, coupled with national laws and policies, do play a significant role in resolving mining disputes.

VI. Conclusion

African countries have not effectively benefited from their mineral resources due to various factors, including unfavourable previous mining laws, political instability in some resource-rich countries, corruption and poor governance. As such there is a need to ensure: the enaction or amendment of relevant laws with the effect of giving the states more powers in the mining sector; the revision of tax laws and the reduction of tax incentives so that governments can get sufficient revenue from the mining sector; and the effective formalisation and legalisation of ASM. With respect to land use, it is essential that the host governments implement the numerous environmental laws and requirements. This will ensure that the mining companies abide by the environmental and land use requirements including mining closures, rehabilitation, and restoration, to mention but a few.

4

Land Access from the Perspective of the Energy Sector

I. Introduction to Energy Law

Concerned with the management of energy resources, energy law has gained a lot of attention in recent years following the need to tackle climate change by, among other means, reducing reliance on fossil fuels and embracing Renewable Energy (RE) and Energy Efficiency (EE).[1] Regulation of nuclear power, an arguably low-carbon energy source, attracted legal developments after the Second World War (post-1945), with the evolution of renewable energy sources including solar, biomass, wind and other low-carbon sources from the 1970s onwards. Of course, hydropower, a renewable source of energy, has been constructed and legislated for since the 1800s. Scholars have identified energy law and policy as being influenced by economics (finance), politics (energy security) and environment (climate change mitigation) – this is what has been termed 'the energy law and policy triangle' or the 'energy trilemma'.[2] Energy law and policy are therefore influenced by the need to tackle economic, political, environmental and social issues. In essence, effective and efficient energy law and policy should aim at balancing the various needs of the society.

Regulation of the energy sector is at the fore now, given the crucial role of energy in our everyday life. The sector is essential for every country's economic development. Energy has also been at the centre of various regional and international organisations and instruments. For instance, the European Union (EU) was founded upon two treaties – the European Coal and Steel Community Treaty and the Euratom Treaty – that were used to manage the natural resources and energy assets of countries within the initial group of Member States, and to bond nations together in peace through this important sector.

Energy law has also become internationally important given the increasing level of investment and the establishment of transboundary energy infrastructure such as oil and gas pipelines, oil refineries, and electricity transmission lines, just

[1] Nalule, VR, 'How to Respond to Energy Transitions in Africa: Introducing the Energy Progression Dialogue' in Nalule (ed), *Energy Transitions and the Future of the African Energy Sector* (Palgrave Macmillan 2021) pp 3–35.

[2] Heffron, RJ, *Energy law: an introduction* (Springer 2014) p 3.

to mention but a few.[3] Additionally, energy investments are expensive ventures requiring large amounts of capital; as such, both host communities and international energy companies are often eager to develop energy laws and policies that favour both parties.[4] The main driver behind the formulation of energy policies and energy legislation has been to tackle or address some issues that are seen as being pertinent in society. For instance, the twenty-first century is characterised by the need to transition to a low-carbon economy and tackle climate change. Besides the 2015 Paris Agreement, several countries have enacted laws aimed at promoting RE, EE and the deployment of electric vehicles and energy storage.[5] But when comparing the current drivers behind energy legislation with the drivers a few decades back, it can be seen that energy law is progressive in nature and, as such, legislators and policy-makers have to be willing to adjust energy law to meet current societal changes and developments.[6] For instance, some energy legislation has focused on the need to increase energy infrastructural developments. A case in point is the 2005 Energy Policy Act of the US, the main aim of which was to initiate several hundred billion dollars' worth of new energy infrastructure projects. Similarly, the UK government declared that the goal of its Energy Act 2013 was to initiate £110 billion of new energy infrastructure.

Energy law is influenced by various other areas of the law, including environmental law. Whereas energy law is focused on regulating the natural resources that yield energy, environmental law is mostly concerned with protection of the environment, forestry and wildlife, although incidences of overlap between the two types of law can and do occur (eg forestry 'products' for energy generation. Nevertheless, the link between energy law and environmental law lies in the fact that in the development of energy infrastructure, there are various environmental issues of concern including pollution (gas flaring and oil spills), and damage to the biodiversity and habitats. This explains why most energy laws require that companies meet the requirements of various environmental laws including: complying with national Environmental Impact Assessment requirements; decommissioning (for oil and gas); mining closure and land rehabilitation (for mining). This is a clear connection between energy law and environmental law. However, we note that environmental protection is part of land management. As defined in Chapter two, land includes not only the tangible property but also the intangible rights. In this respect, any disruption to the environment negatively impacts

[3] Roeben, V and Mete, G, 'What do we mean when we talk about international energy law? in Cameron, PD, Mu, X and Roeben, V (eds), *The Global Energy Transition Law, Policy and Economics for Energy in the 21st Century* (Hart Publishing 2020).

[4] Cameron, P, *International energy investment law: the pursuit of stability* (Oxford University Press 2010).

[5] Nalule, VR, *Energy Poverty and Access Challenges in Sub-Saharan Africa: The Role of Regionalism* (Palgrave Macmillan 2018).

[6] Nalule, VR, 'Extractives and Beyond: Managing the Energy Transition in Africa' in Nalule (ed), *Energy Transitions and the Future of the African Energy Sector* (Palgrave Macmillan 2021) pp 469–72.

land use. For instance, oil spills and gas flaring make it impossible for local farmers to continue with their agricultural and fishing activities, hence not only affecting the environment but also limiting land use. This therefore, is one of the examples of the inter-connection between extractives, land use and environmental protection. Additionally, energy law and policy is also influenced by other disciplines including economics, project management, strategy and finance. The next sub-section briefly discusses the nature of energy law.

A. The Nature of Energy Law

Energy law is derived from four levels: international, regional, national and local.

(i) Energy Law at an International Level

International treaties have long influenced the development of energy law. Although mostly focused on environmental protection and tackling climate change, these treaties have undoubtedly influenced the development of energy law. For instance, the UN-driven agreements on climate change have been ongoing since the Declaration of the United Nations Conference on the Human Environment, adopted in Stockholm on 16 June 1972. These treaties have influenced the enactment and adoption of new energy law legislation focused on tackling climate change by, among other means, reducing reliance on fossil fuels and advocating for the deployment of renewables. Table 4.1 provides a summary of some notable international treaties.

Table 4.1 International Treaties for Energy Issues

Vienna convention for the protection of the ozone layer (Vienna, 22 March 1985)
Montreal protocol on substances that deplete the ozone layer (Montreal, 16 September 1987)
United Nations framework convention on climate change (Rio, 9 May 1992)
Kyoto protocol to the United Nations framework convention on climate change (Kyoto, 11 December 1977)
Aarhus convention on access to information, public participation in decision-making and access to justice in environmental matters (Aarhus, 25 June 1988)
Convention on environmental impact assessment in transboundary context (Espoo, 25 February 1991)
2015 Paris Agreement
Energy Charter Treaty (Lisbon, 17 December 1994, updated 2015)

As illustrated in Table 4.1, most of the international treaties are focused on environmental protection or tackling climate change. This implies that member countries must comply with the treaty requirements of reducing GHG emissions by, among other things, reducing reliance on fossil fuels and embracing RE. The Kyoto Protocol and the 2015 Paris Agreement are among the international treaties that directly have an impact on the regulation of the energy sector, specifically considering their requirements for signatory countries to reduce their reliance on fossil fuels. Besides the international instruments, various international and regional organisations have greatly contributed to energy research, which to some extent forms the basis for these international instruments.[7]

(ii) Energy Law at a Regional Level

At the regional level, countries have embraced regional treaties aimed at ensuring that member countries address energy poverty and energy security issues. The EU is a good example of the influence of supranational organisations in shaping energy law. The EU Commission sets policy and legislative goals in the energy sector that are followed by the Member States. In Africa there are various regional organisations which also play a role in developing regional energy policies and laws, although these are not necessarily binding on their member states. In the EU, a notable example of a regional energy instrument is the Energy Charter Treaty (ECT), although this was modernised in 2015 to ensure that it applies to other countries outside the EU, hence the adoption of the 2015 International Energy Charter (IEC). In Africa, the 2003 ECOWAS Energy Protocol is a good example of a regional energy instrument.

(iii) Energy Law at the National and Local Level

At the national level, governments set the energy policy in their countries, with various goals and targets to be met. These policies are backed by energy laws and regulations aimed at meeting set policy goals. For instance, in Tanzania, they have the 2015 National Energy Policy; and in Rwanda there is the 2011 National Energy Policy and Strategy.

At a local level, local legislators from districts also contribute to the formulation of energy law and policy. They also often directly deal with the energy companies that wish to invest in their communities. Local governments can also offer some benefits and, above all, they are key in ensuring the acquisition of a social licence to operate. For instance, Victoria County in the US State of Texas granted Exelon some benefits for developing its plans to build a nuclear plant there.[8]

[7] Some of the energy organisations include: IEA; UNEP; International Atomic Energy Agency; and European Commission Energy Department.

[8] Heffron, RJ, *Energy law: an introduction* (Springer 2014).

B. Sustainable Development Goals 7 and 13 as Drivers of New Energy Law Development

The need to tackle energy access challenges as stipulated in SDG 7, together with the need to tackle climate change as stipulated in SDG 13, are some of the main drivers for energy governance and energy law. In this respect, this sub-section expounds on the issues of energy access and climate change. This is important as these two play a role in shaping the current and future energy dialogue at both the national and international levels.

(i) SDG 7 on Energy Access

There is no agreed definition of the term 'energy access'. However, different international organisations have endeavoured to define the term. For instance, in 2014, the IEA defined energy access by directly connoting it to the term 'modern', thus defining modern energy access as 'household having access to electricity and to a relatively clean, safe, means of cooking'.[9] In this definition the quality and quantity of electricity are considered, as elaborated below:

> According to the IEA energy modelling results, 250 kilowatt-hours (kWh) per year is assumed to be the electricity consumption for rural households, while 500 kWh is for urban households. Both are calculated based on an assumption of five people per household, this assumed electricity consumption is also influenced by the various purposes of electricity.[10] Recognizing the fact that traditional biomass is mostly relied on in rural areas for cooking, the IEA stretches the definition of modern energy access, to also include access to cooking facilities that are considered safer, more efficient and more environmentally sustainable than the traditional facilities that make use of solid biomass which is common practice across sub-Saharan Africa.[11]

The above IEA definition brings into play aspects of quality, quantity and use of energy. It also highlights different areas of habitation, including rural and urban, and how these consume energy differently. The term 'modern' is also introduced in the access discourse to make a distinction between traditional forms of energy like firewood or agricultural residues and commercial forms of energy like electricity or Liquefied Petroleum Gas (LPG).[12] On the one hand, modern energy can be distinguished from traditional energy by looking at the quality of energy used, for instance with regard to traditional energy, candles, kerosene, and lamps are

[9] IEA, *World Energy Outlook – Methodology for Energy Access Analysis*, 2014 www.worldenergyoutlook.org/media/weowebsite/EnergyAccess_Methodology_2014.pdf, last visited on 6 October 2015.

[10] For instance, whereas in rural areas it might be used to mostly provide light, in urban areas it might stretch to refrigeration uses.

[11] IEA, *World Energy Outlook – Methodology for Energy Access Analysis*, 2014 www.worldenergyoutlook.org/media/weowebsite/EnergyAccess_Methodology_2014.pdf.

[12] Brew-Hammond, A, 'Challenges to increasing Access to Modern Energy Services in Africa', codlogics_ff_201312 30_1388442782.report on West African energy ministers conference 2007.

used for lighting, and firewood for cooking. On the other hand, with regard to modern energy, electricity, natural gas, and LNG are used for lighting and cooking, respectively.[13]

It is well known that energy is key to our everyday life. The former UN Secretary General Ban Ki-moon rightly described it as follows: 'Energy is the golden thread that connects economic growth, increased social equity, and an environment that allows the world to thrive'.[14] Energy is not only essential for the provision of basic social services such as education and healthcare services, it is also essential for industrialisation and general economic development. Although there are various initiatives to ensure the achievement of universal energy access, many people, especially in developing countries, lack access to modern energy. It is estimated that 1.2 billion people worldwide have no access to modern energy such as electricity and nearly 3 billion people rely on traditional biomass (such as wood and charcoal) for cooking and heating.[15]

There have been various initiatives to tackle the challenge of energy access. Despite this, it persists in the Global South.[16] The challenge of energy access is rampant in various developing countries in Asia and Africa. However, Asia has made some significant progress, as the electrification rate in the region increased to 89 per cent in 2016, up from 67 per cent in 2000. Comparatively, the electrification rate in SSA is only 43 per cent, making it the least electrified region in the world.[17] The persistent problem of energy access in Africa has been attributed to the fact that it was not given international attention in the past compared to other development topics such as human sanitation and access to clean water. In this regard, access to energy received much less interest and limited investment and political backing. As such, the challenge of energy access persists especially in developing countries, where the majority of people still rely on traditional forms of energy such as charcoal and firewood for cooking and lighting.

The challenge of energy access was initially escalated due to the growing energy demand resulting from: geometric population growth; the rise in urbanisation and industrialisation; technology gaps; oil price volatility and reduced levels of finance

[13] Nalule, VR, *Energy Poverty and Access Challenges in Sub-Saharan Africa: The Role of Regionalism* (Palgrave Macmillan 2018).

[14] UN Secretary-General Ban Ki-moon, 'Sustainable Energy for All', retrieved at www.se4all.org/our-vision/. Last visited on 2 November 2015.

[15] United Nations Foundation, 'Achieving Universal Energy Access', www.unfoundation.org/what-wedo/issues/energy-and-climate/clean-energy-development.html.

[16] In recent years, there has been an increase in initiatives – bilateral, multilateral and non-governmental initiatives – some of which work closely with SSA governments and regional bodies such as the AU, the African Development Bank and the New Partnership for Africa's Development among others in order to tackle the challenge of energy access. These initiatives include among others: Sustainable Energy for All initiative, Japan's power infrastructure support programme, the US Power Africa initiative, and the EnDev programme (Germany, the Netherlands, the UK, and others).

[17] See IEA, 'Energy Access Outlook 2017: World Energy Outlook Special Report', p 11.

for energy projects; as well as the rising impacts of climate change on energy infrastructure.[18] This situation has now been exacerbated by the outbreak of the COVID-19 global pandemic in 2019, which has resulted in significant disruptions to global energy markets across the world, hence forcing many fossil fuels companies into bankruptcy.[19] The impact of COVID-19 has also emphasised the crucial role of renewables.

Although the concept of energy access has only recently gained academic momentum, different terms with virtually the same effect were highlighted as far back as the 1970s, with discussion on issues such as shortages of firewood in developing countries[20] and RE, particularly solar energy, being tackled.[21] The connection between topics discussed in the 1970s, such as the use of firewood for energy purposes, and the current concept of energy access relates to the fact that firewood is now considered a traditional form of energy; in the recent definitions of energy access, there is an emphasis on the need to shift from traditional to modern energy.[22] There are similar terms which often have the same message as energy access, and these are briefly discussed below.

(ii) Energy Poverty

Energy poverty is defined as the absence of sufficient choice in accessing adequate, affordable, reliable, quality, safe and environmentally benign energy services to support economic and human development.[23] Energy poverty can take different forms, including a lack of access to modern energy services, a lack of reliability, and concerns about affordability of access. The energy poverty term is mostly used interchangeably with that of energy access. However, it is worth noting that, although this chapter focuses on energy poverty in developing countries, specifically those in SSA, energy poverty has also been documented as a challenge in developed countries. Recent literature points to the fact that even countries which

[18] Olawuyi, DS, 'Can MENA extractive industries support the global energy transition? Current opportunities and future directions', *The Extractive Industries and Society*, 4 March 2020.

[19] Some of these companies include: Pacific Exploration & Production – US$5.3 billion in debt; Samson Resources – US$4.3 billion in debt; Ultra Petroleum – US$3.9 billion in debt; Sabine Oil & Gas – US$2.9 billion; Energy XXI – US$2.8 billion. There are many other companies with huge debts. For further information, please see Helman, C, 'The 15 Biggest Oil Bankruptcies (so far)', *Forbes*, 9 May 2020, www.forbes.com/sites/christopherhelman/2016/05/09/the-15-biggest-oil-bankruptcies-so-far/#61e1f4c67ff9. Last accessed on 15 October 2020.

[20] Eckholm, E, *The other energy crisis: firewood. Worldwatch Paper 1* (Worldwatch Institute 1975).

[21] Gergacz, JW, 'Solar Energy Law: Easements of Access to Sunlight' (1980) 10(1) *New Mexico Law Review* 121.

[22] Modern energy also includes renewables such as wind and solar, and traditional energy is often regarded as meaning traditional biomass, which definitely includes the reliance on firewood, mostly in rural areas.

[23] See, Cecelski, E, 'Enabling equitable access to rural electrification: current thinking and major activities in energy, poverty and gender' (University of Capetown 2002): quoting 'World Energy Assessment 2000: Energy and the Challenge of Sustainability' (UNDP September 1999 draft).

have acquired universal and reliable access to modern energy, still encounter affordability challenges.[24] The IEA, based on the methodology of the spending measure[25] and on survey responses on whether households are able to keep their homes sufficiently warm, estimates that over 15 per cent of the total population in developed economies suffers from energy poverty.[26]

In this regard, looking at the issue of affordability which limits or makes it hard for people in developed countries to enjoy already accessible and reliable energy services, it can be concluded that energy poverty is indeed a global challenge which needs to be given more attention both in developing and developed countries. Developed countries have successfully tackled the issue of accessibility and reliability to modern energy services, and as such they are now only working towards addressing the issue of affordability. In most developing countries, however, they are still struggling to address all aspects of energy access including accessibility, reliability, affordability and sustainability.

(iii) Energy Security

Whereas in the past energy security was primarily associated with oil supply, as a consequence of the increasing complexity of energy systems the term has been expanded. In this regard, the IEA defines energy security as 'the uninterrupted availability of energy sources at an affordable price'.[27]

(iv) Impact of SDG 7 on Other SDGs

Access to energy or electricity is key in achieving all the other UN SDGs including goal 3 on health, goal 4 on quality education, and goal 5 on gender equality, just to mention a few. For instance, with respect to SDG 5, women are the main users of energy especially in developing regions including Asia and Africa.[28] This is due to the social roles of women including cooking. Estimates indicate that women spend on average 1.4 hours a day collecting fuel wood and four hours for cooking. Therefore, access to electricity is key in improving the livelihood of these women.[29]

[24] The IEA, referring to the UK Fuel Poverty Strategy in 2001 and the subsequent review in 2012, highlights three main reasons for energy poverty in developed countries, including: low incomes; high energy costs; and energy inefficient dwellings. See IEA, 'Energy Access Outlook 2017: World Energy Outlook Special Report', p 24. It can be accessed at, www.iea.org/reports/energy-access-outlook-2017. Last accessed on 6 March 2021.

[25] The spending measure methodology takes into account the proportion of households spending more than 10% of their income on energy. For a full discussion on this, see IEA, 'Energy Access Outlook 2017: World Energy Outlook Special Report' p 24.

[26] See IEA, 'Energy Access Outlook 2017: World Energy Outlook Special Report' p 24.

[27] IEA, www.iea.org/topics/energysecurity/subtopics/whatisenergysecurity/ last visited on 30 January 2018.

[28] Nalule, VR, *Energy Poverty and Access Challenges in Sub-Saharan Africa: The Role of Regionalism* (Palgrave Macmillan 2018).

[29] ibid.

With respect to SDG 3, the connection between energy and healthy living lies in the fact that electricity is key in healthcare services, including hospitals. Additionally, lack of access to electricity implies that many people in the developing world will use traditional energy such as firewood for cooking and this definitely has various negative effects on the lives of people due to indoor air pollution. Research shows that household air pollution due to over-reliance on traditional energy is responsible for 2.8 million premature deaths every year.[30] The health sector is also arguably the most important sector in the current COVID-19 pandemic. However, although the developed countries are not burdened with lack of access to electricity in their hospitals, this is a big issue in many developing countries. The current COVID-19 crisis requires countries to be ready to adequately respond to health challenges, but this is hard for regions with insufficient healthcare services, and lack of access to electricity in these countries definitely escalates and aggravates the health challenges.[31] Given the important role of electricity in our everyday life, it would be understandable to treat access to electricity as a basic human right. However, economically, treating electricity as a human right would undercut electricity access and reliability, holding back economic growth.

(v) SDG 13 (Climate Change): Impact on SDG 7

Current global efforts to transition to a low-carbon economy and tackle climate change, as stipulated in SDG 13 and the 2015 Paris Agreement, have created a lot of tension regarding fossil fuel developments in recent years. This has resulted in various protests, which have led to a decline in finances for fossil fuel projects. In Norway, for instance, there has been a halt in fossil fuel investments. In June 2020, the Norwegian Parliament recommended that the country's Sovereign Wealth Fund sell off more than US$10 billion of stocks in companies related to fossil fuels.[32] In practice, this implies that the country is shifting from fossil fuels to clean energy. In this respect, the Sovereign Wealth Fund can no longer invest in companies that mine more than 20 million tonnes of coal annually or generate more than 10,000 MW of power using coal.[33] Besides Norway, in November 2019, The European Investment Bank (EIB) approved a policy to ban funding for oil, gas and coal projects by the end of 2021.[34] Since 2013, the EIB has funded €13.4 billion worth of fossil fuel projects, and in 2018 alone, it funded approximately €2 billion

[30] ibid.

[31] Nalule, VR, 'Extractives and Beyond: Managing the Energy Transition in Africa' in Nalule (ed), *Energy Transitions and the Future of the African Energy Sector* (Palgrave Macmillan 2021) pp 469–72.

[32] *Forbes*, 'Norway Wealth Fund to dumb fossil fuels stock', 12 June 2020. Can be accessed at, www.forbes.com/sites/davidnikel/2019/06/12/norway-wealth-fund-to-dump-fossil-fuel-stocks-worth-billions-in-environmental-move/#4dbb5c9748a3.

[33] ibid.

[34] BBC News, 'European Investment Bank drops fossil fuel funding', 14 November 2019. Can be accessed at, www.bbc.co.uk/news/business-50427873.

worth of projects.[35] With the ban, however, no more fossil fuel projects will be funded post-2021, although gas projects could still be funded as long as they utilise clean technologies such as carbon capture and storage, combined heat and power generation, or mixing in renewable gases with fossil natural gas.[36]

The issue of climate change will be expounded on in this book. The next sub-section analyses the impact of regionalism and globalism in the energy sector. Prior to that discussion, however, it is worth noting that there are different energy policy concepts, which although not fully discussed in this chapter, deserve some recognition. These include among others: electricity policy; competition policy; energy waste management policy; planning policy; environmental policy; heritage policy; energy security; national energy policy; and international energy policy.[37]

C. Influence of Regionalism and Globalism in Energy Law

(i) Introduction to Regionalism

Recognising the fact that most regions in SSA face similar energy challenges, including unreliable electricity supply and reliance on traditional biomass, these challenges can be tackled by employing common initiatives and mechanisms through regionalism.

In essence, regionalism is defined as the expression of a common sense of identity and purpose, combined with the creation and implementation of institutions that express a particular identity and shape collective action within a geographical region.[38] Although most regional blocs in Africa, including SADC, East African Community (EAC), and ECOWAS, have a geographical perspective underlying their establishment, it is imperative to note that there are some regional blocs which do not purely consider geography as the basis for inclusion of new members. A case in point is the League of Arab States (LAS), which essentially applies linguistic-cultural aspects as the basis for the inclusion of members rather than geographical conditions.[39] The Organization of Islamic Cooperation (OIC) also focuses on religious identity in defining its membership rather than geography.[40] Furthermore,

[35] ibid.

[36] ibid.

[37] For a detailed discussion on these policies, see Heffron, RJ, *Energy law: an introduction* (Springer 2014) p 35.

[38] Ethier, W, 'The international commercial system' (Essays in International Finance No 210). (International Finance Section, Princeton University Dept of Economics 1998) p 11.

[39] The Arab League is a regional organisation of Arab countries in and around North Africa, the Horn of Africa and Arabia. It was established in Cairo on 22 March 1945 with six members; to date, it now includes 22 Member States.

[40] The OIC is the collective voice of the Muslim world, established upon a decision of the historical summit which took place in Rabat, Kingdom of Morocco on 12 Rajab 1389 Hijra (25 September 1969) following the criminal arson of Al-Aqsa Mosque in occupied Jerusalem. The OIC is the second-largest inter-governmental organisation after the UN with a membership of 57 states spread over four continents.

other regional blocs are basically driven by a specific function and purpose.[41] A case in point is the North American Free Trade Agreement (NAFTA)[42] and the Asia-Pacific Economic Cooperation (APEC)[43] which are mostly focused on economic integration. Moreover, the creation of some regional blocs was initially driven by security concerns as in the case of the North Atlantic Treaty Organization (NATO)[44] and the Shanghai Cooperation Organization (SCO).[45]

Historically, the notion of regionalism was influenced by various changes to the international system including the Cold War and its ending, the post-hegemonic era and the processes of decolonisation and globalisation.[46] Regionalism dates back as far as the 1950s and 1960s with the establishment of Western Europe – this is understood as the old regionalism, which was mostly influenced by the Cold War logic. The Cold War is indeed seen as having been essential in providing an arena for the selective development of regional organisations and as a foundation for later regional building.[47] In the 1980s, the global community experienced another form of regionalism typically referred to as 'new regionalism'.[48]

New regionalism has also been associated with the EU and there is a general consensus that the success story of EU integration has provided both the inspiration and normative model for the new wave of regionalism found throughout the world.[49] Regional blocs including EAC and ECOWAS have been trying to imitate the EU model, and in some instances the EU policies in these regions have acted as an external driver to regionalism.[50] Besides the influence of the EU, other external

[41] Fawcett, L, 'Region-Building Debates in a Global Context' in Levine, DH and Nagar, D (eds), *Region-Building in Africa* (Palgrave Macmillan US 2016) pp 21–36.

[42] NAFTA is an agreement signed by Canada, Mexico and the United States, creating a trilateral trade bloc in North America.

[43] APEC was established in 1989 in response to the growing interdependence of Asia-Pacific economies, and it currently has 21 members.

[44] NATO is an intergovernmental military alliance consisting of 29 member countries across North America and Europe.

[45] SCO is a Eurasian political, economic and security organisation with eight member states: China, Kazakhstan, Kyrgyzstan, Russia, Tajikistan, Uzbekistan, India and Pakistan. Although SCO was officially created in 2001, its origin dates as far back as the 1990s, with the signing of the Treaty on Deepening Military Trust in Border Regions in Shanghai, China by the heads of state of China, Kazakhstan, Kyrgyzstan, Russia and Tajikistan.

[46] In past centuries, however, regionalism was influenced by powerful states and empires that sought to build and develop regions as an extension or demonstration of their power or as a means of balancing the power of others. For a full discussion on this, see Fawcett, L, 'Region-Building Debates in a Global Context' in Levine, DH and Nagar, D (eds), *Region-Building in Africa* (Palgrave Macmillan US 2016) pp 21–36.

[47] Fawcett, L, 'Region-Building Debates in a Global Context' in Levine, DH and Nagar, D (eds), *Region-Building in Africa* (Palgrave Macmillan US 2016) pp 21–36.

[48] Nalule, VR, 'Regionalism in Addressing Energy Access Challenges' in Nalule (ed), *Energy Poverty and Access Challenges in Sub-Saharan Africa* (Palgrave Macmillan 2018) pp 41–89.

[49] Telò, M (ed), *European Union and new regionalism: regional actors and global governance in a post-hegemonic era* (Ashgate Publishing, Ltd 2013).

[50] Although the European form of regionalism has had an impact on current trends in the African continent, it is worth noting that the desire for regionalism and advocacy for togetherness and oneness of all Africans has been in existence since long before the success story of the EU regionalism. Regionalism in Africa has always been based on the desire to unite a continent which was divided by

drivers have been felt from international organisations such as the UN, World Bank and multilateral institutions such as the GATT and the World Trade Organization (WTO).[51] Besides external drivers, there are also internal drivers, which of course reflect the specific concerns of the states involved, unlike the external drivers which mostly focus on the interests of international organisations.[52]

(ii) Regionalism in the Energy Sector

The relevant legal provisions that form the basis for regional cooperation in the energy sector are contained in the establishing regional treaties. For instance, Article 2 of the EAC Treaty establishes the East African Community (EAC), with the main objective of widening and deepening cooperation among the Partner States in political, economic, social and cultural fields.[53] With regard to the energy sector, Article 101(1) encourages Partner States to jointly adopt policies and mechanisms to promote the efficient exploitation, development, joint research and utilisation of various energy resources available within the region.[54] Article 101 further provides the different forms by which the Partner States can cooperate in the energy sector, including: promoting the least cost development and transmission of electric power; joint planning, training and exchange of information on the exploration, exploitation, development and utilisation of available energy resources; development of integrated policy on rural electrification; and joint efforts in the construction of oil and gas pipelines.[55]

In West Africa, ECOWAS was established under Article 2 of the ECOWAS Treaty, with the main aim of promoting cooperation and integration.[56] With respect to the energy sector, in 2003, ECOWAS created an Energy Protocol with the aim of promoting further cooperation in the energy sector among the member states.[57]

In Southern Africa, SADC was established under Article 2 of the 1992 Treaty, with various objectives including achieving development, economic growth and alleviating poverty through regional integration.[58] The Treaty encourages member

former colonialists. Historically, regionalism in Africa and the desire for regional cooperation has been evident since the independence of most African states and has its roots in political Pan-Africanism, which required a lot of solidarity to achieve the various goals of the liberalisation movements. The fundamental purpose for Pan-Africanism was national independence leading to African unity. For a detailed discussion on regionalism, see, Nalule, VR, 'Regionalism in Addressing Energy Access Challenges' in Nalule (ed), *Energy Poverty and Access Challenges in Sub-Saharan Africa* (Palgrave Macmillan 2018) pp 41–89.

[51] Fawcett, L, 'Region-Building Debates in a Global Context' in Levine, DH and Nagar, D (eds), *Region-Building in Africa* (Palgrave Macmillan US 2016) pp 21–36.

[52] Nalule, VR, 'Regionalism in Addressing Energy Access Challenges' in Nalule (ed), *Energy Poverty and Access Challenges in Sub-Saharan Africa* (Palgrave Macmillan 2018) pp 41–89.

[53] Article 5(1) of the Treaty for the Establishment of the East African Community, 1999.

[54] Article 101(1) of the Treaty for the Establishment of the East African Community, 1999.

[55] Article 101(2) of the Treaty for the Establishment of the East African Community, 1999.

[56] Article 3(1) of the ECOWAS Revised Treaty.

[57] ECOWAS Energy Protocol, 2003.

[58] Article 5(1)(a) of the 1992 SADC Treaty.

states to cooperate in areas such as infrastructure, natural resources and the environment.[59] The SADC Protocol on Energy was passed in 1996 with the main aim of ensuring regional cooperation in the energy sector.[60] These regional blocs have greatly influenced regional cooperation in the development of energy projects, including regional energy infrastructure and the establishment of regional energy laws.[61] The next sub-section will briefly discuss the concept of globalism in the energy sector, with a focus on the case study of the ECT.

(iii) Globalism in Energy Law: Focus on the Energy Charter Treaty

The ECT is one of the unique multilateral instruments found in the energy sector. The origins of the ECT need to be understood in the European countries' interest to trade with countries in the East following the collapse of the Soviet Union in 1991. Although the ECT initially covered a limited number of countries, recent developments have seen the expansion of the principles of the ECT to various regions including Asia, Africa, and Latin America. This expansion was made possible following the adoption of the International Energy Charter. Basically, the IEC is a political declaration on energy cooperation which does not bear any legal or financial obligation, and has been adopted and signed by over 80 countries and organisations including, among others, the US, China, Burundi, Uganda, Chad, ECOWAS, EAC and the EU.

In contrast, the ECT is a legally binding text providing rules regarding the areas of investments, trade and transit and energy efficiency. It provides dispute resolution mechanisms, while explicitly recognising and protecting national sovereignty over natural resources.[62] The purpose of the ECT as provided for in its provisions is to promote cooperation in the field of energy.[63] For more than a decade, the ECT has attracted a lot of literature from different scholars and this can be attributed to its unique focus on the energy sector, one which is at the heart of every country's economic development.[64]

Recent developments in the RE sector have also increased the relevance of the ECT. Notably, solar photovoltaic (PV) energy investors instituted claims against

[59] Article 21(3) of the 1992 SADC Treaty.

[60] SADC Protocol on Energy, 1996.

[61] For a detailed discussion on regionalism in the energy sector, see Nalule, VR, *Energy Poverty and Access Challenges in Sub-Saharan Africa: The Role of Regionalism* (Palgrave Macmillan 2018).

[62] Article 18 of the ECT provides for national sovereignty over energy resources. The ECT and the Energy Charter Protocol on Energy Efficiency and Related Environmental Aspects were signed in December 1994 and entered into force in April 1998.

[63] See, Article 2 of the Energy Charter Treaty.

[64] Some of the literature on the ECT include: Konoplyanik, A and Wälde, T, 'Energy Charter Treaty and its role in international energy' (2006) 24(4) *Journal of Energy & Natural Resources Law* 523; Wälde, T (ed), *The Energy Charter Treaty: An East-West Gateway for Investment and Trade* (Kluwer Law International 1996); Hobér, K, 'Investment arbitration and the energy charter treaty' (2010) 1(1) *Journal of International Dispute Settlement* 153–90; Taheri, S and Sharify, SK, 'An analysis of the method of dispute settlement in Energy Charter Treaty compared with World Trade Organization' (2016) 8(2S) *Journal of Fundamental and Applied Sciences* 3669–87.

some ECT member states (such as Italy, Spain and the Czech Republic). These claims were as a result of the domestic legislative revisions of incentive schemes for RE in those countries (initially the RE sector in general and the PV energy generation sector had benefited from large national incentive schemes and many EU countries subsidised the sector).[65] Some of the claims included that the reforms of some national supporting schemes breached the fair and equitable treatment standard and ECT treaty provisions prohibiting indirect expropriation. This claim was based on the fact that the reforms had the effect of making their businesses less profitable, contrary to pre-reform legislative and regulatory commitments. The ECT was modernised in 2015, hence adopting the 2015 IEC which seeks to expand the principle of the ECT to all countries globally. In this respect, the IEC is a global instrument promoting globalism in the energy sector, specifically given its provisions on energy investment, energy infrastructure and dispute resolution.[66] The IEC and ECT will not be discussed in detail in this short sub-section. However, what is key here is the influence of international instruments in shaping the energy sector globally. The next section will discuss the nexus between petroleum projects and land access.

II. Petroleum Projects and Land Access

A. Types of Fossil Fuels

(i) Oil

As with other types of fossil fuels, including coal and gas, oil is associated with various environmental impacts. Unlike coal and gas, however, oil is used to a limited extent for electricity production, although its major role in the transport sector cannot be underestimated. Safety is also a major concern following a number of various accidents related to the oil sector. The most well-known of these accidents is the BP Deepwater Horizon oil spill accident in the Gulf of Mexico in 2010. Oil spills have also been a major concern in different countries including Nigeria.

(ii) Gas and Shale Gas

Natural gas is becoming increasingly important as a source of energy in this energy transition era. Although considered as a fossil fuel, compared to coal and oil, gas produces fewer GHG emissions than the rest. Consequently, it is seen as a transitional solution replacing the other types of fossil fuels and thereby reducing CO_2 emissions. Drilling for gas can take place both onshore and offshore, and

[65] For a full discussion on this, see De Luca, A, 'Renewable Energy in the EU, the Energy Charter Treaty, and Italy's Withdrawal Therefrom', *Bocconi Legal Studies Research Paper No. 2657395* (January 2015).

[66] Nalule, VR, 'Regionalism in Addressing Energy Access Challenges' in Nalule (ed), *Energy Poverty and Access Challenges in Sub-Saharan Africa* (Palgrave Macmillan 2018) pp 41–89.

gas has been used in many countries for electricity generation. However, various safety concerns have been highlighted regarding the extraction of gas and, as such, accidents relating to gas extraction are common.

'Fracking' for shale gas has also been a marked feature of the twenty-first century, presenting many opportunities in different countries. Although common in the US, the hydraulic fracturing (or fracking) of shale gas has been banned in some European countries such as France and Scotland.

(iii) Coal

Coal has been a dominant source of energy for many centuries, and greatly contributed to the economic and social development of many developed countries in the 1800s and 1900s. Whereas there have been various efforts to reduce reliance on coal globally, many developed countries such as Poland are still utilising coal for electricity generation. Coal extraction is associated with both environmental and safety concerns. For instance, in New Zealand, 29 people died in a methane explosion in the Pike River mine in 2010.

B. Energy Infrastructure and Related Land Issues

Access to land is essential in the establishment of energy infrastructure. As such, there are various advantages and disadvantages that local communities are bound to experience in the development of various energy projects. On the positive side, developmental infrastructure such as roads and healthcare services are often established in resource-rich areas, not to mention the creation of employment opportunities for local people. However, a negative aspect in the establishment of energy infrastructure is that many people are displaced or resettled in different places. It is also important not to forget the inadequate compensation given to some locals for accessing their land.

Further, energy resources are unequally distributed across the globe and this has necessitated the trans-national character of extraction and utilisation of these resources, including the establishment of energy infrastructure. Energy infrastructure is crucial as it enables both producing and consuming countries to benefit from various energy resources.[67] Although fundamental for tackling the challenge of energy access, the establishment and development of energy infrastructure generally raise a lot of concerns both nationally and regionally. At the national level, for instance, concerns over consumer privacy have arisen;[68] protests by

[67] See Goldthau, A, 'Rethinking the governance of energy infrastructure: Scale, decentralization and polycentrism' (2014) 1 *Energy Research & Social Science* 134–40.

[68] In 2008, a debate on the privacy consequences of the diffusion of smart grid and smart metering technologies gained some momentum. Suggestions were made on how to address the privacy threat posed by new energy infrastructure. See Quinn, EL, 'Privacy and the new energy infrastructure', *EES Working Paper No 09-001* (2008), https://papers.ssrn.com/sol3/papers.cfm?abstract_id=1370731, last accessed on 14 February 2017.

local communities have also been experienced and these are mostly driven by the discontent felt by local people over the combined environmental and economic harm caused by some energy infrastructure.[69] At a regional level, complex issues regarding legal frameworks and the financial contribution of the member states in a regional organisation have been experienced.

Critical energy infrastructure includes: utilities associated with energy transport and management such as: electricity generation and transmission; oil and gas production and pipeline systems; LNG facilities; coal transport trains; and management technology such as advanced electricity metering and distribution systems; modern power plant control systems and smart building technologies. These different kinds of energy infrastructure are important in addressing SDG 7, which is focused on energy access. The next section explores the various energy infrastructure.

Table 4.2 Energy Infrastructure

Country/ Countries	Energy Infrastructure Type	Details
Nigeria, Benin, Togo and Ghana	West African Gas Pipeline (WAGP)	WAGP, based on the Treaty of the West African Gas Pipeline Project, was established with the main purpose of constructing a 600 km pipeline. The pipeline is owned and operated by West African Gas Pipeline Company Limited (WAPCo), with a regulatory body based in Abuja, the West African Gas Pipeline Authority. The pipeline is anticipated to reduce overall production costs of electricity generation using fossil fuels, improve energy access and reduce gas flaring which is associated with environmental pollution.
Uganda-Tanzania	Crude Oil Pipeline	The main aim is to transport crude oil from the Ugandan fields to Tanga, Tanzania, a port on the Indian Ocean. The 1,445 km East African Crude Oil Pipeline is estimated to cost US$3.5 billion.

(continued)

[69] For instance, in Nigeria, one of the largest oil-producing countries in SSA, there has been socio-political unrest due to the exploration and production of oil; this has also affected the energy infrastructure in the region. These conflicts include, among others, the Ogoni environmental conflict (1992–95), and the Warri crisis (1997–99). For a detailed discussion on the subject, see Yeeles, A and Akporiaye, A, 'Risk and resilience in the Nigerian oil sector: The economic effects of pipeline sabotage and theft' (2016) 88 *Energy Policy* 187–96.

Table 4.2 ***(Continued)***

Country/ Countries	Energy Infrastructure Type	Details
Uganda	Oil Refinery	This project is to be developed under a public private partnership and the EAC countries are expected to have a stake in this US$2.5 billion project.[70]
Niger-Benin	Oil Pipeline	The pipeline is 1,950 km in length and is being constructed by the China National Petroleum Corporation. It is set to transport crude oil to global markets, via the port of Seme on the coast of Benin from Niger's oil-prolific Agadem basin.
Tanzania	LNG Liquefaction Plant	Plans were made for the construction of an LNG liquefaction facility, spanning 5,119 acres in Likong'o Village, outside the town of Lindi. Key players include Equinor, Shell, ExxonMobil, Ophir Energy and Pavilion Energy. Estimated cost US $30 billion.
Mozambique	Rovuma LNG Liquefaction Plant	The project is estimated to cost US $22.4 billion.
Mozambique	Mozambique LNG Project	Estimated at a cost of US $15 billion. Key players include Total, Mitsui & Co, ONGC, ENH, Bharat PetroResources, PTTEP and Oil India Ltd. Total is leading the project after taking over Anadarko's 26.5 per cent interest in September 2019.
Nigeria	Dangote Refinery and Polypropylene Plant	Estimated at a cost of US $11 billion. This is a major downstream facility in Nigeria's Lekki Free Trade Zone. It is planned to refine 650,000 barrels per day; produce 153,000 barrels per day of gasoline; 104,000 barrels per day of diesel; 73,000 barrels per day of jet fuel; 4,109 barrels per day of LPG and 12,300 barrels per day of fuel oil.
Angola	Namibe Refinery Complex	Estimated at a cost of US $12 billion, this 400,000 barrel-per-day refinery was proposed by local partners in 2017.

[70] Previously, Uganda had considered partnering with Kenya to construct an oil pipeline (the Uganda-Kenya Crude Oil Pipeline); however, this idea was abandoned due to security and cost concerns, making Uganda opt for a route in Tanzania.

All the fossil fuel energy infrastructure projects discussed above require massive land for them to be operational. The nexus between energy and land use will be expounded on in this chapter, but prior to that, the next section spotlights the various renewable energy infrastructure in different countries.

III. Renewable Energy Projects and Land Access

By definition, renewable energies are typically energy sources that are continually replenished by nature and derived directly from the sun (such as thermal, photo-chemical, and photo-electric), indirectly from the sun (such as wind, hydropower, and photosynthetic energy stored in biomass), or from other natural movements and mechanisms of the environment (such as geothermal, wave and tidal energy).[71]

A. Sources of Renewable Energy

The global effort and campaign to reduce GHG emissions have seen developed countries such as Spain achieve 100 per cent electrification from renewables. This is indeed a goal shared by many developing countries in SSA, as evidenced in their pledge in 2016 during the United Nations Climate Change Conference in Morocco. Although the SSA region still faces the challenges of energy poverty, there is potential to meet these challenges by utilising the enormous renewable resources in the region. There is no doubt that SSA is very rich in RE resources, with solar power potential totalling about 10,000 GW, wind potential totalling about 109 GW (found mostly in the coastal countries), geothermal capacity estimated at 15 GW (especially in the East African Rift Valley), and exploitable hydropower estimated at about 350 GW (mainly located in Angola, Cameroon, Ethiopia, Gabon, and the Democratic Republic of Congo (DRC)).[72]

Despite such enormous resources and the global commitment to increase the proportion of renewables in the energy mix, there are some basic requirements that need to be fulfilled if the vision is to be attained. These requirements include among others: an enabling legal and regulatory framework; policies that incentivise RE deployment; innovative financing mechanisms that allow decentralised solutions to thrive and be integrated into future grid expansion; electricity supply strategies that prioritise the diversity of resources such as dispatchable renewables and storage that negate the need for fossil fuels and play a role to ensure supply security.

[71] Ellabban, O, Abu-Rub, H and Blaabjerg, F, 'Renewable energy resources: Current status, future prospects and their enabling technology' (2014) 39 *Renewable and Sustainable Energy Reviews* 748–64.

[72] Avila, N, Carvallo, JP, Shaw, B and Kammen, DM, 'The energy challenge in sub-Saharan Africa: A guide for advocates and policy makers', Technical report (OXFAM 2017).

RE sources basically include biomass, geothermal energy, hydropower energy, marine energy, solar energy, and wind energy. These are briefly discussed below:

(i) Biomass

Biomass is a source of energy through plants, crops, and trees and it entails the collection and storage of the sun's energy through photosynthesis. The biomass process also involves the conversion of biomass into useful forms of energy such as heat, electricity, and liquid fuels.

(ii) Geothermal Energy

Geothermal energy is an efficient way to extract RE from the earth, and it originates from the formation of the planet and the radioactive decay of materials.

(iii) Hydropower Energy

Hydropower is power derived from the energy of moving water. It is generated from water moving in the hydrological cycle, which is driven by solar radiation. Dams are the most prevalent form of hydropower.

(iv) Marine Energy

Marine energy, sometimes referred to as ocean energy, comes from six distinct sources – namely: waves, tidal range, tidal currents, ocean currents, ocean thermal energy conversion, and salinity gradients – each with different origins and requiring different technologies for conversion.

(v) Solar Energy

Solar energy is produced through sunlight. Solar energy generation involves the use of the sun's energy to provide hot water via solar thermal systems, or electricity via solar PV and Concentrating Solar Power systems. Solar energy is mostly used for lighting purposes through photovoltaic conversion in rural areas. Although developing at an increased rate, the challenge with solar energy technology is that it does not permanently tackle the challenge of energy poverty, especially considering the limited lifespan of solar panels. Nevertheless, many people are embracing solar energy since it is increasingly being localised, with more individuals able to own solar panels.

(vi) Wind Energy

Wind energy is produced by harnessing wind power and converting it into a useful form, eg using wind turbines to make electricity, windmills for mechanical power, wind-pumps for pumping water or drainage, or sails to propel ships. Although increasingly important in the transition to a low-carbon economy, the development of wind energy and the construction of wind turbines have faced significant protests in the past by local communities in countries such as Germany and Ireland.[73] In an effort to address such opposition, some countries such as Denmark embraced community ownership of the wind energy projects by local residents and towns.

B. Advantages and Challenges of Renewable Energy

On the one hand, there are various advantages of RE sources, for instance, hydro resources have considerable potential to be utilised for power generation. And solar and wind energy resources are excellent for applications such as water pumping, water heating, and power generation through centralised schemes, mini-grids, and stand-alone systems.

Notwithstanding the advantages associated with RE sources, there are some shortcomings related to the reliance on renewables to expand the supply of electricity. For instance, RE sources such as solar, wind and hydro are prone to the impacts of climate change; the intermittency and variability of solar and wind; and the risk of over-generation and curtailment. Additionally, Table 4.3 provides a general summary of both the benefits and barriers of each type of RE source.

Table 4.3 Advantages and Disadvantages of Renewable Energy

RE Source	Advantages	Disadvantages
1. Biomass	• Abundant and renewable	• Burning biomass can result in air pollution • May not be cost effective
2. Geothermal	• Unlimited supply of energy • Produces no air or water pollution	• Costly to establish and maintain
3. Marine	• Ideal for an island country • Captures energy that would otherwise not be collected	• Construction can be costly • Has negative impact on wildlife • Takes up lots of space

(continued)

[73] In November 2019, there were protests in Germany, with locals opposing the construction of new wind turbines in their areas. In September 2019, Norway put a halt to new wind power projects following public protests. In 2014, more than 100 opposition groups sprung up against new wind farms in the rural areas of Ireland.

Table 4.3 ***(Continued)***

RE Source	Advantages	Disadvantages
4. Solar/Wind	• Potentially infinite energy supply • Causes no air or water pollution	• May not be cost effective[74] • Storage and backup are necessary • Variable and intermittent[75]
5. Hydropower	• Abundant, clean and safe • Easily stored in reservoirs • Relatively inexpensive way to produce electricity • Offers recreational benefits like boating and fishing	• Can cause flooding • Can threaten livelihoods • Poses social and ecological risks • Affected by drought and lack of water • May negatively impact wildlife

Reflecting on the discussion above, it can be argued that although RE is now central to tackling climate change, energy access and energy security, the disadvantages and challenges associated with the development of RE sources pose a big barrier to their development. With regard to biomass, it has the advantage of being abundant; however traditional biomass is associated with air pollution; further, certain types of biomass produce significant GHG emissions, at times producing higher amounts than natural gas in terms of CO_2 per kWh output.[76] Solar and wind energy are also variable and intermittent implying that their reliability depends on availability of sunlight or wind. Other RE sources such as hydropower are abundant, safe and inexpensive but they cause flooding, and dammed reservoirs can result in stagnant reservoir water, high sedimentation and algae growth that impact wildlife. A case in point is the development of the Akosombo Dam on the Volta River in Ghana, which led to the resettlement of about 80,000 people from 740 villages. It also led to biodiversity loss and floods that increased the risk of water-borne diseases.[77]

C. Energy Efficiency in SSA

Energy Efficiency (EE) refers to the use of less energy to achieve the same services. EE and various technological advancements in the energy sector represent some

[74] There has, however, been a decline in renewables, implying that high economic costs may no longer be the primary constraint to deploying renewables. For instance, the cost of utility-scale installed solar PV dropped from about US$5 per watt in 2009, to about US$2 per watt in 2015: consequently, Africa added about 800 MW of solar PV in 2014 and 750 MW in 2015. See IRENA, Renewable Energy Statistics 2016; Avila, N, Carvallo, JP, Shaw, B and Kammen, DM, 'The energy challenge in sub-Saharan Africa: A guide for advocates and policy makers', Technical report (OXFAM 2017).

[75] Reliability depends on availability of sunlight.

[76] For a detailed discussion of this issue, see Wood, G, 'Policy risk, politics and low carbon energy' in Considine, J and Paik, K-W (eds), *The Handbook of Energy Politics* (Edward Elgar 2018).

[77] See Avila, N, Carvallo, JP, Shaw, B and Kammen, DM, 'The energy challenge in sub-Saharan Africa: A guide for advocates and policy makers', Technical report (OXFAM 2017).

of the available options for the reduction of carbon emissions. Moreover, EE is also regarded as a complementary approach to RE – given that the reduction of energy demand through EE can improve the financial feasibility of RE options.

Various countries have embraced EE. Besides national initiatives, there are also regional initiatives focused on both RE and EE deployment. For instance, in West Africa, the ECOWAS Regional Centre for Renewable Energy and Energy Efficiency legally came into existence via the adoption of Regulation C/REG 23/11/08 in 2008 at the 61st Session of ECOWAS Council of Ministers – and the secretariat of the Centre was established in Praia, Cape Verde in 2010.[78] Although the West African renewables centre has been in existence for more than a decade, in East and Southern Africa preparations are still under way to establish regional RE centres. In EAC, for instance, the East African Centre for Renewable Energy and Energy Efficiency (EACREEE) was approved during the 33rd Meeting of the Council of Ministers held on 29 February 2016 (in fact, Makerere University College of Engineering, Art, Design and Technology was designated as a Centre of Excellence for EACREEE). In Southern Africa, the establishment of the SADC Centre for Renewable Energy and Energy Efficiency was approved by the SADC energy ministers on 24 July 2015.

Whereas the objectives of RE and EE centres are promising, it is imperative to note that these will not be achieved by the mere establishment of such centres. There is a need not only to strengthen regional institutions such as regional regulatory associations, but also to establish and strengthen national institutions.[79] These are necessary to adopt and implement regional RE and EE projects.

Despite the recent efforts to deploy RE and EE technologies, there are some limitations which cannot be ignored. These are briefly highlighted in Table 4.4.

Table 4.4 Challenges in Renewable Energy and Energy Efficiency Development

Poor baseline information
Lack of political will in some African countries
Lack of skilled manpower
High initial capital costs
Low maintenance capacity
Inadequate planning
Poor institutional framework and infrastructure
Inadequate data collection and analysis capability

[78] ECOWAS Centre for Renewable Energy and Energy Efficiency, www.ecreee.org/page/overview-ecreee, last visited on 5 June 2020.

[79] SADC Renewable Energy and Energy Efficiency Strategy and Action Plan (REESAP 2016–2030), p 35.

The above challenges can be grouped into three categories: policy/regulatory barriers; financial/investment barriers; and research/technology barriers. However, with recent technological advancements and support from the international community, these barriers are being addressed.

D. Low-Carbon Energy Infrastructure

With the global move to tackle climate change, there have been massive investments in low-carbon energy infrastructure, including wind power projects, solar power plants, hydropower plants and many others. Some of these are briefly outlined in Table 4.5.

Table 4.5 Low-Carbon Energy Infrastructure

Renewable Energy Project	Country	Details
Lake Turkana Wind Power Project	Kenya	The 310 MW facility is Africa's largest wind farm. It is made up of 365 turbines, each with a capacity of 850 kilowatts
Parc Eolien Taiba N'Diaye Wind Project	Senegal	The 158.7 MW wind farm is Senegal's first utility-scale wind energy project. A 46-turbine facility, it is estimated to generate more than 450,000 MW hours of energy annually
Noor Solar Power Plant	Morocco	At 510 MW, it is the world's largest concentrated solar power plant
KaXu Solar Plant	South Africa	The 100 MW plant is located in the Northern Cape Region of South Africa
Kathu Solar Park	South Africa	The 100 MW project is located in the Northern Cape Region of South Africa
Rwamagana Solar Power Station	Rwanda	This is a 8.5 MW solar power plant
Nasho Solar Power Plant	Rwanda	This is a 3.3 MW solar power plant
Bujagali Hydropower Station	Uganda	The 250 MW project is found in Bujagali, Buikwe District
Grand Ethiopian Renaissance Dam	Ethiopia	This is a 6,450 MW project
Koeberg Nuclear Power Station	South Africa	Africa's only nuclear power station, with a 1,860 MW capacity

As illustrated in the table above, there is considerable low-carbon energy infrastructure in various African countries. Table 4.5 is not exhaustive; rather it highlights some of the key infrastructure in Africa. In the establishment and development of various energy infrastructure, land disputes might arise, not to mention protests from the local communities. The next section therefore spotlights some of the energy disputes in different countries.

IV. Energy Disputes Related to Land

Energy disputes are not only limited to disputes between host states and energy companies, but also include disputes and protests from the local communities. In this section, various key community protests will be highlighted. It is important to note that some of these protests are triggered by land use (which also broadly includes environmental protection).

For instance, there have been various protests targeting solar power plants in the different parts of the globe. Native Americans protested the 1,500-acre Invenergy's Horseshoe Solar project. The land use concerns with respect to this protest were due to the indigenous people being uncomfortable with the solar farm being built on sacred land in the Genesee Valley. Additionally, there were concerns that the solar farm would harm the environment.[80] In the UK, the 2,300-acre Sunnica Energy Solar Farm also attracted some protests from local people.[81] Additionally, the Cleve Hill Solar Park, UK, also attracted attention from protesters who were concerned about the impact of the project on the environment, specifically that the site is said to sustain thousands of migrating birds and is recognised as providing essential feeding and nesting grounds for many threatened species, including Brent geese, reed-buntings, nesting skylarks, and marsh harriers. The protesters were also concerned that the project would industrialise a natural landscape of considerable value for recreation, tourism, and wildlife.[82]

Protests targeting wind turbine projects have also been visible across the world. For instance, the people on the Hawaiian island of Oahu protested a wind energy project being built near the small village of Kahuku. The project is planned to include eight turbines standing 568 feet high. These protests took place in Hawaii, a State that has pledged to generate 100 per cent of its electricity from renewable sources by 2045. In Norway, people protested the construction of a 60 MW wind project on Frøya Island.[83] In Germany, local populations have often protested

[80] For more information, see 'Native Americans Protest Planned Livingston County Solar Plant', 12 October 2020 (spectrumlocalnews.com). Last accessed on 10 December 2020.

[81] The farm was planned to be built on the west Suffolk and east Cambridgeshire border, on 2,300 acres of land stretching from Burwell to Snailwell, Newmarket, Freckenham, Worlington and Isleham. See 'Worlington villagers plan protest walk over Sunnica solar farm proposals', 31 October 2020 (suffolknews.co.uk). Last accessed on 10 December 2020.

[82] The project would be located just one mile northeast of Faversham, in Kent, situated close to the village of Graveney. It is being developed as part of a joint venture between Hive Energy and Wirsol, and is expected to cost £450 million. See, 'Last chance to stop massive solar power plant – *Faversham Life*, 21 April 2020. Last accessed on 10 December 2020.

[83] As a result of the protests, the Norwegian government announced it was scrapping plans for a national roll-out of wind projects.

wind power projects, which they refer to as 'Verspargelung', roughly translated as 'pollution with giant asparagus spears'.[84] Besides protests targeting wind power projects, Germany has also been at the centre of anti-coal protests. The Garzweiler mine and nearby power plants have been a focus of protests for several years, due to the negative environmental impacts associated with the burning of coal.[85] In Australia, Adani Mining's Carmichael coal mine in Queensland has attracted a lot of controversy due to environmental concerns. The project is under construction as it was approved by both the Queensland and Federal Governments in 2019. It is expected to produce 10 million tons of thermal coal per annum. Worth mentioning is that the project has attracted global protests even outside Australia.[86]

Protests targeting oil and gas pipeline projects have also been experienced in different parts of the globe, again also associated with land use. For instance, in the US, a range of protests began in 2016 against the construction of the Dakota Access Pipeline across four States of the northern US. One of the reasons against the project was that the pipeline constitutes a serious threat to the region's water. The construction was also seen as a direct threat to ancient burial grounds and cultural sites of historic importance.[87]

The examples above paint a clear picture about the impact of energy projects on land use. As noted above, most of the protests are based on environmental concerns and land use including protecting sacred land and avoiding pollution. Pollution is not only limited to fossil fuels: low-carbon energy such as wind power has attracted public discomfort due to the noise pollution associated with wind turbines.

A. Negotiating Petroleum Projects: Dispute Resolution

One way of avoiding energy disputes is to ensure effective negotiations throughout the project life cycle. Negotiations can also play a crucial role in resolving energy disputes. Although there are various issues to be taken into consideration with respect to negotiating energy projects and resolving related disputes, this subsection will focus on stabilisation and arbitration clauses.

[84] For a full discussion, see 'Hawaii protests show why wind energy can't save us from climate change', *The Hill*, 13 November 2019. Last accessed on 10 December 2020.

[85] Environmental groups oppose the German government's decision to allow the mining and burning of coal in the country until 2038, a deadline the activists say is too late to effectively tackle climate change. For a full discussion, see ABC News, 'Hundreds of anti-coal campaigners protest at German mine', *ABC News* (go.com), 26 September 2020. Last accessed on 10 December 2020.

[86] For instance, protests erupted in Germany aimed at halting German engineering giant Siemens' support for the Adani Mining's Carmichael coal mine in Queensland. Siemens has a contract worth €18m (£15m; US$20m) to supply railway signalling equipment for the mine. For more information, see, BBC News, 'Siemens resists climate protests over Australia coal project' – *BBC News*, 13 January 2020. Last accessed on 11 December 2020.

[87] The pipeline was projected to run from the Bakken oil fields in western North Dakota to southern Illinois, crossing beneath the Missouri and Mississippi Rivers, as well as under part of Lake Oahe near the Standing Rock Indian Reservation.

Simply defined, negotiation refers to the process of holding a discussion with the main aim of reaching an agreement. With respect to petroleum projects, the host government and the international oil companies must negotiate the terms of the petroleum agreement. There are various issues to be considered when negotiating the petroleum agreement, including: the fiscal regime; accounting standards; contract termination provisions; social impact including land access, compensation and relocations; local content provisions; environmental and health issues; and many others. In negotiating petroleum agreements, there are some unique features that must be considered and thought about. These include, among others: the cost of exploration and development; the ever-changing market conditions; the possible field size, including the possibility of dry holes; and the difficulty of recovery.

Of interest to this sub-section, is the issue of stabilisation and arbitration clauses. These clauses have raised a lot of concern in the twenty-first century. As such, these will be briefly explored here. Prior to this discussion, however, it is imperative to highlight the main phases of the petroleum life cycle, as this will give us an understanding of the physical nature of oil operations and the related risks. These phases are briefly highlighted in the table below:

Table 4.6 Petroleum Field Life Cycle

Phase	**Brief**
Acquisition of a licence or concession	Granted by the host government to an oil company to prospect for oil
Exploration	Seismic surveys; drill an exploration well; if oil is found, then testing is carried out
Appraisal	This follows discovery of oil/gas. Reservoir appraised to ascertain its characteristics
Development	If the field is commercially viable, the company goes into the development phase; agree on the development technology for exploiting the reserves
Production	Production wells are drilled to access as high a proportion of the field reserves as possible; it's at this stage where both operating revenues and operating costs occur
Abandonment	This happens when the field is no longer profitable, and it is decommissioned

Each stage of the production field life cycle outlined in Table 4.6 above presents unique risks and challenges. The complexity of petroleum projects has been the basis for including stabilisation clauses in developing countries.[88] For instance,

[88] Nakhle, C, *Petroleum taxation: sharing the oil wealth: a study of petroleum taxation yesterday, today and tomorrow* (Routledge 2008).

during the exploration phase, a lot of capital is invested and this could cost tens or hundreds of millions of dollars, and yet there is a risk of encountering a dry well.[89] Consequently, if the well proves dry, the exploration costs of the dry hole are written-off. Conversely, if oil is found, then the company proceeds to the testing phase. A well is considered commercially viable if it can produce enough oil or gas to justify the costs of drilling and placing it in production. As such exploration activities are not only expensive but also high-risk; hence international oil companies (IOCs) will devise all means to protect their investments and minimise the related risks. In the appraisal stage, the risks are also inevitable. The appraisal phase follows discovery, which necessitates the need to appraise the reservoir in order to ascertain its size, structure and quality. Although the odds of success are higher at this stage, there are aspects of risk, especially in instances where the technology required to produce oil or gas is too expensive; or where there is not enough oil or gas to be commercially attractive. After the development and production phases, the last phase is abandonment. This point is reached where production levels fall to a level which ceases to cover operating costs. Abandonment costs cover the plugging of wells and removal of well equipment, production tanks and associated installations.

The above briefly outlines the complexity of petroleum projects and the risks associated with these projects. In the next sub-section, petroleum agreements are discussed in detail. This discussion will be followed by an analysis of stabilisation clauses.

B. Types of Petroleum Agreements

There are several petroleum agreements that a government has to choose from. These include: a concession or licence agreement, a production-sharing agreement (PSA), a joint venture (JV) or a service agreement. These agreements govern the relationship between governments and oil investors. These are briefly discussed below:

(i) Concession (or Licence) Agreements

Concession or licence agreements grant an oil company a right to explore, develop, sell and export the oil extracted in a specified area, for which the company has received exclusive development and production rights for a prescribed period of time. All this is done against payment of a royalty to the host state.

[89] The costs vary depending on some key factors such as the location of the possible oil reserves, whether it is near land or in deep water; how large the oil field is expected to be, etc. The most common method used in exploration is geophysical and seismic surveys. However, in the distant past, early explorers relied on looking at surface rock formations for clues about the rocks below – a hit and miss approach.

(ii) Production-Sharing Contracts/ Agreements (PSCs/ PSAs)

PSAs were first introduced in Indonesia in 1966. Under this type of agreement, the host government, as the owner of the resources, engages an IOC as a contractor to provide technical and financial services for exploration and development operations. As a reward for the risks taken, the IOC acquires an entitlement to a stipulated share of the oil produced.

(iii) Risk Service Agreements

Here, the host state merely hires the service of a petroleum company or consortium to benefit from its financial and technical expertise, with the company or consortium assuming the risk and liability after which it is reimbursed through a service fee, usually paid in cash.

(iv) Joint Venture Contracts (JVC)

A JV arises if two or more parties wish to pursue a joint undertaking. It is a partnership-based arrangement between the two parties with a view to jointly running an extractive venture. The agreement provides a structured means for shared decision-making.

The discussion above is not exhaustive, as there are other key issues that ought to be discussed with respect to petroleum agreements. This sub-section, however, will focus on stabilisation clauses, as discussed below.

C. Stabilisation Clauses in Petroleum Agreements

Stabilisation clauses have increasingly become an important subject given their impact on the sovereignty of a state over its natural resources. The resource curse notwithstanding, the discovery of petroleum resources generally ignites national dreams of riches and economic prosperity. Indeed, there are countries that have benefited significantly from these resources, including Norway, the United Kingdom, the United States, The United Arab Emirates and Kuwait, to mention but a few.

Different stakeholders have different expectations from these resources. For instance, the host government is most concerned about revenues; the IOCs are concerned about protecting their investments and making profits. On the other hand, the citizens and host communities are more interested in developmental infrastructure and employment opportunities. Meeting the needs of all the stakeholders is impossible and, as such, host governments must strike a balance.

The risks associated with transforming locked underground assets (oil and gas) into cash cannot be ignored. As noted earlier, the different phases of a petroleum field life cycle present various risks. These risks may differ depending on the region or country in question. Often, politically unstable countries present greater risks for IOCs. In order to mitigate some of these risks and protect their investments, the IOCs often negotiate to have stabilisation clauses inserted into the petroleum agreements. Before a discussion on stabilisation clauses, it is important to understand what exactly 'Stabilisation' means. Professor Peter Cameron in his book *International Energy Investment Law: The Pursuit of Stability*, asserts:

> In the context of an international energy contract, the term stabilization applies to all of the mechanisms, contractual or otherwise, which aim to preserve over the life of the contract the benefit of specific economic and legal conditions which the parties considered to be appropriate at the time they entered into the contract.[90]

Depending on the type of stabilisation clause (including the wording), IOCs may seek protection against unilateral modifications to the contract and against taking the rights of the investor.[91]

Energy investments are very expensive ventures requiring a large amount of capital which is often beyond the reach of host governments. In this respect, host governments must attract the participation of international companies with the resources and expertise to help them exploit and market their energy resources. IOCs often demand for inclusion of stabilisation clauses in their contracts (these demands are made in developing countries only). The past experiences of IOCs with host governments have played a major role in shaping the current stabilisation mechanisms, particularly the nationalisation of IOCs' assets and the failure of the early stabilisation clauses to act as a deterrent in the nationalisation movements which were experienced in the Middle East and North Africa.

Basically, these clauses target risks that have the impact of causing losses to the investors. Such risks include direct expropriation; a gradual loss of investment value by a series of measures over time (creeping expropriation); or the loss of anticipate future opportunities.[92] Stabilisation clauses are, in essence, contractual assurance of negotiated terms against future legal or regulatory chances. This is achieved by providing legal and fiscal stability.[93]

Moving forward, there is no guarantee that these clauses will mitigate the political risks. Nevertheless, they have the capacity to limit the scale of economic loss that results. Consequently, investors often use these clauses to deter host governments from embracing major changes in their laws and fiscal regime.

[90] Cameron, P, *International energy investment law: the pursuit of stability* (Oxford University Press 2010) p 69.

[91] It is imperative to note that the way in which these 'rights' are viewed and interpreted matters. For instance, if the investors' rights as stipulated in the Petroleum Agreement are viewed as a form of property, then the legal issue will be whether interference by a state with these rights amounts to expropriation? See, Cameron, P, *International energy investment law: the pursuit of stability* (Oxford University Press 2010) p 69.

[92] Cameron, P, *International energy investment law: the pursuit of stability* (Oxford University Press 2010).

[93] There are states that provide legislative support for the stability provisions of a contract. This can be either of a procedural kind (by legislative approval of the contract itself) or a substantive kind (by incorporating specific stabilisation guarantees for investment contracts in domestic law).

This prima facie is advantageous to the investors, who might rely on stabilisation clauses to threaten arbitration proceedings, hence persuading the host state to reach a settlement favourable to the investor. Indeed, the presence of a stabilisation clause in an investment contract can have an important effect on the outcome of an arbitral proceeding.

It is important to note that, despite the fact that IOCs operate in both the developed and developing countries, these companies do not apply the same standards in both with respect to negotiating stabilisation clauses. For instance, some countries don't offer stabilisation guarantees at all. These include, among others, the UK, Brazil, Colombia, Libya, Norway and Saudi Arabia.[94] It is believed that countries that don't offer stabilisation guarantees have effective legal remedies for changes in the contract under a domestic legal system that is independent from the executive branch of government. As should be the case in all countries, the national parliament should not bind itself as to how it might legislate in future, and as such countries in the Global South should pick a leaf from these developed countries before negotiating stabilisation clauses.

Historically, stabilisation clauses date as far back as the 1930s, when they were introduced in the new oil provinces of the Middle East. These were also used as a defence against expropriation and nationalisation, which characterised the 1970s and 1980s. Evidence from arbitration cases relating to expropriation indicates that the even though stabilisation clauses exist in a petroleum agreement, the state can still use its sovereign power to revise its relationship with the investor unilaterally. However, the impact of this is that the state is liable for the payment of damages.[95]

(i) Instability and the Quest for Stabilisation Clauses

The petroleum sector is unpredictable, especially with the unstable markets. Additionally, the COVID-19 pandemic has proved that uncertainties in the energy sector can no longer be ignored. For instance, the pandemic has had an impact on all spheres of life. In the energy sector, oil demand and consumption has decreased consequently leading to drastic drop in oil prices to below zero as of 21 April 2020. This led many to question the future of fossil fuels especially in this energy transition era.

On Monday 20 April 2020, the world experienced a drop in the US crude oil price for May, falling below 0 and turning to negative. This caused a lot of bankruptcy panic among various oil companies, especially US shale companies. The drop in oil prices was mainly due to the March 2020 oil price wars. Additionally, the COVID-19 pandemic, which had reduced oil demand in the transport

[94] The bargaining power of a country plays a major role in negotiating on whether to include stabilisation clauses or not. The bargaining power is often rooted in a state's character as a capital-exporting country or its extensive control over the domestic energy industry and large domestic resources of fossil fuels.

[95] Cameron, P, *International energy investment law: the pursuit of stability* (Oxford University Press 2010) p 89.

sector and manufacturing industry, also significantly contributed to the low oil prices. Consequently, there were massive stresses in the oil industry with many companies losing their value, including Halliburton, Noble Energy, Marathon Oil and Occidental (OXY) – which lost more than two-thirds of their value.[96] Furthermore, for the first time, renewables overtook coal-fired power generation in OECD. According to the IEA April 2020 report, electricity produced from natural gas in 2019 increased by 4.8 per cent and was responsible for 29 per cent of the total electricity production. Comparatively, coal production in the same year was 13.4 per cent lower than in 2018, contributing to 22.1 per cent of the total electricity production.[97]

The above market uncertainties affect both developed and developing countries. However, for the countries in the Global South, they are often viewed by IOCs as being unstable with ineffective rule of law. For these reasons, IOCs often persuade and bully host governments in the Global South into accepting stabilisation clauses.

The above notwithstanding, it is imperative to note that legal and fiscal instabilities are not confined to developing countries. For instance, the fiscal instabilities in the UK cannot be ignored. Since the establishment of the UK Continental Shelf tax system governing exploration for, and production of, oil and gas, in 1975, the regime has been repeatedly reviewed and many amendments applied. There are various factors that may cause the host state to revise the fiscal terms to which they originally agreed with investors. As spotlighted by Dr Carole Nakhle, these include:[98]

(a) Oil Prices

Typically, when the oil price is high, the government has the upper hand. Governments often change their fiscal terms to respond to oil prices. For instance, the high oil prices experienced in the period between 2002 and 2008 influenced different countries to increase the tax rate paid by companies. Some of these countries are Angola, Ecuador, India, Libya, Nigeria, among others.

(b) Investment

A significant rise in petroleum investments may encourage the host government to introduce a tax increase. However, an unexpected decline in investment may trigger the opposite response.

[96] Egan,M, 'Oil prices turned negative. Hundreds of US oil companies could go bankrupt', *CNN Business* (21 April 2020). Can be accessed at, https://edition.cnn.com/2020/04/20/business/oil-price-crashbankruptcy/index.html. Last accessed on 22 April 2020.

[97] IEA, 'Key electricity trends' (14 April 2020). Can be accessed at, www.iea.org/articles/key-electricity-trends-2019. Last accessed on 20 April 2020.

[98] Mansour, M and Nakhle, C, 'Fiscal stabilization in oil and gas contracts – evidence and implications', *Oxford Institute for Energy Studies paper: SP 37* (2016).

(c) Production Life Cycle

Whereas governments are keen to attract investments before a discovery, by among other means, providing a favourable tax regime; often the same government will increase the taxes once commercial discoveries are made.

(d) Regional Trend and Neighbourhood Effect

A change in the fiscal regime of one country can influence neighbouring countries to do the same. This is so because most of the countries in the region are competing for the same few petroleum investors, so they endeavour to have similar tax policies.

(e) Changes in Political Conditions

Once a new government is ushered into the country, they often change the legal, regulatory and fiscal frameworks. As such, the petroleum fiscal regime designed by the previous administration will invariably be reviewed critically by a successor with a different political persuasion or ideology.

(f) Deteriorating Government Finances

When a country is going through an economic crisis, the government will take all measures to raise revenue, including increasing taxes for IOCs. In this respect, a country will make changes to the general fiscal regime, affecting not only the local industry and other sectors, but also the IOCs. Besides, the extractive sector may be an easy target for increased revenue, since companies in this business cannot simply move abroad because the resource is immobile.

(ii) Types of Stabilisation Clause

There are stabilisation clauses of a fiscal nature and stabilisation clauses of a legal (or regulatory) nature. Fiscal stabilisation clauses relate to government revenue: taxes, royalties, and customs duties to mention but a few. Legal stabilisation clauses on the other hand, cover laws and regulations of a non-fiscal character, such as the statutes that govern operations at the project site on a day-to-day basis (mining laws, labour laws, environmental laws, etc). The inclusion of stabilisation clauses in contracts dates as far back as the early 1930s. There are various types of stabilisation clauses, as will be discussed below. However, the impact or purpose of these clauses is the same; that is, to offer assurance that the terms of the investment at its core on the date of signature will remain the same over the life of the agreement. Stabilisation clauses are drafted differently: some clauses focus on the fiscal impacts, while other clauses include the right to monetise; the right to develop a petroleum discovery site to be commercial; an exchange regime and the governance of the project itself.[99]

(a) Freezing Clauses

In the legal profession, these are also referred to as stabilisation clause *stricto sensu*. Freezing clauses are to the effect that the governing laws – general and special – applicable to operations under a contract between a company and a sovereign state should be those of the state at the time the contract was executed. When applied strictly, these clauses prohibit the host state from changing its laws, by effectively freezing the laws which were in force on the date that the contract came into effect, hence shielding the IOC from any changes in legislation occurring after this date. Freezing clauses may be used in different ways. Besides being applied strictly, they may also be used to prevent the host state from applying changes in its law, made after the effective date of the contract, to the specific investment contract. Alternatively, the contract may be granted an enclave status by making it exempt from any legal changes occurring in the wider legal regime of the host state. These clauses are not often acceptable to the host governments, since it is unconstitutional to completely restrain the sovereign authority of the host state from amending its laws. In this respect, host governments prefer to limit the applicability of the freezing clauses to a few aspects of the contract (taxes for instance). As such, freezing clauses have increasingly been replaced with the 'Economic Equilibrium' clauses.

(b) Economic Equilibrium/ Economic Stabilisation Clauses

These seek to re-establish the economic position – the economic equilibrium – of the contract following changes in law which have an economic impact on the bargain struck between the host state and its contractual partner. They provide protection through a renegotiation mechanism. Whereas the investors are supposed to comply with the new laws, they are entitled to compensation so that they remain in the same economic situation they would have been in had the laws not changed. These function as indemnity clauses which provide balance to the economic equilibrium of the contract by ensuring that appropriate remedies are available to the investor if the host state's actions adversely affect the underlying economics of the relevant project. The common form of remedy is compensation; this can take such forms as adjusted tariffs, extension of the concession, tax reductions, or monetary compensation.

With economic equilibrium clauses, the parties must define the 'trigger event', which can either be widely defined (for example, 'any change in law') or narrowly defined (for example, 'any change in tax law'). However, these clauses do not apply

[99] The right to monetise may include the right to export products, and sell interests in the investment. For a detailed discussion, see Cameron, P, *International energy investment law: the pursuit of stability* (Oxford University Press 2010) p 60.

to issues that are considered to be of public interest including health, safety, environment, national security or other issues.

Economic balancing/equilibrium is more complex to administer than freezing-style mechanisms. Besides offering different terms to different countries, the fact that the policy tools subject to stabilisation are not identified implies that the parties must know the outcome at any point in time. Often the IOCs have an information advantage, thus limiting effective and fair implementation of economic equilibrium clauses. It would therefore be prudent for the host government to have the same model for stabilisation clauses for all IOCs, albeit this also presents challenges, as the clauses are often negotiated in different years.

(c) Rebalancing of Benefits

These clauses are similar to economic equilibrium. They basically envisage automatic adjustments or renegotiation of contract terms in the event the specified circumstances occur. They stipulate that if the host state adopts a measure subsequent to the conclusion of the contract that is likely to have damaging consequences to the economic benefits of the original bargain for one or both parties, a re-balancing must take place. It has been observed that although most stabilisation clauses cover tax policy parameters, there those that extend coverage to exogenous shocks – which presumably relate to market conditions but can be anything that affects the return on investment.

(d) Hybrid Clauses

These seek to combine the unambiguous nature of freezing clauses with provisions commonly found in economic equilibrium clauses.

(e) Allocation of Burden Clauses

These seek to allocate the fiscal and related burdens created by a unilateral change in the law. It is common for the resultant burden to be borne by the National Oil Company or the state.

(f) Prohibition on Unilateral Changes

This is also referred to as an 'intangibility clause'. It prohibits unilateral changes to the investment agreement and requires the consent of both parties before any changes may be made. Unlike the freezing clauses which freeze the law, this type of clause only freezes the contract. It tries to limit the state's capacity by requiring mutual consent to contract changes.[100]

[100] Examples of this type of clause can be found in different PSCs. For instance, Article 18.2: Mayfair Production-Sharing Agreement between the Ministry of Oil and Natural Resources and Yemen Mayfair

(g) Good Will Clause

This is similar to the 'intangibility clause', although the scope of its application might differ. Basically, as the name suggests, the 'good will' clause is to the effect that the parties shall perform the contract with 'good will' or 'good faith'; hence the clause precludes unilateral modification or termination of the contract.

(h) Combined Stabilisation Clauses

It is common for a regime or PSC to contain a combination of all the different types of stabilisation clause. Scholars have identified the example below from Azerbaijan's Shah Deniz contract:[101]

> The rights and interests accruing to Contractor (or its assignees) under this agreement … shall not be amended, modified or reduced without the prior consent of Contractor [intangibility]. In the event that any Governmental Authority invokes any present or future law, treaty, inter-governmental agreement, decree or ministerial order which contravenes the provisions of this Agreement or adversely or positively affects the rights or interests of Contractor hereunder, including, but not limited to, any change in tax legislation, regulations or administrative practice, or jurisdictional changes pertaining to the Contract Area, the terms of this Agreement shall be adjusted to re-establish the economic equilibrium of the Parties [balancing], and if the rights or interests of Contractor have been adversely affected, the SOCAR (the NOC) shall indemnify contractor for any disbenefit, deterioration in economic circumstances, loss or damages that ensue therefrom [allocation].

Moving forward, we note that, all the stabilisation clauses are incompatible with the state's permanent sovereign power to enact and amend laws. The sovereignty of the state should not be limited by contractual mechanisms: and yet these clauses in effect can be described as the limits of non-alienation of state prerogatives, or as self-limitation of its legislative competences.[102] Additionally, these clauses are as a result of negotiations between the host country and the IOCs. As such, it is common to find that a host government has negotiated different stabilisation clauses with different companies. Consequently, this leads to administrative complexity – as the government will have to apply to each project the law existing at the time of concluding the relevant contract. Consequently, the tax authority ends up administering different tax procedures and forms, which could become quite complex with the accumulation of contracts.[103]

Petroleum Corporation (Al Zaydiah, Block 22, Tihama Area), dated 29 July 1992. This provision is to the effect that the petroleum agreement may be altered or amended only by the mutual agreement of the parties.

[101] Cameron, P, *International energy investment law: the pursuit of stability* (Oxford University Press 2010) p 81.

[102] Mansour, M and Nakhle, C, 'Fiscal stabilization in oil and gas contracts – evidence and implications', *Oxford Institute for Energy Studies paper: SP 37* (2016).

[103] Mansour, M and Nakhle, C, 'Fiscal stabilization in oil and gas contracts – evidence and implications', *Oxford Institute for Energy Studies paper: SP 37* (2016).

(iii) Examples of Stabilisation Clauses

Stabilisation mechanisms can be in different forms. Some are provided for in a law (for instance foreign investment laws). However, the common form of stabilisation clause is found in petroleum agreements or it may be 'contractualised' by way of a law referencing the petroleum contract. Regardless of the form the stabilisation mechanism takes, the stabilisation clause must be properly entered into by the state; and it must be enforceable in the domestic law of the host state. The table below spotlights the different types of stabilisation clauses in different countries:

Table 4.7 Examples of Stabilisation Clauses

Liberia stabilisation clause:[104]

> For the avoidance of doubt, any amendments, additions, revisions, modifications or other changes on the Tax Corpus made after the Amendment Effective Date shall not be applicable to the CONCESSIONAIRE. Furthermore, any future amendment, additions, revisions, modifications or other changes to any Law (other than the Tax Corpus) applicable to the CONCESSIONAIRE or the Operations that would have the effect of imposing an additional or higher tax, duty, custom, royalty or similar charge on the CONCESSIONAIRE will not apply to the CONCESSIONAIRE to the extent it would require the CONCESSIONAIRE to pay such tax, duty, royalty or charge.[105]

Egypt stabilisation clauses:[106]

> In case of changes in existing legislation or regulations applicable to the conduct of Exploration, Development and production of Petroleum, which take place after the Effective Date, and which significantly affect the economic interest of this Agreement to the detriment of CONTRACTOR or which imposes on CONTRACTOR an obligation to remit to the ARE (Arab Republic of Egypt) the proceeds from sales of CONTRACTOR's Petroleum, CONTRACTOR shall notify EGPC (the NOC) of the subject legislative or regulatory measure. In such case, the Parties shall negotiate possible modifications to this Agreement designed to restore the economic balance thereof which existed on the Effective Date.
>
> The Parties shall use their best efforts to agree on amendments to this Agreement within ninety (90) days from aforesaid notice.
>
> These amendments to this Agreement shall not in any event diminish or increase the rights or obligations of CONTRACTOR as these were agreed on the Effective Date. Failing agreement between the Parties during the period referred to above in this Article XIX, the dispute may be submitted to arbitration, as provided in Article XXIV of this Agreement.[107]

(continued)

[104] The Mineral Development Agreement between the Government of the Republic of Liberia and Mittal Steel Holdings NV dated 17 August 2005, and the Amendment thereto dated 28 December 2006.

[105] This is an example of a freezing stabilisation clause.

[106] Concession Agreement for Petroleum Exploration & Exploitation between Egypt & The Egyptian General Petroleum Corporation & Dover Investments Ltd (East Wadi Araba Area Gulf of Suez) (2002). Source: Cameron, P, *International energy investment law: the pursuit of stability* (Oxford University Press 2010) p 77.

[107] This is an example of the type of stabilisation clause which is referred to as 'Rebalancing of benefits'.

Table 4.7 ***(Continued)***

Uganda Negotiated Stabilisation Clause:[108]

Article 33.1 This agreement shall be governed by, interpreted and construed in accordance with the laws of Uganda.

33.2 The Parties agree that the terms and conditions of this Agreement are based on the existing laws of the Republic of Uganda and the terms contained in this Agreement. If after the Effective Date, there is any change in any law in Uganda dealing with income tax which substantially and adversely alters the economic benefits accruing to the Licensee, the Licensee may within five (5) calendar years from the date on which any such change has legal effect, notify Government accordingly and thereafter the Parties shall negotiate in good faith to agree upon the effect of the changes in law and the necessary adjustments and modifications to the Agreement in order to maintain the economic benefit of the Licensee which existed at the Effective Date of this Agreement PROVIDED that the Licensee shall comply with the requirement of the law and then notify the Government about the substantial and adverse effect of the change in the law.

33.3 In the event that within ninety (90) days of receipt of notification, the parties are unable to agree that the Licensee's economic benefits have been substantially and adversely affected and /or are unable to agree on the modifications required to maintain the economic benefits of the Licensee which prevailed at the Effective Date, then either Party may refer to the matter for expert determination pursuant to paragraph 26.2.

33.4 For the avoidance of doubt, the provisions of paragraph 33.2 above are intended for maintaining the original economic benefits of the Agreement and shall not prevent the Government from enacting laws intended to levy additional profit tax on additional profits.

33.5 For purposes of this Article, the term 'economic benefits' means the project's Net Present Value (NPV) for the Licensee.

Tanzania[109]

Article 30: If at any time or from time to time there should be a change in legislation or regulations which materially affects the commercial and fiscal benefits afforded by the Contractor under this contract, the Parties will consult each other and shall agree to such amendments to this Contract as are necessary to restore as near as practicable such commercial benefits which existed under the Contract as of the Effective Date.[110]

[108] Production Sharing Agreement for Petroleum Exploration Development and Production in the Republic of Uganda by and between The Government of The Republic of Uganda and Tullow Uganda Limited in respect of the Kanywataba Prospect Area February, 2012. Accessed from UGANDA-KANYWATABA-PSC-FOR-TULLOW.pdf (africaoilgasreport.com).

[109] Art 30: Change in Legislation, Tanzania Model PSC of November 2004, in *Barrows Basic Oil Laws and Concession Contracts*, Supplement 161 – Series on South & Central Africa.

[110] As an example of a change of law provision. The triggering event will usually be a change in the law that materially affects the interests of a party or parties to the contract, and typically that party will be the foreign investor.

In the table above, it can be noted that there is no universally accepted form of stabilisation clauses. These differ in content and wording depending on the country concerned. Additionally, the breadth of protection offered by the stabilisation clauses also differs depending on how they are drafted. In the next table, I further highlight the provisions offering for stabilisation clauses in other African countries.

Table 4.8 Summary of Other Stabilisation Clauses[111]

Country	Legislation/Contract	Provision for Stabilisation
Uganda	Uganda Model Contract 1999 Model Production Sharing Contract	Article 31
	The Petroleum (Exploration, Development and Production) Act, 2013	Part XVII Section 190 (Transitional provision)
	Production Sharing Agreement for Petroleum Exploration Development and Production in the Republic of Uganda by and Between the Government of the Republic of Uganda and Tullow Uganda Limited in respect of Exploration Area 1, February 2012	Article 33
Tanzania	The Petroleum (Exploration and Production) Act 1980, The United Republic of Tanzania (No 27 of 1980)	Second Schedule Section 95 (Transitional provision)
	Model Production Sharing Agreement Between the Government of the United Republic of Tanzania and Tanzania Petroleum Development Corporation and Abc Oil Company, November 2004	Article 30(b)
	Petroleum Act 2008	Section 56 (Transitional provision)
Sierra Leone	Petroleum Exploration and Production Act 2001	Section 66(2) (Transitional provision)
	Petroleum Agreement between the Government of Sierra Leone and Oranto Petroleum Limited (2003)	Article 26
	Model Petroleum agreement (2011 (Open Oil estimate))	Article 26

(continued)

[111] Data partly drawn from Mansour, M and Nakhle, C, 'Fiscal stabilization in oil and gas contracts – evidence and implications', *Oxford Institute for Energy Studies paper: SP 37* (2016).

Table 4.8 ***(Continued)***

Country	Legislation/Contract	Provision for Stabilisation
Papua New Guinea	No 33 of 2000. Resource Contracts Fiscal Stabilization Act 2000	Section 2
Mozambique	Petroleum Law Nº 3/2001 of 21 February	Article 26 (Transitional provision), Article 27 (dispute resolution)
	Law no 21/2014	Article 68 (Transitional provision), Article 69 (dispute resolution)
	Exploration and Production Concession Contract between the Government of the Republic of Mozambique and ENI East Africa SpA and Empresa Nacional di Hidrocarbonetos, EP for Area 4 Offshore of the Rovuma Block, Republic of Mozambique 2006	Articles 27.12, 27.14

As illustrated in the two tables above, there is no internationally recognised format or content for stabilisation clauses. However, there are some common aspects, especially in fiscal stabilisation, which include stability covering all taxes and levies on the sector. This can be provided expressly by referring to the taxes themselves (as the case in Uganda, which limits the coverage to income tax); or implicitly by reference to various (arguably, economically equivalent) notions of 'benefit'. Most stabilisation clauses are also broadly drafted, and as such they offer the investors appropriate protection. This is especially so, considering the fact that some of the terms used in these clauses are ambiguous. Although some of these terms might have different legal interpretations and impact, economically, they refer to the share of the parties from the oil rent.[112] Some of these broad terms include notions such as 'economic balance', 'original situation of the parties' 'economic benefits', 'commercial and fiscal benefits', and 'balance in the interest of the parties'.

There is therefore an urgent need for host governments to narrow down on these ambiguous notions. It would be good practice for the host state to limit the coverage and timeframe for these stabilisation clauses. Where possible, host states in the twenty-first century should not accept these stabilisation clauses. Most of these developing countries are politically stable with an effective rule of law. In this respect, they should be able to protect all kinds of investments

[112] Daniel, P and Sunley, E, 'Contractual Assurances of Fiscal Stability' in Daniel, P, Keen, M and McPherson, C (eds), *The taxation of petroleum and minerals: principles, problems and practice* (IMF/ Routledge 2010). 'Oil rent' being the difference between the value of crude oil production at world prices and the total costs of production.

(including petroleum), through a combination of their national investment laws, regional energy laws such as the 2003 ECOWAS Energy Protocol, BITs and MITs. All these are alternative avenues for protecting IOCs from nationalisation and expropriations, which were the main trigger for stabilisation clauses in the early 1970s.

Further, it is no secret that IOCs continue to invest in countries which don't have stabilisation clauses. One of the curiosities of stabilisation clauses in petroleum agreements is that no developed country will offer them to investors. So, why do developing countries with stable political, fiscal and regulatory climates offer them? Additionally, history shows that these stabilisation clauses have not deterred host governments from expropriating petroleum investments. While governments may be able to make commitments of their own, they cannot bind the legislative competence of the state into the future. As such, IOCs should embrace other mechanisms of protecting their investments. On the other hand, the host governments should be more concerned about establishing a competitive and stable legal, regulatory, and fiscal regime.

(iv) Concluding Remarks on Stabilisation Clauses

It is clear that stabilisation clauses in effect limit the normal prerogatives of any legislature and government, such as their right to enact and issue protective environmental, labour and other regulatory laws. These clauses make the tax regime, financial and commercial concessions, environmental regulations, as well as other contractual provisions, permanent for a 20-year, if not a 40 to 60-year period – depending on the petroleum project life cycle. In essence, stabilisation clauses ensure that the terms and conditions of a contract (and their effects) are 'frozen' from the time of signature over the life of the contract.[113] Although the state has the sovereign power to revise its relationship with the foreign investor unilaterally, the consequence of a stabilisation mechanism is that the government has to compensate an oil company for any change in a nation's laws, rules or regulations that adversely affect the company or its operations there.

A stabilisation clause is a contractual risk-mitigating device to protect investments from variations in the legal environment. This would include risks deriving from a possible exercise of host state sovereignty such as: expropriation, the obsolescence bargain, or any other change which the government might utilise in order to impose new requirements on investors.[114] In summary, a fiscal stability clause only favours the IOCs, as it is only applicable in instances of tax increment but not tax reductions.

113 Dias, D, 'Stability in International Contracts for Hydrocarbons Exploration and Some of the Associated General Principles of Law: From Myth to Reality' (2010) 4 *Oil, Gas & Energy Law*.

114 Mansour, M and Nakhle, C, 'Fiscal stabilization in oil and gas contracts – evidence and implications', *Oxford Institute for Energy Studies paper: SP 37* (2016).

Societies are constantly progressing economically, socially and politically. In this respect, a government should be able to respond to these changes by, among other means, enacting new laws or amending outdated laws. With stabilisation clauses, however, the state's right and ability to modernise its legal system is limited by IOCs. As such, host governments in developing countries often find themselves in a position where they have to negotiate with IOCs before modifying their tax regimes and safety standards. Since these clauses are not found in developed countries such as Canada or Norway, they have been described as 'contractual colonialism', the modern world's legal answer to a discredited system.[115]

Given the growing dissatisfaction with stabilisation clauses, what host governments can do is negotiate these to be in effect for a short period of time only. Often these clauses run for the entire lifetime of the petroleum project, which can last around 20–30 years. This is problematic as it restrains the government from reforming and enacting laws and policies within this period. Some developed countries have proved that it is not necessary for stabilisation clauses to run for many years. For instance, in Norway, in the early years of petroleum projects, the country offered some model of fiscal stability with a favourable tax regime of ordinary or standard taxes and only a 10 per cent royalty and licence fee. This was done to attract investment in the country's petroleum sector. However, the country did not offer these for the entire lifetime of petroleum projects. As such, Norway was able to nearly double the maximum royalty rate to 18 per cent just three years after the discovery. Drawing from the Norwegian example, it is important for developing countries to limit the timeframe for these stabilisation clauses. But as earlier mentioned, developing countries which are politically stable should not be persuaded to provide stabilisation clauses at all; these countries can still offer protection to petroleum investments by relying on their national laws, regional investments laws and protocols, BITs, MITs and even arbitration clauses. The next sub-section briefly explores other ways of protecting investments including BITs, MITs, Regional Investment protocols, national investment laws, and international arbitration in the African energy sector.

D. Other Avenues for Protecting Energy Investments

Besides the stabilisation clauses discussed above, there are other avenues for protecting energy investments. These include national investment laws; national constitutions – specifically provisions which prohibit expropriation without adequate compensation; and International Investment Agreements (IIAs), which comprise of Bilateral Investment Treaties (BITs), Multilateral Investment Treaties (MITs), and Free Trade Agreements (FTAs). This sub-section will focus on the BITs and MITs.

[115] Radon, J, 'How to negotiate an oil agreement' in M Humphreys, M, Sachs JD and Stiglitz, JE (eds), *Escaping the resource curse* (Columbia University Press 2007) pp 89–113.

(i) Bilateral Investment Treaties (BITs)

BITs are agreements between two countries protecting investments made by investors from one contracting state in the territory of the other contracting state. The purpose of BITs is to stimulate foreign investments by reducing political risk. Many countries rushed to sign BITs in the 1990s. For instance, by 2008, South Africa had signed 44 BITs of which 26 had been ratified. By signing these BITs, South Africa had agreed to subject its exercise of public power to international arbitration.

Although BITs have been relied on by many countries to attract foreign investment, they have proved to be replaceable in the twenty-first century. In South Africa for instance, in July 2010, a review of the BITs was conducted which enabled the South African government to make changes in the country's investment sector, including cancelling BITs with several European countries. Among the issues noted by the review committee was that, 'the inexperience of negotiators at time and the lack of knowledge about investment law in general resulted in agreements that were not in the long-term interest of the Republic of South Africa'.[116] Consequently, at the beginning of October 2012, South Africa cancelled its BITs with Belgium-Luxembourg, Spain, Germany, Switzerland, the Netherlands, and Denmark. Following the review of these BITs, the South African cabinet also decided to refrain from entering BITs in the future.[117]

The South African example is important as it highlights the dilemma of protecting foreign investments and redressing historical injustices. Often countries take initiatives and measures to address the injustices suffered by their people during colonialism. Some of these measures are perceived as being directly inconsistent with BITs' and MITs' provisions. In South Africa, the implementation of the policy of Black Economic Empowerment (BEE) had implications for the energy and mining investments. For instance, in the mining sector, the minister was required to abstain from issuing out mining licences which were not compliant with the BEE policy. Section 9 of the Mineral and Petroleum Resources Development Act, 2002 (MPRDA), is to the effect that the relevant institution can take legislative and other measures designed to protect or advance persons disadvantaged by unfair discrimination.[118] Consequently, some claims were brought against South Africa on the basis of the BEE policies in the MPRDA. In the case of *Piero Foresti, Laura di Carli and Others v Republic of South Africa*,[119] based on South Africa's BITs with Italy and the Belgo-Luxembourg economic union, the claimants argued that the

[116] Republic of South Africa Department of Trade and Industry, Bilateral Investment Treaty Policy Framework Review: Government Position Paper (2009) at 5.

[117] ibid.

[118] Mineral and Petroleum Resources Development Act, 28 of 2002 (MPRDA), Laws of South Africa.

[119] *Piero Foresti, Laura di Carli and Others v Republic of South Africa*, ICSID Case No ARB (AF)/07/1 (2010).

MPRDA had extinguished the ownership of the investor's South African mineral rights without providing prompt, adequate and effective compensation as required by the BITs. They also claimed that the violation of the BIT requirement to grant investors 'fair and equitable treatment' took place when they were required to divest 26 per cent of their investments to historically disadvantaged South Africans. They also argued that they had suffered discrimination in favour of those historically disadvantaged South Africans, which violated the BITs' requirements to accord fair and equitable treatment to investors.

The above case is just an example of the complications of implementing BITs in different African countries. Nevertheless, it is worth outlining some of the BITs that directly impact (have impacted) energy investments. These are spotlighted in Table 4.9 below:

Table 4.9 Examples of Bilateral Energy Agreements

Parties	Treaty
Republic of Chad and the Republic of Cameroon	Agreement relating to the Construction and Operation of a Transportation System of Hydrocarbons by Pipeline. Signed on 8 February 1996
Government of the Republic of Turkey and the Government of the Republic of Azerbajian	Intergovernmental Agreement concerning the Trans Anatolian Natural Gas Pipeline System. Signed on 26 June 2012
Government of the Turkish Republic and the Government of the Iraqi Republic	Crude Oil Pipeline Agreement (Kirkuk-Ceyhan Agreement). Signed on 27 March 1973
Government of the Republic of Austria and the Government of the Russia Federation	Agreement on Cooperation in the Construction and Operation of the Natural Gas Pipeline on the Territory of the Republic of Austria. Signed on 24 April 2010
The Government of the Republic of Slovenia and the Government of the Russian Federation	Agreement on Cooperation in Construction and Operation of the Gas Pipeline on the Territory of the Republic of Slovenia. Signed on 14 November 2009
Federal Republic of Nigeria and the Democratic Republic of São Tome and Principe	Treaty on the Joint Development of Petroleum and other Resources, in Respect of Areas of the Exclusive Economic Zone of the Two States. Signed by Nigeria and Sao Tome and Principe on 21 February 2001
Federal Republic of Nigeria and the Republic of Equatorial Guinea	Treaty concerning their Maritime Boundary. Signed by Guinea and Nigeria on 23 September 2000

Source: Data partly drawn from Leal-Arcas, R and Nalule, V, 'Multilateral and Bilateral Energy Investment Treaties' in Chaisse, J, Choukroune, L and Jusoh, S (eds), *Handbook of International Investment Law and Policy* (Springer 2019) pp 1–13.

As illustrated in the table above, BITs can be specific to a particular energy project. However, in the absence of BITs, a state can still rely on MITs and national laws to protect investors. Some of the examples of MITs in the energy sector include the Energy Charter Treaty. There are also regional protocols focused on protecting energy investments. For instance, in West Africa, the 2003 ECOWAS Energy Protocol has the same impact as the Energy Charter Treaty. The provisions relating to investment protection are fully outlined in the Appendixes of this book. In the next sub-section therefore, some of the national laws aimed at protecting investments will be explored.

(ii) National Laws Protecting Investments

Most countries provide for investment protection in their constitutions, and in their investment laws. These laws have the same impact as BITs, and they have been used to replace the BIT regime in some countries (for instance in South Africa). Basically, in the absence of a stabilisation clause, these laws are sufficient to protect petroleum investments.

In South Africa, as an alternative to BIT protections, the country enacted the Protection of Investment Act, 2015. This Act contains different provisions aimed at protecting both national and foreign investments. The main purpose of Act is provided for under Section 4, which states that:

> The purpose of this Act is to—
>
> (a) protect investment in accordance with and subject to the Constitution, in a manner which balances the public interest and the rights and obligations of investors;
>
> (b) affirm the Republic's sovereign right to regulate investments in the public interest; and
>
> (c) confirm the Bill of Rights in the Constitution and the laws that apply to all investors and their investments in the Republic.[120]

In the section above, the country emphasises its sovereign right to regulate investments. In doing so, the Republic of South Africa must balance the public interest and at the same time protect the rights and obligations of the investors. With respect to foreign investments, the Act, under Section 8, provides for 'National treatment'. It states that, 'foreign investors and their investments must not be treated less favorably than South African investors in like circumstances'.[121] However, under Section 8(4), there are limitations on the national treatment requirement. As such, this provision states that:

> Subsection (1) must not be interpreted in a manner that will require the Republic to extend to foreign investors and their investments the benefit of any treatment, preference or privilege resulting from—
>
> (a) taxation provisions in any international agreement or arrangement or any law of the Republic.[122]

[120] Section 4 Protection of Investment Act, 2015 (No 22 of 2015).
[121] Section 8(1) Protection of Investment Act, 2015 (No 22 of 2015).
[122] Section 8(1) Protection of Investment Act, 2015 (No 22 of 2015).

With respect to stabilisation clauses, the above provision may be interpreted to infer that South Africa discourages the preferential treatment which IOCs often enjoy through fiscal stabilisation clauses. Additionally, the Act requires that the parties to a dispute first utilise mediation before the matter is referred to international arbitration. In this respect, Section 13 states that:

> (1) An investor that has a dispute in respect of action taken by the government, which action affected an investment of such foreign investor, may within six months of becoming aware of the dispute request the Department to facilitate the resolution of such dispute by appointing a mediator.
>
> ...
>
> (5) The government may consent to international arbitration in respect of investments covered by this Act, subject to the exhaustion of domestic remedies. The consideration of a request for international arbitration will be subject to the administrative processes set out in section 6. Such arbitration will be conducted between the Republic and the home state of the applicable investor.[123]

The provisions above seem to depart from most BITs and arbitration clauses, which don't recognise the need to utilise all available domestic remedies before a matter is referred to international arbitration.

(iii) Arbitration as a Way of Resolving Energy Disputes in Africa

Arbitration is an alternative dispute resolution mechanism that provides a final and binding outcome. The parties agree to present their dispute to an arbitrator or a panel of arbitrators (tribunal). With the existence of a valid arbitration clause (arbitration agreement), the parties opt for a private dispute resolution procedure instead of going to court. The arbitration agreement should clearly specify the number of arbitrators, the legal place or seat of the arbitration, and the procedural rules that will govern the arbitration. In the agreement, the parties must decide on whether the arbitration will be conducted in accordance with the rules of a particular arbitration institution, or will be 'ad hoc'.

The main difference between arbitration and other forms of dispute resolution such as mediation or conciliation is that a mediator or conciliator can only recommend outcomes and the parties can choose whether or not to accept those recommendations. By contrast, an arbitration tribunal has the power to make decisions that bind the parties. Additionally, arbitral awards can be easily enforced in the courts of most countries without rehearing of the issues. However, the timeframe and complexity of enforcement will vary depending on a number of factors including but not limited to: the jurisdiction in which enforcement is likely to be sought; and the status of the party against whom enforcement is sought (for instance, certain assets may be immune from execution if the award is against a state).

[123] Section 13 Protection of Investment Act, 2015 (No 22 of 2015).

Energy investments are capital-intensive; as such they attract international investors who often prefer resolving any future disputes through international arbitration. In this respect, international arbitration is key in resolving cross-border disputes. There are various international arbitration institutions including: the London Court of International Arbitration (LCIA), the International Chamber of Commerce (ICC), the Singapore International Arbitration Centre, the Hong Kong International Arbitration Centre, and the Stockholm Chamber of Commerce, just to mention but a few.[124]

African countries significantly contribute to the cases decided under international arbitration. For instance, according to the 2019 records for the London Court of International Arbitration (LCIA), African parties were involved in slightly more than 10 per cent of the cases (up from 8 per cent in 2018).[125] According to the International Chamber of Commerce (ICC), 130 parties from sub-Saharan Africa accounted for approximately 5 per cent of all parties in its 2019 caseload, with Nigerian (19), South African (13) and Mauritian (10) parties taking the lead.[126] Various African cases also made up the caseload at the International Centre for Settlement of Investment Disputes (ICSID). Accordingly, in investor–state arbitrations, 15 per cent of the 2019 combined caseload involved disputes from sub-Saharan Africa, while the Middle East and North Africa accounted for 11 per cent of disputes.[127]

In the petroleum sector, arbitration clauses are often included in the Petroleum Sharing Agreements or Concessions. For instance, in the Ugandan PSA Article 26.1 provides for arbitration. It states:

> Subject to Article 14.2, any dispute arising under the Agreement which cannot be settled amicably within sixty (60) days, shall be referred to Arbitration in accordance with the United Nations Commission for International Trade Law (UNCITRAL) Arbitration Rules. The arbitration shall be conducted by three (3) arbitrators appointed in accordance with the said Rules. The said arbitration shall take place in London, England. Judgement on the award rendered may be entered in any court having jurisdiction or application may be made in such court for a judicial acceptance of the award and an order of enforcement, as the case may be. The Arbitration award shall be final and binding on the Parties to this Agreement.[128]

[124] Lack of diversity in international arbitration has prompted many developing countries, especially those in Latin America and Africa, to establish their own centres of arbitration. For instance, several Latin American countries, including Bolivia, Ecuador, and Venezuela, have in recent years announced their withdrawal from the ICSID Convention, and a regional institution with the same effect has been suggested.

[125] LCIA, 2019 Annual Casework Report, available at, www.lcia.org/media/download.aspx?MediaId=816, 'Parties', pp 10–11.

[126] ICC News, 11 June 2019, at https://iccwbo.org/media-wall/news-speeches/icc-arbitration-figures-reveal-new-record-cases-awards-2018/.

[127] The ICSID Caseload Statistics, Issue 2020-1, available at, https://icsid.worldbank.org/sites/default/files/publications/Caseload%20Statistics/en/The%20ICSID%20Caseload%20Statistics%20%282020-1%20Edition%29%20ENG.pdf, p 12.

[128] Article 26.1 of the Production Sharing Agreement for Petroleum Exploration Development and Production in the Republic of Uganda by and between The Government of The Republic of Uganda and Tullow Uganda Limited in respect of the Kanywataba Prospect Area, February, 2012. Accessed from UGANDA-KANYWATABA-PSC-FOR-TULLOW.pdf (africaoilgasreport.com).

In the above provision, it is clear that the preferred seat of arbitration for the parties is London. Additionally, the parties expressly agree to rely on the UNICITRAL Arbitration Rules. In the African energy sector, treaty claims concern various issues, including breach of stabilisation clauses; transfer of concession rights; interruption of midstream LNG operations; licence revocations; just to mention but a few. Some of the energy disputes in Africa are highlighted below:

Table 4.10 African Energy-Related Disputes

Energy Dispute	**Brief**
Ampal-American Israel Corporation and others v Arab Republic of Egypt (ICSID Case No ARB/12/11)	The investment related to a shareholding in a consortium that held a long-term natural gas supply contract with the Egyptian General Petroleum Corporation and the Egyptian Natural Gas Holding Co. The dispute is a result of claims arising out of alleged breaches of the contract between the parties, including the prolonged interruption of gas supply and failure to deliver the agreed volume of gas.
Unión Fenosa Gas, SA v Arab Republic of Egypt (ICSID Case No ARB/14/4)	The dispute was a result of claims arising out of the alleged suspension of gas supplies by an Egyptian state-owned enterprise to the claimant's liquefied natural gas plant, in contravention of the gas purchase agreement. The case was decided in favour of the investor.
Total E&P Uganda BV v Republic of Uganda (ICSID Case No ARB/15/11)	The dispute related to claims arising out of an allegedly unlawful tax levied by the Ugandan Government.
Texaco Overseas Petroleum Co et al v The Government of the Libyan Arab Republic, Award, 17 ILM 1 (1978)	The case related to the breach of stabilisation provisions. This case is fully discussed in the next sub-section.
Shell Nigeria Ultra Deep Limited v Federal Republic of Nigeria (ICSID Case No ARB/07/18)	The dispute related to the transfer of oil and gas concession exploration and development rights to third parties. Specifically, the claims were as a result of an alleged breach of a production-sharing contract concluded between Shell Nigeria and Nigeria's state oil company (NNPC), after the state ordered NNPC's portion of the venture to be handed over to a private company, Malabu Oil and Gas, with which the claimant had farmed the relevant exploration block.
WalAm Energy Inc v Republic of Kenya (ICSID Case No ARB/15/17)	The dispute related to the revocation of a licence granted to the Canadian claimant to explore and develop geothermal resources at the Suswa Geothermal Concession in Kenya.
Togo Electricité and GDF-Suez Energie Services v Republic of Togo (ICSID Case No ARB/06/7)	The dispute related to the termination of an electricity concession.

The list in the table above is not exhaustive. There are several other international arbitration cases relating to African energy disputes, which ought to be considered, including among others: *African Petroleum Gambia Limited (Block A1) v Republic of the Gambia* (ICSID Case No ARB/14/6), relating to the Gambia's revocations of an Australian IOC's two offshore oil licences on the basis that the licences violated the state's national petroleum law; *Société d'Energie et d'Eau du Gabon v Gabonese Republic* (ICSID Case No CONC/18/1), concerning water services and electric power concession; and *Puma Energy PNG Supply Ltd and Puma Energy PNG Refining Limited v Independent State of Papua New Guinea* (ICSID Case No ARB/17/26), concerning an oil refinery. In the Libyan case below, the concepts of state sovereignty and contract internationalisation are explored.

(iv) The Example of the Libyan Arbitration Case

The case of *Texaco Overseas Petroleum Company (TOPCO) and the California Asiatic Oil Company (Calasiatic) v The Government of the Libyan Arab Republic*,[129] (hereinafter TOPCO) relates to expropriation of oil investments. The arbitration originates from 14 Deeds of Concession concluded between 1955 and 1968 between Libya and two United States companies, Texaco Overseas Petroleum Company and California Asiatic Oil Company (hereafter called the Companies). The majority of the Deeds of Concession were modified by consent of all parties in 1963, 1966, 1970 and 1971.

In 1973, however, 51 per cent of the properties, rights and assets relating to the Deeds of Concession of the Companies, as well as of seven other oil companies were nationalised by a legislative Decree. In the following year, on 1 September 1974, a Decree was issued, directed only to the Companies. By this Decree the entirety of all the properties, rights and assets relating to the 14 Deeds of Concession, of which the Companies were holders, was nationalised.

Of relevance to this chapter is the stabilisation provision contained in Clause 6 of the Concession. This reads as follows:

1. The Libyan Government, the (Petroleum) Commission and the competent authorities in the Provinces shall take all the steps that are necessary to ensure that the Company enjoys all the rights conferred upon it by this concession, and the contractual rights expressly provided for in this concession may not be infringed except by agreement of both parties.
2. This concession shall be interpreted during the period of its effectiveness in accordance with the provisions of the Petroleum Law and the Regulations issued thereunder at the time of the grant of the concession, and any amendments to or cancellations of these Regulations shall not apply to the contractual rights of the Company except with its consent.

[129] *Texaco Overseas Petroleum Company (TOPCO) and the California Asiatic Oil Company (Calasiatic) v The Government of the Libyan Arab Republic*, Award, 17 ILM 1 (1978).

It is also worth noting the arbitration clauses. The choice of law provision in Clause 28(7) was as follows:

> [t]his Concession shall be governed by and interpreted in accordance with the principles of law of Libya common to the principles of international law and in the absence of such common principles then by and in accordance with the general principles of law, including such of those principles as may have been applied by international tribunals.

Following the nationalisation, the Companies notified the Libyan Government that recourse would be taken to arbitration. The Libyan government, however, abstained from designating its arbitrator. Consequently, the President of the International Court of Justice appointed the French Law Professor René-Jean Dupuy as sole arbitrator. The arbitrator fixed Geneva as the place of the arbitral tribunal. The sole arbitrator held that Libya's actions relating to nationalisation were illegal. The decision in this case throws more light on various concepts, including: state sovereignty versus stabilisation clauses; and internationalisation.

With respect to the concept of sovereignty, the key issue was whether a state can disregard its international commitments assumed by it within the framework of its sovereignty. In other words, can states bind themselves by contract? The arbitrator decided that a state may contract not to exercise its power of nationalisation at all in respect of a particular enterprise for a limited period of time. In essence, the state can bind itself by contract. Professor René-Jean held that, 'the undoubted right of a state to nationalize' could not prevail over a stabilisation clause in the contract between the state and the foreign private investor, and was therefore illegal per se, regardless of the issue of compensation.

The arbitrator further noted that,

> the recognition by international law of the right to nationalize is not sufficient ground to empower a State to disregard its commitments, because the same law also recognizes the power of a State to commit itself internationally, especially by accepting the inclusion of stabilization clauses in a contract entered into with a foreign private party.

In other words, once a state makes an international commitment, then it shouldn't regard such a commitment as a negation of its sovereignty.

With respect to the concept of internationalisation, it was noted that a private party has an international capacity; as such, contracts between states and private parties can be internationalised by making them subject to public international law or international arbitration. Scholars have also asserted that the character of the contract itself could also be international in both the economic sense (where it involves interests of international trade); and the legal sense (where it includes factors connecting them to different states).[130] The TOPCO case basically opens the possibility of internationalising a concession. Other cases have also emphasised the issue of internationalisation. In the *Lena Goldfields* case, for instance, the

[130] Cameron, P, *International energy investment law: the pursuit of stability* (Oxford University Press 2010) p 116.

tribunal held that the concession was subject to the general principles of law as far as the contractual provisions safeguarding Lena's interests were concerned.[131] The same decision was taken in the *Sapphire* case,[132] where it was held that the general principles of law applied to a prospecting agreement between the North Iranian Oil Company and the Canadian investor, and not Iranian law alone.[133]

Taking stock of the above, it is worth noting that arbitration clauses have been effective in protecting the rights of investors – especially by ensuring that the aggrieved party is compensated for any breach of the provisions of the petroleum agreements. However, it is worth noting that investors are mostly concerned about the fiscal stability of a country. In this respect, the next sub-section briefly discusses petroleum taxation.

E. Petroleum Taxation

Taxation of the petroleum industry has some unique aspects, considering that often the resources are owned by the state. So, in simple terms, petroleum taxation can be considered as the owner's claim to net resource value. This is understood as the net value of revenues from the sale of the recovered product after deduction of all claimed production costs.[134]

The main functions of oil taxation include: distribution of benefits; rent extraction; financing government expenditure; demand management; impact on the economic environment. The revenues generated from the sector have often contributed to financing government expenditures in resource-rich countries such as Nigeria, South Sudan, Angola and many others. Additionally, petroleum taxation has the potential to positively impact the economic environment. This is so because the government is in a position to use taxation as an instrument to control economic decisions and outcomes. For instance, when threatened by the 'Dutch disease',[135] the government can use taxation to mitigate this problem.

[131] Nussbaum, A, 'The Arbitration Between the Lena Goldfields Ltd. and the Soviet Government' (1950) 36 *Cornell Law Quarterly* 31.

[132] *Sapphire International Petroleum Co v National Iranian Oil Company* (1963) 35 ILR 136.

[133] The principle of contract internationalisation in the TOPCO case, followed in *Revere Copper Inc v Overseas Private Investment Corporation* (1978) 17 ILM 1321; 56 ILR 258. In this case, the tribunal had to determine the proper law of an agreement between the Jamaican government and an American company, Revere Copper and Brass Inc. The agreement did not contain a choice of law clause or an arbitration provision, but it did contain a stabilisation clause, which guaranteed that the taxes paid on the company's bauxite/alumina plant in Jamaica would remain unchanged over a fixed period. The government of Jamaica, however, imposed a tax on bauxite at a rate to be decided from time to time. The tribunal, in examining whether the levy constituted a breach of the agreement, noted that all the elements found in the TOPCO award to characterise an economic development agreement were found to be present in the Revere agreement.

[134] Daniel, P, Keen, M and McPherson, C (eds), *The taxation of petroleum and minerals: principles, problems and practice* (IMF/Routledge 2010).

[135] In economics, the Dutch disease is the apparent causal relationship between the increase in the economic development of a specific sector (for example, natural resources) and a decline in other sectors (like the manufacturing sector or agriculture).

This can be achieved by using the taxation regime to moderate the pace of exploration and exploitation of petroleum and at the same time reduce the depletion rate.[136] Taxation is also key in capturing the economic rent from oil production. In this climate change era, taxation can also be used appropriately to control pollution emissions from the energy sector. This can be achieved through the various 'Green taxes' on carbon emissions.

A good tax regime should possess some attributes including stability, efficiency, equity, neutrality, risk sharing, clarity and simplicity.[137] With respect to stability, the tax system should be stable for a foreseeable future. This not only boosts the confidence of petroleum investors who are often worried about the future of their long-term projects; stability of a tax system also offers the government some level of predictability and reliability to plan for the petroleum revenue.[138]

With respect to equity, two concepts ought to be understood. Horizontal equity implies that taxpayers with equal means should pay the same amount of tax. In contrast, vertical equity requires that taxpayers with a greater financial capacity should pay more tax. Another concept is that of intergenerational equity, which aims to discourage rapid depletion of resources at the expense of future generations. In essence, an equitable tax will ensure that future generations get a fair share of the resources or compensation for those that are depleted. Provisions on petroleum taxation are often included in the PSAs, as in the Ugandan example below:

> Uganda PSA: Article 10: Royalty[139]
>
> 10.1.1 In respect of the requirements of Section 47 of the Act, Licensee shall pay to Government the following Royalty on the Gross Total Daily Production in Barrels of oil per day (BOPD) for each Contract Area, such Gross Total Daily Production defined as the total output of crude oil (including liquid petroleum gas) less all water and sediments produced and all amounts of hydrocarbons re-injected into the Petroleum Reservoir.

Gross Total Daily Production (BOPD)	Royalty
(i) Where the production does not exceed 2,500	5%
(ii) Where the production is higher than 2,500 but does not exceed 5,000	7.5%
(iii) Where the production is higher than 5,000 but does not exceed 7,500	10%
(iv) Where the production exceeds 7,500	12.5%

> 10.1.2 The Royalty stipulated in paragraph 10.1.1 shall be received by Government on a monthly basis whether in kind or in cash depending on Government's preference. Government shall have the right to receive Royalty in cash US Dollars, on a Monthly

[136] Nakhle, C, *Petroleum taxation: sharing the oil wealth: a study of petroleum taxation yesterday, today and tomorrow* (Routledge 2008).

[137] An ideal tax should be simple to understand and inexpensive to administer.

[138] Nakhle, C, *Petroleum taxation: sharing the oil wealth: a study of petroleum taxation yesterday, today and tomorrow* (Routledge 2008).

[139] Production Sharing Agreement for Petroleum Exploration Development and Production in the Republic of Uganda by and between the Government of the Republic of Uganda and Tullow Uganda Limited in respect of the Kanywataba Prospect Area February, 2012. Accessed from UGANDA-KANYWATABA-PSC-FOR-TULLOW.pdf (africaoilgasreport.com).

basis, notifying the Licensee of its choice thirty (30) days in advance. If such notification is not made by Government, the Royalty shall be collected by Government in kind at the point of collection.

10.1.3 Royalty shall be calculated on a daily basis on an incremental basis and not on total daily production.

10.1.4 The BOPD calculation shall be done monthly on the basis of daily production.

10.1.5 Save for the Additional Royalty referred to in Article 10.2.1(B), Royalties on gas (Gas Royalty) will be negotiated upon the discovery of gas.

The above example shows how petroleum taxation is provided for in PSAs. This sub-section is not exhaustive on taxation issues. It rather points out the importance of petroleum taxation in ensuring that host governments benefit from their national resources.

Besides income taxes, an oil company is often subject to corporate income tax at established (normally progressive) rates. Other taxes include: a profits tax, which is, effectively, only a tax on the profits earned from the services and equipment utilised in converting the oil into a liquid or cash asset. Basically, oil taxation can take many forms and various tax instruments are employed by host governments to ensure that they reap the benefits that accrue from the sector. Some of these taxes have been a cause of disputes in various resource-rich countries. For instance, in Uganda, a case was brought by Tullow Uganda Limited against the Uganda Revenue Authority (URA). In this case, Tullow was challenging the initial assessments of income tax of US$472,748,128 by the URA in respect of a transfer of Tullow's interests in Exploration Areas EA1, EA2 and EA3 to China National Offshore Oil Corporation and Total, for the consideration of US$2,933,330,400. These assessments were eventually revised by the URA to US$467,271,971, being capital gains tax. This was the springboard for the tax dispute between the parties.[140] There are various petroleum taxation disputes which cannot be fully covered in this sub-section. Important to note, however, are the various tax instruments relevant in the petroleum sector, as outlined below.

(i) Examples of Tax Instruments[141]

(a) Gross Royalty

A royalty is a payment made for the right to use another's property for the purposes of gain. The Gross royalty is determined with reference to the volume

[140] *Tullow Oil v Uganda Revenue Authority* (TAT Application No 4 OF 2011) [2011] UGTAT 1 (16 June 2014).

[141] For a detailed discussion on petroleum taxation, see Nakhle, C, *Petroleum taxation: sharing the oil wealth: a study of petroleum taxation yesterday, today and tomorrow* (Routledge 2008); Daniel, P, Keen, M and McPherson, C (eds), *The taxation of petroleum and minerals: principles, problems and practice* (IMF/Routledge 2010).

of production or to gross revenues. A royalty can be a per-unit tax or an ad-valorem tax.[142]

(b) Brown Tax

The Brown Tax involves the payment of a proportional subsidy or tax credits on annual cash losses and an equivalent tax on annual cash profits.[143]

(c) Resource Rent Tax (RRT)

This is a modified version of the Brown Tax – but instead of paying tax credits in years with negative cash-flows, the government allows such negative amounts to be carried forward and deducted from positive cash-flows in later periods.

(d) Income Tax

This applies to the company's profits and it is sometimes referred to as 'corporation tax'. The tax is levied at a corporate rather than oil field level.

There are various issues with respect to petroleum taxation. All these cannot be exhausted in this short section. However, what remains clear is that, the state, without such an effective tax regime, would have sold its asset at too low a price; and thus the citizens would not reap any benefits from the petroleum sector. Additionally, given the negative impacts associated with petroleum activities on land use, it is essential that the host government negotiates a favourable tax regime that will benefit the host communities.

V. Conclusion

As discussed in this chapter, access to land is essential for the successful establishment and development of energy projects and energy infrastructure. Local communities where these projects are situated often suffer the negative social and environmental impacts associated with energy projects, including: noise pollution (wind turbines); encroachment on sacred or burial land (solar power project); gas flaring (gas projects); oil spills and accidents (oil projects); air pollution (coal burning, biomass). Additionally, displacements and resettlement of the people in resource-rich areas have attracted a lot of controversy in recent years, especially

[142] A per-unit tax is a uniform fixed charge levied on a specified level of output. On the other hand, an ad-valorem tax is a fixed charge levied on the *value* of the output.

[143] Brown tax is levied as a fixed proportion of a project's net cash-flow in each period. Named after the US economist E Cary Brown.

where issues of inadequate or no compensation have been highlighted. The disputes and demonstrations of discontent by the local communities have influenced the embracement of Social Licence to Operate (SLO) and Corporate Social Responsibility (CSR), alongside the need to strengthen local content provisions. All these are aimed at ensuring that the local communities benefit from the energy resources in their area.

5

Conclusion: Pertinent Issues in the African Extractive Industries

I. Social Licence to Operate (SLO), Extractives and Land Access

Inspired by different motives, the bulk of which focus on protecting their investments, companies have long been eager to establish a good relationship with local communities through acquiring a SLO. Once secured, SLO facilitates smooth operations amongst stakeholders, hence ensuring the success of energy and mining projects by reducing project risks. Whereas on the one hand companies benefit from enjoying the profitable operations of their business without interruption, host communities and other stakeholder groups, on the other hand, may benefit from social amenities such as developmental infrastructure, training and employment opportunities.[1]

SLO is a representation of the societal acceptance of ongoing projects formally undertaken by companies. It is unwritten and as such differs from the legal licences typically granted by governments to energy companies. The informal character of SLO implies that companies are at liberty to decide what obligations to fulfil with respect to SLO. These obligations do obviously have financial and economic implications and companies will only commit to SLO activities that fit in their budget. Nevertheless, SLO is a non-permanent right and as such it may be granted, withdrawn or subject to change as new information about the project is acquired.

The impacts of SLO are similar to the objectives of CSR. CSR refers to a business approach that contributes to sustainable development by delivering economic, social and environmental benefits for all stakeholders. For companies, the overall aim is to achieve a positive impact on society while maximising the creation of shared values for the owners of business, their employees, shareholders and stakeholders. When social responsibility is recognised as part of a company's business model, it can attract positive publicity, help attract and retain top talent, and

[1] Njenga, N and Nalule, V, 'What is the Future of Social Licence to Operate in the Extractive Industries post the COVID-19 Pandemic in East Africa?' (2020) 1(2) *Global Energy Law and Sustainability* 156–63.

improve relationships with customers and their communities. The benefits can be far and wide, including client retention, improved sales and financial success.

There are four types of CSR that have been exercised by companies over the years and these include: environmental sustainability initiatives; direct philanthropic giving; ethical business practices; and economic responsibility. Given the negative impacts associated with the mining industry – including environmental degradation, pollution, child labour, and violence – mining companies are embracing CSR as a way of addressing some of these impacts.

CSR by its nature is supposed to be voluntary and as such mining contracts and mining legislations do not expressly provide for it. However, given the hostilities from various local communities, it has become imperative for mining companies to improve their image by enhancing CSR. Consequently, there are now legal provisions for CSR. These are visible at both the national and regional level. Nationally, countries such as South Sudan make it mandatory for mining companies to implement CSR programmes.[2] Mozambique also has provisions on CSR as stipulated in Resolution No 21/2014.[3] Regionally, ECOWAS requires all member states to ensure that CSR is part of the conditions for granting a mining licence.[4] In contrast to the past, where companies concerned themselves with small projects as part of their CSR efforts, in recent years, given the economic challenges faced by most African countries, there have been suggestions to redefine CSR to include developmental infrastructure such as roads, schools and hospitals.

With respect to SLO, CSR, extractives and land access, CSR that is focused on environmental protection necessitates the embracement of initiatives aimed at ensuring local communities are able to utilise their land at the end of mining operations. Also, given the fact that most mining operations take place in rural areas, where most of the host communities rely on agriculture, companies intending to secure SLO are encouraged to invest in projects that can improve the agricultural profitability of the farmers in those host communities. This can include sponsoring executive training programmes for farmers or deploying machinery such as tractors which can be communally used by the local people for agricultural purposes.

II. Local Content, Extractives and Land Access

A. Meaning and Nature of Local Content

Local content requirements (LCRs) are increasingly being introduced in the legal frameworks of different African countries. LCRs are mostly provided for through

[2] Section 128(2) of the 2012 Mining Act.

[3] Resolution No 21/2014 of 16 May 2014 approving the Business Social Responsibility Policy for the Mineral Resources Extractive Industry.

[4] See Article 11(2) of ECOWAS Directive C/DIR 3/05/09 of 27 May 2009 on the Harmonisation of the Guiding Principles and Policies in the Mining Sector.

legislation, regulations, guidelines, industry contracts and bidding practices. Although there are arguably good intentions behind the introduction of LCRs, there have been some arguments against these provisions. Nevertheless, it is imperative that host governments and investors collaborate in implementing LCRs. In the extractive industry, local content can be understood as contractual provisions, laws and policies that entail the use of local workforce and local facilities in the oil, gas and mining industry. Investors are further required to give priority to domestic goods and services, indigenous communities, nationals, and locally produced materials in the procurement of goods and services used in the mining sector. Local service providers include companies involved in the supply, construction and procurement of contracts.

Although LCRs have been common in recent years, the notion of local content requirements dates as far back as the 1970s, where they were first introduced in the North Sea, and ranged from restrictions on imports to direct intervention in the oil sector. In the twenty-first century, different African countries have also embraced LCRs as a way of ensuring the promotion of local skills, economic diversification and local participation.

B. Why are African Countries Advocating for Local Content?

The mining sector, especially for LSM, requires massive capital, which in most cases lies beyond the reach of local people. In this respect, the sector mostly attracts foreign investors, who in the distant past would come with their own personnel and other service providers while carrying out mining activities in Africa. Local content, therefore, is a way to rectify the previous imbalances caused by over-reliance on foreign capital, services and workforce in the mining industry. LCRs are relied on by governments to generate broader economic benefits for the local economy, beyond fiscal benefits, royalties and rents. Besides, by employing nationals, and facilitating the transfer of skills and utilisation of local goods, LCRs are also crucial in the development of endogenous technology and infrastructure, because local content provisions put an obligation on the mining companies to give preference to local service providers, workers and companies – all of which have an effect of enhancing the local economy.

C. Arguments against Local Content

The various arguments against LCRs in developing countries often centre on the inability of some African countries to provide local expertise or even the necessary local goods to be relied on by the foreign companies. Additionally, in some countries, the procurement procedures are frequently not well established. Another argument is that LCRs are sometimes incompatible with international trade measures applicable to members of the WTO. This is so especially with respect to provisions relating to non-discrimination, which in effect reflect the principles of 'national treatment' and 'most favoured nation' obligations. This implies that foreign companies cannot be forced to buy from local suppliers or hire local suppliers if a better alternative in terms of price or quality exists abroad.[5] Despite these concerns, various countries even outside the African continent have embraced LCRs. In Canada, for example, LCRs have been embraced; contractual obligations exist that require 35 per cent of all goods and services to be sourced from aboriginal owned businesses.[6] And Saudi Arabia, through Saudi Aramco, launched its 'In Kingdom Total Value Add' (IKTVA) programme in 2015, with the aim to drive, measure and monitor the 'added value' brought to the country.

D. Legal Provisions for Local Content

Enforcement of LCRs necessitates the backing of national laws and regulations. Some countries like Uganda have gone ahead to draft independent local content Acts while other countries have included local content provisions in their respective mining laws, thus placing an obligation on mining companies to utilise local service providers. Various mining legislation provides for local content. For instance, with respect to locally produced goods and services, these are provided for under: Section 12(1) of the Mines and Minerals Act of Botswana; Section 113(1) of the 2003 Mining Act of Uganda; and Article 101 of Law No 4/2005 of 11 April 2005 Enacting the Mining Code of the Republic of Congo. With respect to the local service providers requirement, these are provided for in: Section 12(1) of the Mines and Minerals Act of Botswana; Article 50 of the 1992 Mineral Prospecting and Mining Act of Namibia; and Article 29 of the Mines and Minerals Act of Swaziland, 2011.

That being said, it is not enough to have good and impressive local content laws on paper. There is a need to ensure the enforcement of such laws. Indeed, the laws have put in place a number of procedures to ensure that local content aspects are practised including: favourable tax regimes; tenders and procurement procedures favouring local people; and encouragement to join operations between foreign and local companies.[7] Some countries such as Ghana have set up local content enforcing units, while other countries have introduced detailed criteria to determine when and how local companies can be involved in the sector. In Guinea, the relevant law, under Article 107, provides in detail how small- and medium-sized

[5] For a detailed discussion, see Olawuyi, DS, 'Introduction' in Olawuyi, *Extractives Industry Law in Africa* (Springer 2018) pp 3–17.

[6] These terms are common in the Canadian provinces of Saskatchewan, Newfoundland and Nova Scotia. See Section 45 of the Canada-Newfoundland and Labrador Atlantic Accord Implementation Act (S.C. 1987, c.3).

[7] This is the case in Mozambique as stipulated under Article 22 of Mining Act No 20/2014 of 18 August 2014.

enterprises owned or controlled by Guineans can be involved in the various stages of mining projects in the country.[8]

Enforceability also necessitates the need to ensure that local people have the necessary skills to take up such entrepreneurship businesses. In this respect, the Minerals Prospecting and Mining Act of Namibia, under Article 50, provides for the enhancement of local entrepreneurship in the mining sector.[9]

In an endeavour to ensure that host countries meet the requirements of qualified personnel, different African governments have sent many of their officials to various developed countries to acquire the necessary knowledge and expertise in the mining sector. Additionally, local universities now offer energy and mining courses. As a result, the issue of a lack of qualified personnel is no longer valid in many African countries. Indeed, African countries are now making bold demands to ensure that qualified nationals are well represented in managerial and senior roles in the mining companies. A case in point is that of Guinea, where the law expressly requires the assistant general manager to be a Guinean and the managing director of the mining company to also be a Guinean (after the lapse of a specified period of time).[10] Additionally, enforceability necessitates clear monitoring programmes and redress in the event that the mining companies fail to comply. In this respect, Guinean companies are required to provide reports on the employment of local personnel as stipulated under Section 108 of the Mining Code.[11]

Taking stock of the above, it can be seen that different African countries have put in place strategies to ensure that the local people actively participate in and benefit from the mining sector. With respect to local content and land access, there are no direct instances of ensuring local content in land use in the extractive industries. However, the requirement focusing on the provision of local services and goods is advantageous to local farmers and other service providers who are well placed to offer direct services such as catering, food stuffs and other agricultural products to extractive companies and their workers.

III. Regionalism, Extractives and Land Access

Regionalism is defined as the expression of a common sense of identity and purpose, combined with the creation and implementation of institutions that express a particular identity and shape collective action within a geographical region.[12] In this book, regionalism is defined in the context of international relations and is

[8] Article 107 of Law No 2011/006/CNT of 9 September 2011 Enacting the Mining Code.

[9] Article 50 of the 1992 Minerals Prospecting and Mining Act, Laws of Namibia.

[10] Article 108 of Law No L/2013/N°053/CNT of 8 April 2013 Amending the Mining Code.

[11] Article 108 of Law No L/2013/N°053/CNT of 8 April 2013 Amending Law No 2011/006/CNT of 9 September 2011 Enacting the Mining Code.

[12] Ethier, W, 'The international commercial system' (Essays in International Finance No 210) (Princeton University Dept of Economics, International Finance Section 1998) p 11.

discussed as one of the three constituents of the international commercial system – the other two being multilateralism and unilateralism. This definition brings into play the component of geography, and mostly connotes the idea of an international region, which is understood to mean a limited number of states linked by a geographical relationship and by a degree of mutual inter-dependence; this can also be called international regionalism, understood as the formation of interstate associations or groupings on the basis of region.[13]

Although the above definition focuses on the issue of geography and territory, it is imperative to note that there are some regional blocks which do not purely consider geography as the basis for inclusion of new members. A case in point is the League of Arab States, which essentially applies linguistic-cultural aspects as the basis for the inclusion of its 22 members rather than geographical conditions. The Organisation of Islamic Cooperation also focuses on religious identity in defining its membership rather than geography.

Regional economic communities are indeed good examples of a regional cooperation mechanism. These have been established in different regions of the globe and in addition to the three mentioned already in this book (EAC, ECOWAS, and SADC) they include the Arab Maghreb Union, the Community of Sahel-Saharan States, the Common Market for Eastern and Southern Africa, and the EU. In this section, the advantages of regional cooperation and regionalism will be discussed under two sub-sections for the purpose of comparing them to isolationism and globalism, respectively.

A. Regionalism versus Isolationism

Isolationism refers to the policies employed by a country to decline from being involved in international agreements, alliances, and commitments. This policy also ensures that the country stays away from the affairs or interests of other groups (especially political affairs), and may be used in a nationalist way with the aim of concentrating the country's efforts to its own advancement. Historically, the doctrine of isolationism can be traced back to the eighteenth century when the US was determined to stay away from the politics in Europe – this, however, ended in the 1890s when the country could no longer ignore the negative effects of the isolationism policy on its security.[14]

The main advantage of regionalism over isolationism in the energy sector is based on the reality that SSA countries are faced with scarce public resources and limited aid in the energy sector. To this end these countries need to cope with

[13] Nye, JS (ed), *International regionalism: Readings* (Little, Brown Co 1968).

[14] For a detailed discussion on isolationism, see Klein, S, 'America first? Isolationism in US foreign policy from the 19th to the 21st century' (Doctoral dissertation, Monterey, CA: Naval Postgraduate School 2017).

their investment needs through cooperation. Moreover, some countries are better endowed with energy resources than others, so again there is a need for cooperation in order to efficiently utilise the resources to benefit neighbouring countries in the region. Taking the example of the DRC, it has a large hydropower potential which is estimated to be sufficient to provide three times as much power as Africa currently consumes.[15] There is therefore a need for regional cooperation to develop and utilise the available energy resources. In this regard, regional cooperation has also been recognised as being a major component of Africa's vision for its future.

B. Regionalism versus Globalism/Multilateralism

When compared to globalism, it has also been observed that the reality of a contemporary world seems to be better expressed in terms of regionalism than globalism. Furthermore, the proponents of regional cooperation identify with its effectiveness in solving new challenges which are typically ignored at the global level. This argument may hold true when comparing regionalism and globalism, for instance, the seriousness of certain problems such as political disintegration or epidemics may be hard to disregard at a regional level since many regional actors are immediately affected in comparison to global actors.[16]

In this case, considering the fact that the challenge of energy access is not a global one but rather a regional one, then regionalism is more suited to tackle such a challenge. Moreover, the lack of politically grounded problem-solving at the global level also makes the regional cooperation mechanism a far better option than globalism. However, the growing interest in solving energy-related investment disputes using international or global avenues and internationally recognised investment treaties should not be ignored. As such, a brief overview of globalism via the lens of international investment treaties is discussed in the next section, with the importance of highlighting the significance of globalism in the energy sector.

As discussed in the previous chapters, regionalism has been embraced in both the energy and mining sectors. However, with respect to land access and administration, it is hard to find common solutions to the different land issues experienced in different countries. There are some internationally accepted principles that have an impact on land use and governance. These principles, as discussed in Chapter one, influence the legislation and administration of land governance in different countries. These principles include, among others: the sovereignty of states and their people over natural resources (including land); and international

[15] Auriol, E and Biancini, S, Powering up developing countries through integration?' (2015) 29(1) *The World Bank Economic Review* 1–40.

[16] Hettne, B and Söderbaum, F, 'Regional cooperation: A tool for addressing regional and global challenges' in *Meeting global challenges: International cooperation in the national interest. Final report. Cross-cutting issues* (International Task Force on Global Public Goods 2006) pp 179–244.

requirements for environmental protection (these directly impact land use). These principles, in essence, play a significant role in advancing land justice in the extractive industries.

IV. Concluding Remarks and Recommendations

The link between energy law and environmental law lies in the fact that in the development of energy infrastructure, there are various environmental issues of concern, including pollution (gas flaring and oil spills) and damage to biodiversity and habitats. This explains why most energy laws require that companies meet the requirements of various environmental laws including: complying with national Environmental Impact Assessment requirements; decommissioning (for oil and gas); mining closure and land rehabilitation (for mining). In the mining sector, the use of dangerous chemicals such as mercury does negatively impact on land use. Additionally, deforestation, displacement of the local people, and land degradation all negatively impact land use by the host communities.

This is a clear connection between energy/mining law and environmental law. However, we note that environmental protection is part of land. As defined in Chapter two, land includes not only the tangible property but also the intangible rights attaching to it. In this respect, any disruption to the environment negatively impacts land use. For instance, oil spills and gas flaring make it impossible for local farmers to continue with their agricultural and fishing activities, hence not only affecting the environment but also limiting land use.

Throughout this book, the concept of land justice has been evident. In the extractive industries, land justice necessitates the distribution of the profits that accrue from energy or mining projects to all the concerned stakeholders. Additionally, there is a need to ensure that people are not displaced from their homes/land because of energy and mining projects. More so, even though various laws provide for compensation, land justice requires that the compensation is fair and reflects the projects in question. For extractive projects, they are capital intensive and are associated with various negative environmental impacts. In this respect, it is necessary that the compensation is calculated in a way that takes into consideration the disturbances people are likely to suffer due to extractive projects.

Appendices

APPENDIX I

THE COMMUNITY LAND ACT No 27 of 2016

PART III: ADMINISTRATION AND MANAGEMENT OF COMMUNITY LAND

15. (1) A registered community shall have a community assembly which shall consist of all adult members of the community.
(2) The quorum for decision making by the community shall not be less than two thirds of the community assembly.
(3) The community assembly shall elect between seven and fifteen members of the community assembly to constitute the community land management committee.
(4) The functions of the community land management committee shall be to—
(a) have responsibility over the running of the day to day functions of the community;
(b) manage and administer registered community land on behalf of the respective community;
(c) coordinate the development of community land use plans in collaboration with the relevant authorities;
(d) promote the co-operation and participation among community members in dealing with matters pertaining to the respective registered community land; and
(e) prescribe rules and regulations, to be ratified by the community assembly, to govern the operations of the community.
(5) Any decision of a registered community to dispose of or otherwise alienate community land shall be binding if it is supported by at least two thirds of the registered adult members of the community, while all other decisions of the registered community shall be by a simple majority of the members present in a meeting.

PART VI: SPECIAL RIGHTS AND ENTITLEMENTS IN THE COMMUNITY LAND

27. (1) A registered community may upon application and with approval of the members of the registered community, allocate part of its registered

community land to a member or a group of members of the community for exclusive use and occupation for such period as the registered community shall determine.

(2) Despite subsection (1), a separate title shall not be issued for such parcel.

(3) An individual entitlement under subsection (1) shall not be superior to community title in any way.

(4) A member granted exclusive use of a parcel of land under this section—

(a) shall pay to the registered community such premium or fees commensurate to the use as may be determined by the community from time to time;

(b) may develop the land subject to the provisions of any laws and regulations relating to land use;

(c) may not assign or lease the land to a third party who is not a member of the community;

(d) shall put the land into lawful use;

(e) shall surrender the land back to the community if the member no longer shall be entitled to quiet enjoyment of the land, requires the land; and

28. (1) The customs and practices of pastoral communities relating to land shall be taken into consideration by a registered community as long as they are consistent with the provisions of this Act or other applicable law.

(2) Community land in a pastoral community shall be available for use by members of the community for the grazing of their livestock, subject to—

(a) such conditions as the respective registered community may impose, including conditions relating to—

(i) the kind and number of livestock that may be grazed;

(ii) the section or sections of the land where livestock may be grazed and the grazing in rotation on different sections; and

(iii) a grazing plan;

(iv) the right of the community to utilize the portion of land in accordance with this Act.

(3) The registered community may upon application by any person who is not a member of the registered community, grant grazing rights and upon such grant, that person shall exercise the rights subject to the conditions referred to in subsection (1):

Provided that the registered community shall subject to the approval of the members of the registered community in a meeting convened for that purpose withdraw a grazing right granted under this subsection if, due to drought or any other reasonable cause, the registered community considers such cancellation to be in the interest of the residents of the community concerned.

(4) Notwithstanding subsection (1), a registered community may withdraw the grazing right of any member who—

(a) fails to observe in a material respect any condition referred to in this Act; or

(b) contravenes any provision of subsection (2).

(5) A person shall not, except with the written authority of the registered community-

(a) erect or occupy any building or other structure on the designated grazing land;

(b) plough or cultivate any portion of the land;

(c) take up abode on or occupy any portion of the grazing land; and

(d) obstruct the access to any watering place on the land, prevent or attempt to prevent any person from drawing water from, or watering stock at a watering place, pollute the water at a watering place or interfere with the operation of any windmill, water pump, water-pipe, dam or storage tank or other appurtenance installed or constructed at such a watering place.

(6) A person who contravenes subsection (5) commits an offence and is liable, on conviction, to a fine not exceeding one hundred thousand shillings or imprisonment for a period not exceeding six months.

29. (1) A registered community may reserve special purpose areas including—

(a) farming areas;

(b) settlement areas;

(c) community conservation areas;

(d) access and rights of way;

(e) cultural and religious sites;

(f) urban development; or

(g) any other purpose as may be determined by the community, county government or national government for the promotion of public interest.

(2) An area designated for special purposes under subsection (1) shall be used exclusively for the designated purposes.

30. (1) Every member of the community has the right to equal benefit from community land.

(2) Equality includes full and equal enjoyment of rights of use and access.

(3) Women, men, youth, minority, persons with disabilities and marginalized groups have the right to equal treatment in all dealings in community land.

(4) A registered community shall not directly or indirectly discriminate against any member of the community on any ground including race, gender, marital status, ethnic or social origin, color, age, disability, religion or culture.

(5) For the avoidance of doubt, every man or woman married to a member of the community shall gain automatic membership of the community and such membership shall subsist until the spouses legally divorce and the woman remarries or the woman remarries after the death of a spouse.

(6) Subject to Article 159 of the Constitution, the culture of each community shall be recognized in accordance with Article 11(1) of the Constitution in the exercise of community land rights.

31. (1) Subject to such exemptions as may be prescribed, or unless any condition attaching to a community land right or a right of leasehold under this Act provides otherwise, a customary land right may be dealt with only with the approval of the registered community in a meeting convened for such purpose.

(2) For the purposes of this Act, contracts and transfers over community land shall be carried out in a manner similar to transactions over private land as provided in the Land Act, 2012 and registered as provided in the Land Registration Act, 2012.

32. (1) A lease over community land shall be on the basis of an agreement between the community and the lessee and subject to such implied conditions, restrictions and covenants as may be contained in any other written law.

(2) Despite section 55 (1) of the Land Act, 2012, unless the agreement contemplated under subsection (1) otherwise provides, the general provisions on leases contained in Part IV of that Act shall apply to leases over community land.

33. In addition to such grounds of cancellation as may be set out in a deed of leasehold, a right of leasehold may be cancelled by a registered community, with approval of the members of the registered community, if the leaseholder fails to comply with the requirements or to adhere to any restrictions imposed by or under any law pertaining to the utilization of the land to which the right relates.

34. (1) Any person who immediately before the commencement of this Act, held a right to use and occupy any part of community land, whether by virtue of any authority granted under any law or otherwise than under a lease, may continue to use and occupy such land under that right, subject to the same terms and conditions until the lease expires, after which the provisions of sections 28 and 29 shall apply.

APPENDIX II

ECOWAS ENERGY PROTOCOL A/P4/1/03

CHAPTER III INVESTMENT PROMOTION AND PROTECTION

ARTICLE 10. PROMOTION, PROTECTION AND TREATMENT OF INVESTMENTS

(1) Each Contracting Party shall, in accordance with the provisions of this Protocol, encourage and create stable, equitable, favorable and transparent conditions for Investors to make Investments in its Area. Such conditions shall include a commitment to accord at all times to Investments of Investors fair and equitable treatment. Such Investments shall also enjoy the most constant protection and security and no Contracting Party shall in any way impair by unreasonable or discriminatory measures their management, maintenance, use, enjoyment or disposal. In no case shall such Investments be accorded treatment less favorable than that required by international law, including treaty obligations. Each Contracting Party shall observe any obligations it has entered into with an Investor or with respect to an Investment.

(2) Each Contracting Party shall endeavor to accord to Investors, as regards the Making of Investments in its Area, the Treatment described in paragraph (3).

(3) For the purposes of this Article, 'Treatment' means treatment accorded by a Contracting Party which is no less favourable than that which it accords to its own Investors or to Investors of any other Contracting Party or, indeed, of any third state, whichever is the most favorable.

(4) Each Contracting Party shall, as regards the Making of Investments in its Area, endeavor to:

   (a) limit to the minimum the exceptions to the Treatment described in paragraph (3);
   (b) progressively remove existing restrictions affecting Investors.

(5) (a) A Contracting Party may, as regards the Making of Investments in its Area, at any time declare voluntarily to the Meeting of Energy Ministers, through the Executive Secretariat of ECOWAS, its intention not to introduce new exceptions to the Treatment described in paragraph (3).

   (b) A Contracting Party may, furthermore, at any time make a voluntary commitment to accord to Investors, as regards the Making of Investments in some or all Economic Activities in the Energy Sector in its Area, the Treatment described in paragraph (3). Such commitments shall be notified to the Executive Secretariat of ECOWAS and shall be binding under this Protocol.

(6) Each Contracting Party shall, in its Area, accord to Investments of Investors and their related activities including management, maintenance, use, enjoyment or disposal, treatment no less favorable than that which it accords

to its own Investors or of the Investors of any third state and their related activities including management, maintenance, use, enjoyment or disposal, whichever is the most favorable.

(7) The modalities of application of paragraph (6) may exclude programs under which a Contracting Party provides to its own national investor's grants or other financial assistance, or enters into contracts, for energy technology research and development. Each Contracting Party shall through the Executive Secretariat of ECOWAS keep the Meeting of Energy Ministers informed of the modalities it applies to the programmes described in this paragraph.

(8) Each state or Regional Economic Integration Organization which signs or accedes to this Protocol shall, on the date it signs the Protocol or deposits its instrument of accession, submit to the Executive Secretariat of ECOWAS a report summarizing all laws, regulations or other measures relevant to:

(a) exceptions to paragraph (2); or
(b) the programs referred to in paragraph (7).

A Contracting Party shall keep its report up to date by promptly submitting amendments to the Executive Secretariat of ECOWAS. The Meeting of Energy Ministers shall review these reports periodically.

In respect of subparagraph (a) the report may designate parts of the energy sector in which a Contracting Party accords to Investors the Treatment described in paragraph (3).

In respect of subparagraph (b) the review by the Meeting of Energy Ministers may consider the effects of such programmes on competition and Investments.

(9) Notwithstanding any other provision of this Article, the treatment described in paragraphs (3) and (6) shall not apply to the protection of Intellectual Property; instead, the treatment shall be as specified in the corresponding provisions of the applicable international agreements for the protection of Intellectual Property rights to which the respective Contracting Parties are parties.

(10) For the purposes of Article 26, the application by a Contracting Party of a trade related investment measure as described in Article 5(1) and (2) to an Investment of an Investor existing at the time of such application shall, subject to Article 5(3) and (4), be considered a breach of an obligation of the former Contracting Party under this Part.

(11) Each Contracting Party shall ensure that its domestic law provides effective means for the assertion of claims and the enforcement of rights with respect to Investments, investment agreements, and investment authorizations.

ARTICLE 11. KEY PERSONNEL

(1) A Contracting Party shall, subject to its laws and regulations relating to the entry, stay and work of natural persons, examine in good faith requests by Investors and key personnel who are employed by such Investors or by

Investments of such Investors, to enter and remain temporarily in its Area to engage in activities connected with the making or the development, management, maintenance, use, enjoyment or disposal of relevant Investments, including the provision of advice or key technical services.

(2) A Contracting Party shall permit Investors which have Investments in its Area, and Investments of such Investors, to employ any key person of the Investor's or the Investment's choice regardless of nationality and citizenship provided that such key person has been permitted to enter, stay and work in the Area of the Contracting Party and that the employment concerned conforms to the terms, conditions and time limits of the permission granted to such key person.

ARTICLE 12. COMPENSATION FOR LOSSES

(1) Except where Article 13 applies, an Investor which suffers a loss with respect to any Investment in the Area of a Contracting Party owing to war or other armed conflict, state of national emergency, civil disturbance, or other similar event in that Area, shall be accorded by the latter Contracting Party, as regards restitution, indemnification, compensation or other settlement, treatment which is the most favourable of that which that Contracting Party accords to any other Investor, whether its own Investor, the Investor of any other Contracting Party, or the Investor of any third state.

(2) Without prejudice to paragraph (1), an Investor which, in any of the situations referred to in that paragraph, suffers a loss in the Area of a Contracting Party resulting from

- (a) requisitioning of its Investment or part thereof by the latter's forces or authorities; or
- (b) destruction of its Investment or part thereof by the latter's forces or authorities, which was not required by the necessity of the situation, shall be accorded restitution or compensation which in either case shall be prompt, adequate and effective.

ARTICLE 13. EXPROPRIATION

(1) Investments of Investors in the Area of any Contracting Party shall not be nationalized, expropriated or subjected to a measure or measures having effect equivalent to nationalization or expropriation (hereinafter referred to as 'Expropriation') except where such Expropriation is:

- (a) for a purpose which is in the public interest;
- (b) not discriminatory;
- (c) carried out under due process of law; and
- (d) accompanied by the payment of prompt, adequate and effective compensation.

Such compensation shall amount to the fair market value of the Investment expropriated at the time immediately before the Expropriation or impending Expropriation became known in such a way as to affect the value of the Investment (hereinafter referred to as the 'Valuation Date').

Such fair market value shall at the request of the Investor be expressed in a Freely Convertible Currency on the basis of the market rate of exchange existing for that currency on the Valuation Date. Compensation shall also include interest at a commercial rate established on a market basis from the date of Expropriation until the date of payment.

(2) The Investor affected shall have a right to prompt review, under the law of the Contracting Party making the Expropriation, by a judicial or other competent and independent authority of that Contracting Party, of its case, of the valuation of its Investment, and of the payment of compensation, in accordance with the principles set out in paragraph (1).

(3) For the avoidance of doubt, Expropriation shall include situations where a Contracting Party expropriates the assets of a company or enterprise in which an Investor has an Investment, including through the ownership of shares.

APPENDIX III

ECOWAS ENERGY PROTOCOL A/P4/1/03

CHAPTER IV MISCELLANEOUS PROVISIONS

ARTICLE 18. SOVEREIGNTY OVER ENERGY RESOURCES

(1) The Contracting Parties recognize state sovereignty and sovereign rights over energy resources. They reaffirm that these must be exercised in accordance with and subject to the rules of international law.

(2) Without affecting the objectives of promoting access to energy resources, and exploration and development thereof on a commercial basis, this Protocol shall in no way prejudice the rules in Contracting Parties governing the system of property ownership of energy resources.

(3) Each state continues to hold in particular the rights to decide the geographical areas within its Area to be made available for exploration and development of its energy resources, the optimization of their recovery and the rate at which they may be depleted or otherwise exploited, to specify and enjoy any taxes, royalties or other financial payments payable by virtue of such exploration and exploitation, and to regulate the environmental and safety aspects of such exploration, development and reclamation within its Area, and to participate in such exploration and exploitation, inter alia, through direct participation by the government or through state enterprises.

(4) The Contracting Parties undertake to facilitate access to energy resources, inter alia, by allocating in a non-discriminatory manner on the basis of published criteria authorizations, licences, concessions and contracts to prospect and explore for or to exploit or extract energy resources.

APPENDIX IV

Nigeria LNG (Fiscal Incentives, Guarantees and Assurances) Act 1990, as amended in 1993

SECOND SCHEDULE

[Section 9.]

Guarantees and assurances to Nigeria LNG limited and its shareholders
The Federal Government of Nigeria (in this Act referred to as 'the Government') in recognition of the magnitude of, and in consideration of the investments which shall have to be made in order to prosecute the venture described in the shareholders' contract dated 19th May, 1989 between the Nigerian National Petroleum Corporation, Shell Gas B.Y., CLEAG Limited and Agip International B.Y., as amended, from time to time (such shareholders' contract, as so amended in this Act referred to as 'the contract') hereby grants to the Company, its successors and to each of the shareholders, from time to time (in their capacity as such), the guarantees, assurances and undertakings following hereunder. These guarantees, assurances and undertakings shall have effect from the date hereof, and so long as the Company, or any successor thereto, is in existence and carrying on the business of liquefying and selling liquefied natural gas and natural gas liquids within and/or outside the Federal Republic of Nigeria.

The guarantees and assurances are as follows–

1. The Government shall do nothing to render invalid unenforceable rights and obligations arising under the contract and the other contracts and arrangements contemplated in the contract, to the extent that such rights and obligations are not illegal in Nigeria and do not offend against Nigerian public policy and provided that such contracts have been kept validly subsisting by the parties thereto, it being understood that such other contracts or arrangements will not be deemed to be illegal or contrary to Nigerian public policy for the sole reason that the requisite government actions referred to in clause 6 hereof have not been effected.
2. The venture shall be subject to the fiscal regime contained in the provisions of this Act. Such fiscal regime shall not be amended in any way, except with the prior written agreement of the Government, the Company and each of the Company's shareholders.
3. Without prejudice to any other provision contained herein, neither the Company nor its shareholders in their capacity as shareholders in the Company, shall in any way be subject to new laws, regulations, taxes, duties, imposts or charges of whatever nature which are not applicable generally to companies incorporated in Nigeria or to shareholders in companies incorporated in Nigeria, respectively.

4. Shareholders who have purchased shares in the Company, with funds originating from outside Nigeria, shall enjoy all benefits of approved status under relevant legislation in respect of their equity shareholding. Such benefits shall include permission to transfer out of Nigeria dividends and capital without undue restriction, provided that there are sufficient foreign exchange reserves in Nigeria to enable such transfers to be made, and that all applicable notifications have been given and relevant regulations complied with.
5. The Government recognises that it is in the interests of the venture that shares in the Company should be freely transferable, subject to the constraints contained in the contract and the applicable laws; accordingly the Government shall facilitate the grant of all permits and other authorisations required for the sale or transfer of shares in the Company.
6. The Government shall take such executive, legislative and other actions as may be necessary so as to effectively grant, fulfil and perfect the guarantees, assurances and undertakings contained herein. In order to afford the degree of security required to enable the Company's investments to be made, the Government further agrees to ensure that the said guarantees, assurances and undertakings shall not be suspended, modified or revoked during the life of the venture except with the mutual agreement of the Government and the shareholders of the Company.
7. The Company shall be permitted to remit funds which shall be carried out through legal channels and to maintain bank accounts outside Nigeria as may be necessary, and retain in such accounts subscription monies for shares, loans, payments and proceeds of sale, for the purpose of making payments in foreign currencies in respect of interests, dividends, loan re-payments, the purchase of natural gas from the production joint ventures, charges and materials, equipment plants, shipping and services acquired abroad. The Company shall be obliged, however to advise the exchange control authorities on a regular basis of the transactions that have taken place and provide any documentation which may be required by the exchange control authorities to support such transactions.
8. Permission shall be given to the Company to declare and pay dividends in United States dollars, after due provision for the payment of tax has been made, without restriction as to time, amount, or the relationship such dividends bear to the share capital of the Company. Such permission shall enable dividends to be paid, without restriction, to resident and non-resident shareholders.
9. The Government shall ensure that the Company is able to receive its finance in Nigeria in the form of either or both money transferred directly from abroad, and plant, machinery, materials, equipment and services imported from abroad; and to convert the money so transferred into Nigerian currency at rates of exchange not less favourable to the Company than those available to any other commercial enterprise in Nigeria.

10. The Government shall treat the venture as a priority project for loan financing purposes and shall reflect this in appropriate public statements and in assurances to the World Bank, the International Monetary Fund, other multilateral and bilateral agencies and financial institutions.
11. The Government, in its capacity as host Government, shall provide assurances and guarantees which may reasonably be required by the Company's lenders, provided such assurances and guarantees are within the scope of the guarantees and assurances contained in this Act.
12. The Government shall not impose constraints on the amount of loan or other financing which may be provided to the venture.
13. The Government shall facilitate–
    (a) the grant of any licence or permit required for the importation or exportation of plant material, equipment and products of the Company;
    (b) the grant of permits, licences required for the construction, start-up and operation of the facilities;
    (c) the customs formalities in respect of imports and exports (not including personal effects) required in connection with the construction, operation and maintenance of the Company facilities and products; and
    (d) the prompt registration and certification by the National Office for Technology Acquisition and Promotion of all contracts for the transfer of technology to the Company by its advisers, contractors and sub-contractors in accordance with the National Office for Technology Acquisition and Promotion Act, accordingly the provisions of subsection (2) of section 6 of the said Act, shall not be applicable to any of the afore-mentioned contracts.
14. The Government shall facilitate the acquisition by the Company of legally sound title to, and vacant possession (for a period of not less than 80 years) of land required by the Company for the venture (including a suitable residential area), together with rights of way, easements and other rights necessary for the implementation of the venture. Such title to and possession of the land shall be on reasonable and non-discriminatory terms.
15. For all practical purposes, the Company shall be treated as an independent, autonomous, commercial entity and its operations, policies, procedures and conditions of services shall be determined by the Board of Directors of the Company.
16. The Government shall facilitate the grant of visas to expatriate staff required by the Company for the implementation, construction, start-up and on-going operations of the venture.
17. Permission for the Company to own and construct jetties and a bonded area for loading and unloading construction equipment and material and for shipment of liquefied natural gas and natural gas liquids shall be granted where these comply with the requirements of the Federal Ministry of Transport, the Nigerian Ports Authority ('NPA') and the relevant Customs authority and

other official bodies in Nigeria. Customs personnel shall be provided at the bonded area at all times. Appropriate facilities for such personnel shall be provided by the Company.

18. (1) The Company and Government shall work together to agree on specifications for marine and port services to be provided at Bonny as regards—
    - *(a)* the capital dredging of the Bonny bar channel by the Company and the maintenance dredging by Government;
    - *(b)* Government's responsibility to provide and maintain the navigational aids for the Bonny bar channel;
    - *(c)* Government's responsibility for providing a fully comprehensive traffic control system for Bonny port;
    - *(d)* Government's responsibility for ensuring that all traffic in the Bonny channel shall carry a pilot and allocation of top graded pilots to the venture;
    - *(e)* the Company's responsibility for ensuring the safety and protection of the designated safety zone around the LNG berth with the assistance and co-operation of the law enforcement agencies;
    - *(f)* the Company's responsibility to provide, operate and maintain the tugs, mooring boats and patrol crafts required for the venture; and
    - *(g)* if, in the Company's opinion, the activities for which the Government is responsible, pursuant to sub-paragraph *(a)*, *(b)* and *(c)* of this paragraph, are not carried out in such a manner as to satisfy the Company's requirements, the Company shall have the right to arrange for the necessary activities to be carried out.

    (2) The Company and the Nigerian Ports Authority acting on behalf of Government shall liaise and co-ordinate their respective activities to ensure the successful implementation of the sub-paragraph (I) of this paragraph.

    (3) The capital costs incurred by the Company in fulfilling the responsibility allocated to it pursuant to sub-paragraph (1) *(a)* of this paragraph and in providing navigational aids for the Bonny bar channel and traffic control facilities to be used by Nigerian Ports Authority on behalf of Government in fulfilling Government's responsibilities pursuant to sub-paragraphs (1) *(b)* and *(c)* of this paragraph and any costs incurred by the Company for activities undertaken by the Company pursuant to sub-paragraph (1) *(g)* of this paragraph shall be borne by the Nigerian Ports Authority and shall be reimbursed to the Company on terms to be agreed between the Nigerian Ports Authority and the Company in good faith.

19. Permission shall be granted by the Government through the Nigerian Electric Power Authority on application by the Company for the Company to construct, own and operate an electricity generating plant with a capacity

of about 200 megawatts as part of the facilities under terms and conditions which govern such power generating plants:

Provided that no conditions shall be attached to any such grant requiring the Company to generate and supply electrical power for any purpose other than to meet the requirements of the venture for power supply to the LNG plant, the Company's other facilities area at Bonny and the Company shall not be obliged to supply power to the Nigeria Electricity Power Authority for local distribution or otherwise.

20. The Company shall, at its own expense, provide itself, in accordance with the Company's Comprehensive and Integrated Telecommunications Network plan, with local telephone and telex services and facilities for international leased circuits and satellite links between its loading terminal near Bonny and ships at sea transporting liquefied natural gas produced by the Company, as well as the receiving terminals of the Company's overseas custom~I'S [sic], provided howsoever that where the~e serviee~ and faeilitie~ CRn b~ [sic] provided by the Nigerian Telecommunications Limited in a timely fashion so as to fulfil the requirements of the venture, the Company shall use reasonable endeavours to use the services and facilities of the Nigerian Telecommunications Limited.
21. The Government hereby affirms its recognition of the shareholders' right to prompt adequate and effective compensation in the event of expropriation of tangible property or property rights or interference with contract rights.
22. In the event of any dispute in respect of a substantial matter arising from the provisions of this Act, the aggrieved shareholder(s) in the Company shall issue a letter of notification to Government, formally notifying Government and the other shareholders of the dispute. The Government's representatives and one or more of the Company's shareholders, as the case may be, shall make serious efforts to resolve amicably such dispute.

    In the event of failure to reach amicable settlement within 90 days of the date of the letter of notification mentioned above, such dispute may be submitted to arbitration before the International Centre for the Settlement of Investment Disputes.

BIBLIOGRAPHY

International Instruments

Charter of the United Nations (Adopted June 26 1945, entered into force on 24 October 1945).

UN General Assembly Resolution 523 (VI) of 12 January 1952 – Integrated economic development agreements commercial agreements.

UN General Assembly Resolution 626 (VII) of 21 December 1952 – Right to Exploit Freely Natural Wealth and Resources.

UN General Assembly Resolution 1314 (XIII) of 12 December 1958 on the Commission on Permanent Sovereignty over Natural Resources.

UN General Assembly Resolution 1803 (XVII) of 14 December 1962 – Permanent Sovereignty over Natural Resources.

UN General Assembly Resolution 2200 A (XXI) of 16 December 1966 – International Covenant on Economic, Social and Cultural Rights.

UN General Assembly Resolution 3281 (XXIX) of 12 December 1974 – Charter of Economic Rights and Duties of States.

OPEC Resolution XVI.90 of 24 June 1968 – Declaratory Statement of Petroleum Policy in Member Countries.

Stockholm Declaration of 1972.

Vienna Convention on the Law of Treaties, 23 May 1969, 1155 UNTS 331.

ECOWAS Energy Protocol, 2003.

ECOWAS Directive C/DIR 3/05/09 of 27 May 2009 on the Harmonisation of the Guiding Principles and Policies in the Mining Sector.

The 1992 SADC Treaty.

SADC Protocol on Energy, 1996.

UNCLOS Convention, United Nations Convention on the Law of the Sea, 1982, 21 ILM (1982), 1261 (adopted on 10 December 1982, and entered into force on November 16 1994).

National Laws

The Constitution of Uganda, 1995, as amended.

Mines and Minerals Act 1999 (Cap 66:01) (No 17 of 1999), Laws of Botswana.

The Mining Act, 2003 (No 9 of 2003), Laws of Uganda.

The 1992 Mineral Prospecting and Mining Act of Namibia.

Law No 4-2005 of 11 April 2005 Enacting the Mining Code of the Republic of Congo.

The 2011 Mines and Mineral Act of Swaziland.

Mining Act No 20-2014 of 18 August 2014, Laws of Mozambique.

Books, Articles and other sources

ACHPR, Communication no 155-96 of 13 October 2001: *Social and Economic Rights Action Center (SERAC) and Center for Economic and Social Rights v Nigeria.*

Adams, M, 'Land tenure policy and practice in Zambia: issues relating to the development of the agricultural sector' (Draft). (Mokoro 2003).

Allison, C, Oriabure, G, Ndimele, PE and Shittu, JA, 'Dealing with oil spill scenarios in the Niger Delta: Lessons from the past' in Ndimele, PE (ed), *The political ecology of oil and gas activities in the Nigerian aquatic ecosystem* (Academic Press 2018).

Amin, M, 'Challenges in reliability, security, efficiency, and resilience of energy infrastructure: Toward smart self-healing electric power grid' in IEEE, *Power and Energy Society General Meeting – Conversion and Delivery of Electrical Energy in the 21st Century* (IEEE 2008) 1–5.

Armar, A, *Building Regional Power Pools. A Toolkit* (The World Bank 2008).

Auriol, E and Biancini, S, 'Powering up developing countries through integration?' (2015) 29(1) *The World Bank Economic Review* 1–40.

Avila, N, Carvallo, JP, Shaw, B and Kammen, DM, *The energy challenge in sub-Saharan Africa: A guide for advocates and policy makers* (Oxfam 2017).

Bazilian, M, Nussbaumer, P, Cabraal, A, Centurelli, R, Detchon, R, Gielen, D, Rogner, H, Howells, M, McMahon, H, Modi, V and Nakicenovic, N, 'Measuring energy access: Supporting a global target' (Earth Institute, Columbia University, NY 2010).

Belguedj, M, 'The West Africa Gas Pipeline and Power Pool Project Building Blocks for Regional Energy Integration'. A report prepared for the International Gas Union (2006).

Bendixen, M, Best, J, Hackney, C, and Iversen, LL, 'Time Is Running Out for Sand' (2019) 571 *Nature International Journal of Science* 29–31.

Bergius, M, Benjaminsen, TA, Maganga, F and Buhaug, H, 'Green economy, degradation narratives, and land-use conflicts in Tanzania' (2020) 129 *World Development* 104850.

Bhatia, M and Angelou, N, 'Beyond Connections Energy Access Redefined' (Energy Sector Management Assistance Program, World Bank 2015).

Binswanger-Mkhize, HP, 'From failure to success in South African land reform' (2014) 9 *African Journal of Agricultural and Resource Economics* 253–69.

Bonafé Martínez, E, *Towards a European energy policy: resources and constraints in EU law* (Doctoral book 2010).

Boschini, AD, Pettersson, J and Roine, J, 'Resource curse or not: A question of appropriability' (2007) 109(3) *Scandinavian Journal of Economics* 593–617.

BP Plc, *BP Energy Outlook, 2019.*

Brew-Hammond, A: 'Challenges to increasing Access to Modern Energy Services in Africa', codlogics_ff_201312 30_1388442782.report on West African energy ministers conference 2007.

Buberwa Kamala, D, 'The Achievements and Challenges of the New East African Community Co-operation' (January 2006), available at, http://www2.hull.ac.uk/hubs/pdf/memorandum58.pdf.

Burrows, E and Bird, L, 'Ghana: Gold, Guns and China-Ghana's fight to end galamsey', *AllAfrica*, 30 May 2017.

Byamugisha, FF (ed), *Agricultural land redistribution and land administration in sub-Saharan Africa: case studies of recent reforms* (The World Bank 2014).

Cameron, P, *International energy investment law: the pursuit of stability* (Oxford University Press 2010).

—— *Legal aspects of EU energy regulation: the consolidation of energy law across Europe* (Oxford University Press 2016).

—— 'Stabilization and the impact of changing patterns of energy investment' (2017) 10(5) *The Journal of World Energy Law & Business* 389–403.

Cameron, PD and Brothwood, M, *Competition in energy markets: law and regulation in the European Union* (Oxford University Press 2002).

Cameron, PD and Stanley, MC, *Oil, gas, and mining: a sourcebook for understanding the extractive industries* (The World Bank 2017).

Cherp, A and Jewell, J, 'The concept of energy security: Beyond the four As' (2014) 75 *Energy Policy* 415–21.

Chimhowu, A, 'The "new" African customary land tenure. Characteristic, features and policy implications of a new paradigm' (2019) 81 *Land Use Policy* 897–903.

Choi, JB, Goo, BK, Kim, JC, Kim, YJ and Kim, WS, 'Development of limit load solutions for corroded gas pipelines' (2003) 80(2) *International Journal of Pressure Vessels and Piping* 121–28.

Choo, J, 'Energy cooperation problems in Northeast Asia: Unfolding the reality' (2006) 23(3) *East Asia* 91–106.

Cochrane, L and Hadis, S, 'Functionality of the Land Certification Program in Ethiopia: Exploratory Evaluation of the Processes of Updating Certificates' (2019) 8(10) *Land* 149.

Cooke, JA and Johnson, MS, 'Ecological restoration of land with particular reference to the mining of metals and industrial minerals: A review of theory and practice' (2002) 10(1) *Environmental Reviews* 41–71.

Dammert, AC, de Hoop, J, Mvukiyehe, E and Rosati, FC, 'Effects of public policy on child labor: Current knowledge, gaps, and implications for program design' (2018) 110 *World Development* 104–23.

Daniel, P, Keen, M and McPherson, C (eds), *The taxation of petroleum and minerals: principles, problems and practice* (IMF/Routledge 2010).

Daniel, P and Sunley, E, 'Contractual Assurances of Fiscal Stability' in Daniel, P, Keen, M and McPherson, C (eds), *The Taxation of Petroleum and Minerals: Principles, Problems and Practice* (IMF/Routledge 2010).

De Luca, A, 'Renewable Energy in the EU, the Energy Charter Treaty, and Italy's Withdrawal Therefrom', *Bocconi Legal Studies Research Paper No. 2657395* (January 2015).

Deininger, K, 'Land Policies for Growth and Poverty Reduction' (World Bank and Oxford University Press 2003).

Deininger, K, Ali, DA, Holden, S and Zevenbergen, J, 'Rural land certification in Ethiopia: Process, initial impact, and implications for other African countries' (2008) 36(10) *World Development* 1786–1812.

Del Rey, E, Jimenez-Martin, S, and Castello, JV, 'Improving educational and labor outcomes through child labor regulation' (2018) 66 *Economics of Education Review* 51–66.

Del Río, P and Janeiro, L, 'Overcapacity as a barrier to renewable energy deployment: The Spanish case' (2016) *Journal of Energy* 1–10.

Department of Defense (US), 'Energy for the Warfighter: Operational Energy Strategy', Assistance Secretary of Defense for Operational Plans and Programs (ed) (Dept of Defense 2011), https://apps.dtic.mil/dtic/tr/fulltext/u2/a544100.pdf.

Dias, D, 'Stability in International Contracts for Hydrocarbons Exploration and Some of the Associated General Principles of Law: From Myth to Reality' (2010) 4 *Oil, Gas & Energy Law*.

Dincer, I and Rosen, MA, 'A worldwide perspective on energy, environment and sustainable development' (1998) 22(15) *International Journal of Energy Research* 1305–21.

Dixon, M, *Modern Land Law*, 11th edn (Routledge 2018).

—— *Modern Land Law*, 12th edn (Routledge 2021).

Downie, C and Drahos, P, 'US institutional pathways to clean coal and shale gas: lessons for China' (2017) 17(2) *Climate Policy* 246–60.

Eastern Africa Power Pool, 'Regional Power System Master Plan 2014: Volume II Data Report' (EAPP 2014), https://www.ea-energianalyse.dk/wp-content/uploads/2020/02/1332_eapp_master_plan_2014_volume_2_data_report.pdf.

ECOWAS Centre for Renewable Energy and Energy Efficiency, http://www.ecreee.org/page/overview-ecreee.

ECOWAS Energy Policy A/DEC 3/5/82. Decision AIDEC 3/5/82 relating to the adoption of the ECOWAS Energy Policy, adopted by the Authority of Heads of State and Government in 1982.

Eckholm, E, *The other energy crisis: firewood. Worldwatch Paper 1* (Worldwatch Institute 1975).

Elwerfelli, A and Benhin, JK, 'Oil a blessing or curse: A comparative assessment of Nigeria, Norway and the United Arab Emirates' (2018) 8(5) *Theoretical Economics Letters* 1136–60.

Ellabban, O, Abu-Rub, H and Blaabjerg, F, 'Renewable energy resources: Current status, future prospects and their enabling technology' (2014) 39 *Renewable and Sustainable Energy Reviews* 748–64.

Engwicht, N, 'After blood diamonds: The moral economy of illegality in the Sierra Leonean diamond market' *MPIfG Discussion Paper, No. 16/9* (2016).

Ershad, AM, Institutional and Policy Assessment of Renewable Energy Sector in Afghanistan.

Estache, A and Wren-Lewis, L, 'Toward a theory of regulation for developing countries: Following Jean-Jacques Laffont's lead' (2009) 47(3) *Journal of Economic Literature* 729–70.

Esteves, AM, Coyne, B, and Moreno, A, 'Local content initiatives: Enhancing the subnational benefits of the oil, gas and mining sectors' Policy Brief (Natural Resource Governance Institute 2013).

Ethier, W, 'The international commercial system' (Essays in International Finance No 210) (Princeton University Dept of Economics, International Finance Section 1998).

EU-Africa Infrastructure Trust Fund, 'Annual Report 2010', http://www.eu-africa-infrastructuretf.net/attachments/Annual%20Reports/eu_africa_infrastructure_trust_fund_annual_report_2010_en.pdf, p 26.

Fainstein, SS, 'The just city' (2014) 18(1) *International Journal of Urban Sciences* 1–8.

Fawcett, L, 'Region-Building Debates in a Global Context' in Levine, DH and Nagar, D (eds), *Region-Building in Africa* (Palgrave Macmillan US 2016) 21–36.

Finer, M, Jenkins, CN, Pimm, SL, Keane, B and Ross, C, 'Oil and gas projects in the western Amazon: threats to wilderness, biodiversity, and indigenous peoples' (2008) 3(8) *PloS one* e2932.

FEWS NET, 'Southern Africa Special Report. 2014/15 EL Niño Event, July 2014' (Famine Early Warning System Network (FEWS NET) July 2014).

Gergacz, JW, 'Solar Energy Law: Easements of Access to Sunlight' (1980) 10(1) *New Mexico Law Review* 121.

Ghouth, ASB, Taleb, MAB, Hadi, AA, Algarzi, MM, Bahartah, AA, Taleb, EHB, Ba-dokhon, KA, Alsayari, MM, Khader, MM, Nasser, KM and Baju, SA, 'Prevalence of Child Labor among Elementary School Students from 5th to 9th Grade in al Mukalla' (2018) 18(6-H) *Global Journal of Human-Social Science Research.*

Gibson, JL, *Overcoming historical injustices: Land reconciliation in South Africa* (Cambridge University Press 2009).

Gippner, O, 'Energy cooperation in South Asia: prospects and challenges' (South Asia Watch on Trade, Economics & Environment (SAWTREE) 2010).

Gnansounou, E, 'Boosting the electricity sector in West Africa: An integrative vision' (2008) 17 *International Association for Energy Economics* 23–29.

Goldthau, A, 'Rethinking the governance of energy infrastructure: Scale, decentralization and polycentrism' (2014) 1 *Energy Research & Social Science* 134–40.

Heffron, RJ, *Energy law: an introduction* (Springer 2014).

Hettne, B and Söderbaum, F, 'Regional cooperation: a tool for addressing regional and global challenges' in *Meeting global challenges: international cooperation in the national interest. Final report Cross-cutting issues* (International Task Force on Global Public Goods 2006) 179–244.

Hettne, B, Sunkel, O and Inotai, A (eds), *Globalism and the new regionalism* (Vol 1) (Springer 2016).

Hilson, G, 'An overview of land use conflicts in mining communities' (2002) 19(1) *Land Use Policy* 65–73.

Hilson, G and Maconachie, R, 'Formalising artisanal and small-scale mining: Insights, contestations and clarifications' (2017) 49(4) *Area* 443–451.

Hilton, I and Kerr, O, 'The Paris Agreement: China's "New Normal" role in international climate negotiations' (2017) 17(1) Special Issue *Climate Policy* 48–58.

Huber, M, 'Carbon Nation: Fossil Fuels in the Making of American Culture. By Bob Johnson' (2017) 22(1) *Environmental History* 151.

Huda, MS and McDonald, M, 'Regional cooperation on energy in South Asia: Unraveling the political challenges in implementing transnational pipelines and electricity grids' (2016) 98 *Energy Policy* 73–83.

International Energy Agency, 'World Energy Outlook Special Report, 2014' (IEA 2014).

—— 'World Energy Outlook – Methodology for Energy Access Analysis', www.worldenergyoutlook.org/media/weowebsite/EnergyAccess_Methodology_2014.pdf.

—— 'Africa Energy Outlook 2019' (IEA 2019), https://www.iea.org/reports/africa-energy-outlook-2019.

Intergovernmental Panel on Climate Change, 'Global Warming of 1.5°C – A Special Report' (IPCC 2018), https://www.ipcc.ch/sr15/.

Isiani, MC and Ihediwa, NC, 'War and Gender: Socio-Economic Reflections on the Sierra Leonean Civil War' (2019) *Cogito: Multidisciplinary Research Journal* 133–59.

James, RW, *Land Tenure and Policy in Tanzania* (East African Literature Bureau 1971), note 3, 93–95.

Jenjekwa, V and Barnes, L, 'Changes in the Linguistic Landscape Resulting from Zimbabwe's Post-2000 Land Reforms: Recasting the First and Second Chimurenga Narratives' (2018) 49(3) *Language Matters* 67–85.

Jenkins, H, 'Corporate social responsibility and the mining industry: Conflicts and constructs' (2004) 11(1) *Corporate Social Responsibility and Environmental Management* 23–34.

Jenkins, H, and Yakovleva, N, 'Corporate social responsibility in the mining industry: Exploring trends in social and environmental disclosure' (2006) 14(3–4) *Journal of Cleaner Production* 271–84.

Jenkins, K, McCauley, D, Heffron, R, Hannes, S, and Rehner, R, 'Energy justice: A conceptual review' (2016) 11 *Energy Research & Social Science* 174–82.

Kanagawa, M and Nakata, T, 'Analysis of the impact of electricity grid interconnection between Korea and Japan – Feasibility study for energy network in Northeast Asia' (2006) 34(9) *Energy Policy* 1015–25.

Kapelus, P, 'Mining, corporate social responsibility and the "community": The case of Rio Tinto, Richards Bay Minerals and the Mbonambi' (2002) 39(3) *Journal of Business Ethics* 275–96.

Karekezi, S, Kimani, J, Mutiga, A and Amenya, S, 'Energy services for the poor in Eastern Africa: sub-regional "Energy Access" study of East Africa'. A report prepared for 'Energy Access' working group of the Global Network on Energy for Sustainable Development (2003).

Keating, M, *The new regionalism in Western Europe: Territorial restructuring and political change* (Edward Elgar 1998).

Kennedy, JL, *Oil and gas pipeline fundamentals* (PennWell Books 1993).

King, R, *Land reform: A world survey* (Routledge 2019).

King, MD and Gulledge, J, 'Climate change and energy security: an analysis of policy research' (2014) 123(1) *Climatic Change* 57–68.

Klein, S, 'America first? Isolationism in US foreign policy from the 19th to the 21st century' (Doctoral dissertation, Monterey, CA: Naval Postgraduate School 2017).

Kriegler, E, Bauer, N, Popp, A, Humpenöder, F, Leimbach, M, Strefler, J, Baumstark, L, Bodirsky, BL, Hilaire, J, Klein, D and Mouratiadou, I, 'Fossil-fueled development (SSP5): an energy and resource intensive scenario for the 21st century' (2017) 42 *Global Environmental Change* 297–315.

Lange, S, and Kinyondo, A, 'Resource nationalism and local content in Tanzania: Experiences from mining and consequences for the petroleum sector' (2016) 3(4) *The Extractive Industries and Society* 1095–1104.

Lazkano, I, Nøstbakken, L and Pelli, M, 'From fossil fuels to renewables: The role of electricity storage' (2017) 99 *European Economic Review* 113–29.

Leal-Arcas, R and Nalule, V, 'Multilateral and Bilateral Energy Investment Treaties' in Chaisse, J, Choukroune, L and Jusoh, S (eds), *Handbook of International Investment Law and Policy* (Springer 2019) 1–13.

Lee, CKF, Duncan, C, Owen, HJF and Pettorelli, N, 2017. 'A New Framework to Assess Relative Ecosystem Vulnerability to Climate Change' 11(2) *Conservation Letters* e12372.

Lovering, J, 'Theory led by policy: the inadequacies of the "new regionalism" (illustrated from the case of Wales)' (1999) 23(2) *International Journal of Urban and Regional Research* 379–95.

Lubell, H, 'Security of supply and energy policy in Western Europe' (1961) 13(3) *World Politics* 400–422.

Mabey, PT, Li, W, Sundufu, AJ and Lashari, AH, 'Environmental impacts: Local perspectives of selected mining edge communities in Sierra Leone' (2020) 12(14) *Sustainability* 5525.

Mansour, M and Nakhle, C, Fiscal stabilization in oil and gas contracts – evidence and implications' *Oxford Institute for Energy Studies paper: SP 37* (2016).

Marcuse, P, Connolly, J, Novy, J, Olivo, I, Potter, C and Steil, J (eds), *Searching for the just city: debates in urban theory and practice* (Routledge 2009).

Mathews, JA and Tan, H, 'Manufacture renewables to build energy security' (2014) 513 *Nature* 166.

McNutt, M, 'Climate change impacts' (2013) 341(6145) *Science* 435.

Menon, N and van der Meulen Rodgers, Y, 'Child labor and the minimum wage: Evidence from India. 46(2) *Journal of Comparative Economics* 480–94.

Migot-Adholla, SE, Place, F and Oluoch-Kosura, W, 'Security of tenure and land productivity in Kenya' in Bruce, JW and Migot-Adholla, SE (eds), *Searching for land tenure security in Africa* (Kendall/Hunt Publishing 1994) 119–40.

Military Advisory Board, 'National security and the threat of climate change' (CNA Corporation 2007).

Mkodzongi, G and Spiegel, S, 'Artisanal gold mining and farming: livelihood linkages and labour dynamics after land reforms in Zimbabwe' (2019) 55(10) *The Journal of Development Studies* 2145–61.

Mwakyusa, A, 'East Africa: Construction of Uganda – Tanga Port Oil Pipeline Starts August', 8 March 2016, *Tanzania Daily News* (dar es Salaam) via *AllAfrica.com*.

Nakhle, C, *Petroleum taxation: sharing the oil wealth: a study of petroleum taxation yesterday, today and tomorrow* (Routledge 2008).

Nalule, VR, 'Achieve Gender Equality and Empower All Women and Girls' in Parra, C, Lewis, B and Ali, SH (eds), *Mining, Materials, and the Sustainable Development Goals (SDGs): 2030 and Beyond* (CRC Press 2020) 39–50.

—— *Mining and the Law in Africa: Exploring the social and environmental impacts* (Palgrave Pivot 2020).

—— *Energy Poverty and Access Challenges in Sub-Saharan Africa: The Role of Regionalism* (Palgrave Macmillan 2018) 104.

—— 'How to Respond to Energy Transitions in Africa: Introducing the Energy Progression Dialogue' in Nalule (ed), *Energy Transitions and the Future of the African Energy Sector* (Palgrave Macmillan 2021) 3–35.

—— 'Extractives and Beyond: Managing the Energy Transition in Africa' in Nalule (ed), *Energy Transitions and the Future of the African Energy Sector* (Palgrave Macmillan 2021) 469–72.

—— 'Energy Access Challenges in the COVID-19 crisis: Is there a future for Extractives in the Energy Transition Era?' *Extractives Hub Research Insight*, May 2020.

—— 'Transitioning to a low carbon economy: Is Africa ready to bid farewell to fossil fuels?' in Wood, G and baker, K (eds), *The Palgrave Handbook of Managing Fossil Fuels and Energy Transitions* (Palgrave Macmillan 2020) 261–86.

—— 'Salt Mining in Uganda', *YouTube*, https://www.youtube.com/watch?v=RKFP5DswMrM&t=564s.

Nalule, VR and Ayebare, RT, 'Uganda: Mineral Policy' in Tiess, G, Majumder, T and Cameron, P (eds), *Encyclopedia of Mineral and Energy Policy* (Springer 2018).

NASA, 'Global Climate Change', https://climate.nasa.gov/effects/.

Nepal, R and Jamasb, T, 'Interconnections and market integration in the Irish Single Electricity Market' (2012) 51 *Energy Policy* 425–34.

Niang, I, Ruppel, OC, Abdrabo, MA, Essel, A, Lennard, C, Padgham, J and Urquhart, P, 'Africa' in *Climate Change 2014: Impacts, Adaptation, and Vulnerability. Part B: Regional Aspects*. Contribution of Working Group II to the Fifth Assessment Report of the Intergovernmental Panel on Climate Change (Cambridge University Press 2014), 1199–1265. Can be accessed at, http://www.ipcc.ch/pdf/assessment-report/ar5/wg2/WGIIAR5-Chap22_FINAL.pdf.

Nizami, AS, Shahzad, K, Rehan, M, Ouda, OKM, Khan, MZ, Ismail, IMI, Almeelbi, T, Basahi, JM and Demirbas, A, 'Developing waste biorefinery in Makkah: a way forward to convert urban waste into renewable energy' (2017) *Applied Energy, 186*.

Njenga, N and Nalule, V, 'What is the Future of Social Licence to Operate in the Extractive Industries post the COVID-19 Pandemic in East Africa?' (2020) 1(2) *Global Energy Law and Sustainability* 156–63.

Nkhonjera, GK, 'Understanding the impact of climate change on the dwindling water resources of South Africa, focusing mainly on Olifants River basin: A review' (2017) 71 *Environmental Science & Policy* 19–29.

Novy, J and Mayer, M, 'As "just" as it gets? The European City in the "Just City" discourse' in Marcuse, P, Connolly, J, Novy, J, Olivo, I, Potter, C and Steil, J (eds), *Searching for the just city* (Routledge 2009) 123–39.

Nussbaum, A, 'The Arbitration Between the Lena Goldfields Ltd. and the Soviet Government' (1950) 36 *Cornell Law Quarterly* 31.

Nye, JS (ed), *International regionalism: Readings* (Little, Brown Co 1968).

Ogwezzy, MC, 'Legal Framework for the Implementation of ECOWAS Energy Programmes: The Energy Protocol, WAPP Agreement and WAGP Treaty' (2017) 15(1) *Oil, Gas & Energy Law Journal (OGEL)*.

Olawuyi, DS, *Extractives Industry Law in Africa* (Springer 2018).

Onditi, F, 'From resource curse to institutional incompatibility: a comparative study of Nigeria and Norway oil resource governance' (2019) 11(2) *Africa Review* 152–71.

Painuly, JP, 'Barriers to renewable energy penetration; a framework for analysis' (2001) 24(1) *Renewable Energy* 73–89.

Parail, V, 'Properties of Electricity Prices and the Drivers of Interconnector Revenue', *Cambridge Working Paper in Economics 1059/ Electricity Policy Research Group 1033* (University of Cambridge 2010).

Pedersen, RH, Jacob, T, Maganga, F and Kweka, O, 'Rights to land and extractive resources in Tanzania (1/2): The history', *DIIS Working paper 2016/11*.

Prosser, T, *Law and the Regulators* (Oxford University Press 1997).

Quinn, EL, 'Privacy and the new energy infrastructure', *EES Working Paper No 09-001* (2008). https://papers.ssrn.com/sol3/papers.cfm?abstract_id=1370731.

Radon, J, 'How to negotiate an oil agreement' in Humphreys, M, Sachs JD and Stiglitz, JE (eds), *Escaping the resource curse* (Columbia University Press, 2007) 89–113.

Roeben, V and Mete, G, 'What do we mean when we talk about international energy law?' in Cameron, PD, Mu, X and Roeben, V (eds), *The Global Energy Transition Law, Policy and Economics for Energy in the 21st Century* (Hart Publishing 2020).

REN21, 'Renewables 2014: Global Status Report' (Renewable Energy Policy Network for the 21st Century (REN21) 2014).

Revised National Land Policy of Rwanda, 2019. It can be accessed at, Revised_National_Land_Policy_2019.pdf (rlma.rw).

SADC Energy Monitor, 2016 – Baseline Study of the SADC Energy Sector (SADC/SARDC 2016).

SADC Renewable Energy and Energy Efficiency Strategy and Action Plan (REESAP 2016-2030) (SARDC 2017).

Sarmiento, HG and Avila Rosales, MA, Issues Associated with International Power Grid Interconnections in Mexico (IEEE 2010).

Saviour, MN and Stalin, P, 'Soil and Sand Mining: Causes, Consequences and Management' (2012) 2(4) *IOSR Journal of Pharmacy (IOSRPHR)* 1–6.

Schiff, M and Winters, LA, 'Regional cooperation, and the role of international organisations and regional integration', *World Bank Policy Research Working Paper 2872* (July 2002).

Schueler, V, Kuemmerle, T, and Schröder, H, 'Impacts of surface gold mining on land use systems in Western Ghana' (2011) 40(5) *Ambio* 528–39.

Soja, EW, 'The city and spatial justice' (2009) 1(1) *Justice Spatiale/Spatial Justice* 1–5.

Sovacool, BK and MH Dworkin, MH, 'Energy Justice: Conceptual Insights and Practical Applications' (2015) 142 *Applied Energy* 435–44.

Spalding-Fecher, R, Joyce, B and Winkler, H, 'Climate change and hydropower in the Southern African Power Pool and Zambezi River Basin: System-wide impacts and policy implications' (2017) 103 *Energy Policy* 84–97.

Stiles, G and Murove, C, 'SADC renewable energy and energy efficiency status report' (REN21 2015) 9.

Tiess, G, *General and International Mineral Policy: Focus: Europe* (Springer Wien 2011).

UN Environment Programme, 'Environmental Assessment of Ogoniland Report, 2011', https://postconflict.unep.ch/publications/OEA/UNEP_OEA.pdf.

Unruh, JD and Turray, H, 'Land tenure, food security and investment in postwar Sierra Leone' *Food and Agriculture Organization Livelihood Support Programme Working Paper 22* (2006).

Van der Walt, AJ, *Property in the Margins* (Bloomsbury Publishing 2009).

Veiga, MM, Angeloci-Santos, G and Meech, JA, 'Review of barriers to reduce mercury use in artisanal gold mining' (2014) 1(2) *Extractive Industries and Society* 351–61.

Vogel, C, Musamba, J, and Radley, B, 'A Miner's Canary in Eastern Congo' (2017) 5(1) *Extractive Industries and Society* 73–80.

Wälde, TW, 'Investment Arbitration Under the Energy Charter Treaty – From Dispute Settlement to Treaty Implementation' (1996) 12(4) *Arbitration International* 429–66.

Wood Mackenzie Energy Transition Outlook: The Scalability Challenge (Wood Mackenzie 2019).

Wood, G, 'Policy risk, politics and low carbon energy' in Considine, J and Paik, K-W (eds), *The Handbook of Energy Politics* (Edward Elgar 2018).

Zabbey, N, Sam, K and Onyebuchi, AT, 'Remediation of contaminated lands in the Niger Delta, Nigeria: Prospects and challenges' (2017) 586 *Science of the Total Environment* 952–65.

INDEX

www.ingramcontent.com/pod-product-compliance
Lightning Source LLC
Chambersburg PA
CBHW071257180926
51613CB00001B/56
9781509938421